The Perfect Host

Entertainment

THE
PERFECT HOST

A Husband's Guide to Home Entertaining

MEL MARSHALL
with photos by the author and Aldine Marshall

WINCHESTER PRESS

This book is for Connie and Steve, in lieu of.

Library of Congress Catalog Card Number: 75-9253
ISBN: 0-87691-174-2

Published by Winchester Press
205 East 42nd St., New York, 10017

Designed by Paula Wiener
Printed in the United States of America

Contents

Acknowledgments

For many kinds of assistance in preparing the text and pictures of this book I'm indebted to friends old and new.

They include Bill Bergner, Les and Billie Boykin, Jim Edwards of Borger Meat Co., Mrs. Syble Holley of Collector's Corner, Amos Miracle of Amarillo Packing Co., Wes Sours of the Wyatt Cafeteria chain, Clint Tidenberg of Southern Union Gas Co., Bill Windsor and Jim Smith of the Handy Dan organization, and W. T. Atkins of the A.I.D. Co.

My thanks to all of them.

—M. M.

Introduction

This is a survival manual for beginning husbands and veterans of matrimony who haven't yet learned to cope.

It is dedicated to the proposition that all men aren't created as chauvinist pigs; that in spite of the image so determinedly projected by a few extremists, men don't spend their time trying to impose menial, thankless tasks on their spouses—or on partners in households whose principals aren't joined in formal matrimony.

Most men are willing to share the job of making the bed as well as the pleasures of sleeping in it; to join in the stand-up kitchen chores as well as sitting down to the dinner table; in short, to carry their part of the household's tasks instead of expecting Her to do all the work.

If they're not willing, they damned soon learn to be. Sooner or later, when domestic tasks rear their ugly little heads and demand attention, She will smile Her sweetest and say in the Family Voice, "But, that's *your* job, dear."

Even novitiates in domesticity quickly come to a recognition that when the Family Voice is used, it's time to act, not to argue. They might not be exactly sure what action to take, but they move to do something—anything—that will preserve the Pax Familiae.

Now, some relationships survive because soon after being established the parties to them agree on what constitutes a proper and fair distribution of labor. Some survive in the absence of such an agreement, but to the creaks and groans of recurring internal friction. Others survive because both He and She are flexible enough to realize that a precise division of labor isn't always possible, and both of them stand ready to rush into whatever breaches might open.

In many households, equilibrium is maintained if the male partner simply does the jobs assigned Him by tradition. For the most part, these are repetitive and essentially uncreative functions such as disposing of the garbage, attending to the lawn and furnace in residences which have such things to tend, and performing minor repairs on items of household equipment that have suddenly become possessed by the Devil and must be exorcised by a handyman.

More creative tasks, such as cooking, are traditionally undertaken by Her, but on occasion these jobs threaten to put a strain on Her above and beyond the normal call of duty. Usually, such an occasion is connected with periods when a family entertainment is being planned. It is at such times that She most often employs the Family Look and the Family Voice. Unhappily, these are the very occasions with which He is most often illequipped to cope.

Equally unhappily, She is often as badly equipped as He is. For the past two decades, the total thrust of food advertising and promotion has been devoted to "instant" substitutes for genuine food and to precooked "convenience foods," many of which are neither convenient nor food when one considers the quantities of chemical additives and water they contain. There is a very strong possibility that She may never have learned really to cook; there's an equally good possibility that She may have been totally turned off on the entire matter of eating by the spectacle of those TV commercials which show ill-mannered individuals cramming great gobbets of indeterminate substances into already overstuffed mouths while grimacing in obviously feigned enjoyment.

Her cry for help, then, is quite probably an honest one, not motivated by female chauvinism. She resorts to the Family Look and the Family Voice out of real need for assistance in dealing with a situation that is causing Her genuine concern, and such honest pleas should bring willing response. As noted, the occasion is usually one involving a family bash. It might be a cocktail party, a reception, a sitdown dinner, or a patio cookout. And it is while the details of the event are being discussed that She will smilingly say, "But, that's *your* job, dear."

What follows might be any one of a number of tasks; She may, for example, conclude the sentence with ". . . to take care of the drinks."

She might well add, ". . . and to give me some help in the kitchen, preparing all that extra food."

Her suasion might include, ". . . and you'll do the carving at the table, of course."

Or, if a cookout is under consideration, be sure She'll remind you it's your job ". . . to handle any outdoor cooking that's done."

Finally, if you're among those whose innocent relaxations include hunting or fishing, or if you have friends who bring you gifts of game and fish, She'll probably begin by admiring these edible trophies of outdoor skill and wind up by mentioning that ". . . it's your job to clean and cook them."

It's with these varied aspects of "your job" that we're going to be concerned in the pages that follow. If along the way you garner a few miscellaneous tidbits of information that will win you the admiration of less-knowledgeable friends, count it as an extra bonus.

The Perfect Host

I

Tending Bar and Cellar

One of the great differences between the sexes—aside from those obvious physical differences for which both male and female readers may now pause to offer a moment of silent thanks—is their approach to the buying and serving of wines and liquors.

Without disparaging any female psychological attributes, there is something in Her mind that inhibits Her from apportioning an adequate share of the family food budget to the beverages that precede, accompany, and follow a meal. She may enjoy them and know as much about them as He does— may be as expert in judging wines and as quick to savor the mellowness of a fine Cognac or whiskey—but at the critical moment She will balk at paying the price attached to the unopened bottle.

It is significant that in the Dark Ages, households were totally controlled by women, and that in them adequate beverages were singularly lacking. The chatelaine kept all household keys, including those to the wine cellar; the man's role was confined to defending the family's domain. He came home bushed, and often didn't even take off his sweat-rusted armor before sitting down to whatever his spouse had caused to be placed on the table in the way of food and drink. Usually, the food was good, the drink mediocre.

Truly civilized dining did not begin until men abandoned knight errantry and crusading, pastimes that took them away from home for extended periods. Only when men began to spend most of their time at home did the quality of beverages served even at royal and noble tables start improving. As long as She controlled the keys to the cellar, the dinner tankards were filled with watery ale, weak cider, and sweetly cloying mead. After the last great Crusade ended at the beginning of the fourteenth century, family life began to be re-established as a matter of sharing household responsibilities. The man of the house took over management of the cellar, and things got better in the beverage department.

At that time the tradition began that persists today. By this tradition, it is His job to see to the beverages served before, during, and after dinner; by extension, the responsibility extends to drinks served at any family entertainment. Since cocktail parties, receptions, buffet or sit-down dinners, patio dining, and other events require different approaches, let's look at each of them separately.

The Cocktail Party

You can chicken out and hire a bartender or you can handle the drink service yourself. For what it's worth, you'll probably see more of your guests if you do your own mixing and serving than you will if you delegate that job to a hired barman and spend your time circulating and mingling. Unless there are more than thirty guests to be looked after, a bartender is an unnecessary expenditure if you're prepared to do a bit of thoughtful planning and to spend most of your time at whatever bar you set up for the occasion.

Realize first that today's drinking tastes and habits make the job of the amateur bartender an easy one. Few people indulge in elaborate mixed drinks any more; the multi-ingredient cocktail became popular during the Prohibition era, when the quality of most liquor was so bad that it had to be mixed with something—almost anything—to be drinkable. Today, the most complicated cocktail you'll be called on to concoct will contain three, at most four, ingredients. There are always a few fad drinks that rise swiftly and fade as rapidly, but the same half-dozen old standbys remain the backbone of the bartender's work at the average cocktail party, and all of them are very easy to mix.

Three out of ten of your guests will ask for straight Bourbon or Scotch on the rocks. Four more will want whiskey and plain water; perhaps one or two of these will ask for a bottled mixer instead of water. Of the remaining three, two will request a Martini in one of its several versions. The tenth guest will likely want one of a few simple mixed drinks—a Screwdriver, Bloody Mary, Manhattan, or Old Fashioned.

You'll probably get an occasional call for whatever fad drink happens to be current, but few guests will ask for anything extraordinary unless there's a professional handling the bar. Professional bartenders at private parties seem to bring out· the worst in some people; they seem determined to challenge the barman's skill by asking for the most bizarre concoctions. Usually, they don't feel this compulsion if the host is doing the mixing.

Fad drinks are almost always created in the back room of an advertising agency's office, and are designed only to promote a proprietary liquor or liqueur, not to taste good. Their popularity endures only as long as they are advertised, and after the ad campaign has run its course, fad drinks tend to drop into the limbo that most of them deserve and are heard of no more. You have two courses open when a guest asks for one of these concoctions. Either level with him and tell him you don't have the ingredients on hand, or give him the treatment professional bartenders tell me they use. Turn your back and create something—anything—on the spur of the moment, and pass it across the bar with a perfectly straight face. The professionals say it's rare that anybody will question the validity of a drink they mix and serve in response to an outlandish request.

At the end of this chapter, where they've been grouped for your convenience, you will find the formulas for the most-often-requested cocktail-party drinks.

For a temporary bar, use masking tape to strap a piece of plywood or
particle board to the top of an adjustable ironing board. You'll need a
piece ⅝ or ¾ inch thick and about 24 by 60 inches. At its highest
adjustment the ironing board is just about the height of a bar. Drape
the setup with a long tablecloth or bedsheet or a sheet of opaque
plastic to hide the ironing board legs. Use space under the bar for
storage of extra ice, bottles, the waste bucket. A small table behind
the bar holds working supplies.

There are several steps you can take in planning your
cocktail party that will ease the strain on time and energy
expended as well as on the budget. Let's consider a few.

Your first problem may well be a suitable place for serving
drinks. While the permanent, built-in home bar has come to be
a popular feature in newly built homes and apartments, chances
are you'll be faced with the need to do some improvising. No
problem. If you lack a bar, even small towns now are apt to have
businesses where you can rent a small roll-around bar for a few
bucks a day. If you'd prefer to improvise, use a single long table
or shove together two small tables of the same height and cover
them with opaque plastic sheeting. If you don't have tables,
maybe there's a bookcase or record cabinet that can be draped.

If you entertain often enough to make the effort worthwhile, get a piece of plywood or particle board about two feet
wide and five feet long, strap it with masking tape to the top of a

folding ironing board, and drape the arrangement with a sheet of opaque plastic to hide what's under the top. This kind of setup has several advantages over cabinets or tables. Most folding ironing boards are adjustable in height, so your bar will be a lot more convenient to use. You'll also have lots of space under the board for a waste bucket, a tub of ice, extra bottles, and other needs. Keep your working bottles of liquor and mixers on a small table back of the bar. Details of this setup are shown in the accompanying pictures.

Two things you'll want to keep in mind when setting up any kind of temporary bar: Keep the liquor service out of the kitchen, where the canapés and snacks are being handled, and locate your bar as far as conveniently possible from the food service areas. If you have both liquor and food service together, your guests will collect around them and form a human traffic jam.

When you set out to buy the liquor for your blowout, give a bit of thought to the drinking habits of the part of the country in which you live. Geography doesn't play the important role in drink preferences that it once did, but there are still some regional favorites. Along both East and West coasts, the whiskey choices now split about evenly between Scotch and Bourbon. Throughout the central sections and on the Gulf Coast—except for Florida—Bourbon is the preferred whiskey; it will be called for three or four times more often than will Scotch. Vodka is ubiquitous; it is today's most-requested liquor and is drunk on the rocks, with water, or with a bottled mixer, and is also the base for a number of popular mixed drinks. Gin will be needed for Martinis, and some still prefer the flavor gin gives a Screwdriver.

There is a small enclave in the northeastern Atlantic area where rye whiskey will be asked for with reasonable frequency, and through the eastern and upper Midwestern areas Canadian whiskeys have a measurable degree of popularity. In the Southeast and in West Coast cities, you'll find regional preferences for Tennessee sour-mash whiskey. Most of those asking for either Canadian or sour-mash will settle for Bourbon without any visible reluctance.

Irish whiskey is a special taste, seldom encountered. If you're at all well acquainted with your guests, you'll be aware if the list includes the one individual out of every hundred who'll ask for Irish, or even drink it if it's offered. A bottle of Irish adds flair to your bar, if you feel like making a long-term investment. Out of deference to a close friend who'd developed a taste of Irish, I bought a bottle ten or twelve years ago. My friend moved away after he'd had only a couple of drinks from the bottle, and since then I've dusted off the Irish bottle and set it out at more than a hundred parties and have called attention to it regularly, but its level is still only three drinks down.

Your cocktail-party bar, then, should be stocked chiefly with Bourbon and Scotch, and if regional tastes are likely to be encountered, with rye or Canadian or sour-mash in small quantities. You'll also need vodka and gin, and a suggestion or so for other options will be offered a bit further on. At the end of the chapter, with the drink formulas, is a list of essential supplies you'll need to handle the most popular cocktails and mixed drinks.

When it comes to bottled mixers, let your conscience, the weather, and your knowledge of your guests' tastes guide you. Club soda tops the list, but there's a growing and deplorable taste for sweet carbonated soft drinks as mixers. These blend well with flavorless vodka, but their composition of chemical flavors with sugar syrup is to my taste incompatible with whiskey. I stock as few bottles of these unhealthy potions as is decently possible, hoping to run out early. In the summertime, tonic water is handy to have on hand, and though a gingerale is about phased out, a few still call for it as a mixer. You'll find it both practical and economical to hold your choice of mixers to the lowest feasible level. There's a happy point between ostentatious lavishness and miserly meanness, and only you can find it for yourself.

Ice must be on hand. The practical way to buy it—assuming your refrigerator produces only standard cubes—is to get one big chunk plus a supply of chips or tiny cubes in plastic bags. There are reasons for getting both kinds, which will be discussed later on. If you need containers, sporting-goods stores carry foam-plastic buckets—used by fishermen for minnows—in several sizes, and also have foam-plastic ice chests in a variety of sizes and shapes. These are very inexpensive. You can, of course, use whatever container you might have on hand:

a dishpan, a stewpot, even a big deep bowl. If you have an otherwise suitable container that would strike a jarring note on a bar, cover it temporarily with metal foil.

Now, let's discuss drinks, especially in terms of liquor quantities. Do two things. For long-term savings, invest in double-sized highball, cocktail, and Old Fashioned glasses. The average standard highball glass holds ten to twelve ounces, the standard Old Fashioned glass holds eight ounces, the standard cocktail glass five to six ounces. Get highball glasses that will hold 26 to 30 ounces, Old Fashioned glasses that will hold 18 to 20 ounces, and cocktail glasses that will hold eight ounces. Then, when serving tall mixed drinks or drinks on the rocks, use a single big chunk of ice, and make your drinks with one ounce of 100-proof liquor or 1½ ounces of 86- or 84-proof. Use the same ratio in mixing oversized cocktails.

Consider the arithmetic. Usually, you'll put an ounce of 84- or 86-proof liquor into a tall drink served in a standard highball glass, and the same quantity in a drink served on the rocks in a standard Old Fashioned glass or standard cocktail. When outsized glasses are used, drinks look a lot bigger and taste a lot more potent than they actually are. Using a single big chunk of ice keeps a drink cold more effectively, dilutes it less, yet reduces the effective capacity of the big glass. The virtue lies in the mental effect big glasses have on those drinking from them. The big glass discourages drink-gulping; few people will empty such a glass in a couple of swallows, as they would a glass of average size. Seasoned topers will, but they'd gulp even if drinking straight liquor from the bottle.

Don't feel you're short-changing your guests by doing this. Their drinks will taste the same if you follow the foregoing suggestions, and though the end result happens to be economy, the savings are a mere by-product. The real virtue of the over-sized glasses is that drinks in them last longer, you mix fewer, and though as another side-effect your guests may drink a bit less, fewer will wind up smashed, and your party will be more pleasant. Almost twenty years ago, when outsized glasses were relatively rare, we bought ours simply because we liked their shape and proportions. Quite by accident, we discovered the fringe benefits their use brings.

Getting back to arithmetic, what you're doing is serving

two drinks for every three you'd serve in average-sized glasses. Your net saving is ½ ounce of liquor per serving—more, if you follow the next suggestion and buy 100-proof Bourbon and vodka and reduce the quantity of liquor to one ounce per drink. The higher proof lets you do this with no loss of flavor, yet the price differential between 84- or 86-proof and 100-proof bottlings is rarely more than two or three cents per ounce of liquor—even less, now that distillers are offering 80-proof bottlings of most spirits. Scotch, except for a few rare straight-whisky bottlings that are very expensive indeed, is only available at 86-proof; gin is usually 90-proof, but you can find 100-proof gins if you'll do a bit of looking.

Remember, all the distillery does in cutting the proof of liquor is to add water. When the distiller performs this elementary chore, you then buy x ounces of water at liquor prices; the water from your home tap costs several thousand times less. Do it yourself and save the difference. Save still more by buying your liquor in half-gallons instead of the customary fifths; the bigger containers will usually save you from 6 to 8 percent per ounce of liquor.

Measure your needs for a party in three dimensions: number of guests, average consumption per guest, length of time your party will last. Allow three drinks per guest per two-hour period. Within that time, heavy drinkers will put away three or four drinks, moderates will consume two, and the cautious drinkers only one.

Count on getting 16 to 18 drinks per fifth, if you serve 1½ ounces of liquor per drink. If you switch to 100-proof, you'll get 25 percent more drinks per fifth because you'll only be pouring one ounce per drink. The fifth is being taken as our unit of measure only because it's the most common liquor-bottle size, not necessarily the most economical. For twenty guests at a two-hour party, then, your absolute minimum need would be a fifth each of Bourbon and Scotch and two fifths of vodka. This would allow you a small margin for errors in pouring, spillage, and a switch by your guests in liquor preferences. It is, however, a figure against which you can work in making up a shopping list.

At every cocktail party there will be a few guests who'll prefer wine to spirits and a few who'll want something nonalcoholic. In addition to liquor, you might have on hand a chilled bottle of dry white wine or a dry rosé. Or, you might elect to offer a fortified wine, a chilled dry sherry or one of the drier Madeiras, Sercial or Rainwater. Sercial Madeira is comparable to a medium-dry sherry, Rainwater is a bit sweeter. The modern affectation of serving sherry on the rocks is a waste of good wine, but no matter how barbarous you consider it, you'll probably follow my example of bowing to the whim of a guest who asks for it.

Guests who feel obliged to hide their teetotalism can be served a Horse's Neck or a Shirley Temple, both quite easy to prepare. The formulas for these nonalcoholic but sinister-looking drinks are included with those for cocktails at the chapter's end. And you will, of course, have on hand both orange juice and tomato juice, either of which appears to be something else at a cocktail party.

There's also a contrivance of my own, which I call Eau d'Ange. Translated, the name has a double meaning, and I suggest you use the more polite, Angel Water. It's made simply by heating a bottle of good robust red or white Burgundy in a saucepan until bubbles begin to appear on the pan's bottom. This indicates the wine has reached the boiling point of alcohol, 148 degrees, and at that point the alcohol evaporates and vanishes. Allow the wine to cool naturally in the pan, then stir in about eight drops of Angostura Bitters, pour the dealcoholized wine into a decanter, and chill. The flavor won't be as satisfying as that of regular wine, but it's a pleasant beverage far superior to carbonated soft drinks, which are universally nothing more than caffeine extract, caramel or aniline dye coloring, and a sugar or saccharin syrup.

Unless the event is a special one or you've just struck a mother lode of gold, sparkling wines are best avoided at cocktail parties. The newest of the family, Cold Duck, is nothing more than an inferior Burgundy subjected to carbonation, and a cheap Champagne insults both guests and host. Sparkling wines are the devil to serve to a crowd, even under the best-controlled conditions, and a successful cocktail party isn't under tight control at any time or it becomes more like a wake. All sparkling wines require stemmed glasses to bring out their best qualities, and though there are now stemmed plastic throwaways available, they somehow seem out of place at a small private gathering. No host with any desire to participate in his own party will serve sparkling wine, anyhow; he finds all his time devoted to opening bottles. And, from the standpoint of outlay, you'll spend less on liquor for a sizable cocktail party than you will on decent Champagne.

That cocktail parties also require edibles isn't being overlooked; you'll find recipes for canapés and tidbits in a later chapter.

The Reception

Sooner or later, into everyone's life a reception comes. If you feel that "reception" is too formal or grandiose a term to describe your welcoming of a large group of guests for light refreshments and idle chatter, call it an open house or an at-home. Whatever the name, you'll still be receiving guests.

Receptions differ from cocktail parties and other forms of home entertaining in that they're usually organized so the guests arrive and leave in shifts, so you have a much more controllable situation. Your invitations should state the span of time your guests are expected, and you can schedule these periods to give you a predictable crowd flow. Refreshments at receptions and kindred bashes are generally fairly simple, and as a rule the quantity of both liquids and solids consumed is on the light side.

By tradition, receptions almost invariably feature a big bowl of punch; sometimes a pair of punch bowls will be used, one alcoholic, the other temperance. It's also the custom to offer coffee or tea, or both. On occasion, these will replace even the single punch bowl, and special-occasion receptions may feature no beverage other than Champagne. Reception foods tend to be simpler and less elaborate than cocktail-party offerings, running to cakes or cookies, paper-thin sandwiches, perhaps a choice of two or three light and nonfilling canapés.

Formulas for several punches, both alcoholic and temperance, will be found with those for cocktails; reception foods are grouped with recipes for canapés and tidbits in the next chapter.

Preparing for a reception is much easier than setting up for most other methods of home entertaining. The rental services mentioned earlier as a source of a temporary bar also have punch bowls and cups for rent. Punch goes a long way, and the base liquid for punches not only can be but should be mixed in advance and refrigerated until ready for use. The final step in preparing punch, addition of sparkling water or Champagne or both, should be done at the last possible moment; the punch should still be effervescing when the first guests arrive.

Since at a reception all service centers around the punch bowl, the host's job is greatly simplified. It's just a matter of keeping an eye on the serving table, rushing out fresh trays of food, replenishing the punch, and keeping the hot coffee or tea coming along. A reception, by the way, is one function at which a helping hand in the kitchen, a maid hired for a half-day, is very much worthwhile. That extra pair of hands relieves the hostess of dishwashing during the affair, and assures a steady flow of clean glasses and dishes without fuss or muss.

As an alternative to the more taxing—and more expensive—cocktail party, you and She might consider a reception the next time you get the urge to entertain a large number of guests. Even if you lack the traditional reason for a reception—a celebrity to introduce or an anniversary to observe—you can call the affair by another name, and discharge a lot of social obligations with a minimum amount of strain on your energies and budget.

Drinks at Table

Foods don't come within the scope of this chapter; you'll find them discussed later. Here, we're concerned with beverages and the function of the host in selecting and serving them. As noted earlier, the choice and handling of wines at dinner belong in his domain, so the cellar's as good a place as any to start, and the first question we might consider is the basic one of whether or not you really need a wine cellar.

Several factors must guide your decision: the frequency with which you serve wine, the ready availability of an ade-

quate source of supply to your home, the degree of sophistication your taste has reached in wine appreciation, the availability of space suitable for storing wine, the condition of the family
budget, and, not least important, your interest in wine as an
adjunct to dining well.

If you serve wine only occasionally, on very special occasions, a cellar is an unnecessary luxury that you will be maintaining only as a status symbol. If you have wine on your table
no more often that a half-dozen times a year, it's much more
practical to buy the occasional bottle you need as you need it.
Just make your purchase a week or so in advance, carry the
bottle or bottles home, and put them on the floor in a corner of a
seldom-used closet or cupboard. Let them rest for several days
before opening; some wines bruise easily.

This bit about bruising is neither a joke nor a part of the
wine mystique. The word "bruising" describes an actual phe-
nomenon; what happens is that some wines cannot be moved
even short distances without being harmed. In an easily bruised
wine the slightest movement upsets the balance of the many
molecules that compose the delicate structure of oils, acids, and

To keep just a few bottles of wine on
hand, set aside space in a closet or
cupboard and use one of the many
kinds of portable racks available to
store ten or a dozen bottles.

esters that have been created by fermentation and brought into harmony by aging. Although experience has labeled some wines as perennially bad travelers, there is no real predictability to the bruising process. It simply occurs, and quite often one bottling of a given wine will be immune to it while another bottling of the same wine will be highly susceptible. The only safe approach is to assume that any bottle of good wine you handle may bruise, and set it aside for a few days of rest and recuperation before serving it.

If you serve wine infrequently, then, and live close to a reasonably well-stocked dealer's shop, a cellar is not a real need. You can quite easily buy for each occasion and have no reason to keep a wine stock on hand at home. However, if you live in an area where there are no dealers with adequate stocks close by, you might want to keep a moderate number of bottles, a dozen or so of your favorites, to have them instantly available. In this case, you can set aside a small space in a closet or cupboard where you can place a portable rack that will accommodate this supply. Many types of small racks are on the market; some of them are modular in construction and can be added to as required.

However, let's suppose that you've become a true oenophile and have cultivated your palate to a high degree of sophistication. In this case, even if a cellar is a luxury, you might be well advised to maintain one for the genuine pleasure you'll get from it as a hobby. If you're fortunate enough to live in or near one of the country's wine-producing regions, your pleasure will be doubled and your cellar an excellent long-term investment, for you will be able to buy good varietal wines in their inexpensive youth and lay them down to mature and increase in value.

Very little is required in either space or facilities to accommodate 200 to 250 bottles of wine. The three great enemies of wine are light, heat, and vibration, and these are what you must guard against in planning your storage area. A closet in a quiet corner, well away from such household appliances as washers, driers, dishwashers, and trash compactors, will do very well indeed. Line its walls with pre-fab shelving that can be divided into bins, and you have room for around 200 bottles.

Before putting in the shelves, take the precaution of cover-

Very little space is required to accommodate 200 to 250 bottles of wine. In a storage cellar, bins are better than notched shelves, which take up a great deal of space when the cellar's primary use is bulk storage.

ing the closet's interior walls and its door with sheets of expanded foam plastic. A one-inch-thick sheet of this is equal to a couple of feet of solid concrete in insulating value, and it will minimize temperature variations within the closet. Actually, extreme coolness in your storage space is not as vital as maintaining an even temperature. The temperature in your closet can go up to 65 or even 70 degrees without harming any but the most delicate Rhines and Moselles. Your wines will age faster at the higher temperature, but will suffer less than they would if the thermometer registered 50 degrees today and 70 or 75 tomorrow.

Rhine and Moselle wines, however, should not be stored for long periods at temperatures above 50 to 55 degrees. Since floor-level temperatures are usually lowest, keep wines of this type on the bottom tier of your shelves. And if you find that the temperature in your wine closet stays consistently in the 70-degree range, keep a close eye on your bottles. Open a bottle of each vintage you've laid away at least once every six to eight months and drink it to determine how greatly its aging is being accelerated. Some wines age and mature faster than others, and a regular sampling will enable you to determine which of yours fall into this category.

How much does it cost to stock and maintain a wine cellar? That's a matter between you and your budget, and Her, of course. She's probably been misled by the articles that recur every six to eight months in women's magazines, purporting to tell you how to establish a wine cellar for $49.95. No way. No way at all. A 200-bottle cellar of good domestic varietals and a sampling of European bottlings will represent an initial outlay of between $750 and $900. To maintain such a cellar, keep it properly stocked, will run to something between $250 and $300 or $400 a year, depending on how selectively and carefully you buy. Of course, there's no law requiring you to stock a cellar at once. Build it up over a period of time, a case this week, another next month, until the bins are filled. But the maintenance cost will stay at a fairly constant level.

A cellar of 200 to 250 bottles can be considered adequate but not elaborate. I try to maintain a 600-bottle cellar, and still don't have the storage capacity for some bottlings of lesser varieties that I'd like to keep on hand. But I don't consider my cellar a luxury for several reasons. Writing about food and cooking is part of my business, and to write about wine means tasting and sampling. Since we live in an area where a 100-mile trip is required to get a reasonably good selection of wines, it's necessary to keep an adequate stock on hand.

Incidentally, because the underground portion of my cellar is not easily accessible from our kitchen, I have a large cabinet adjoining the kitchen, in a utility room, that will accommodate about 150 bottles as well as a supply of jug wine. This makes frequent visits to the cellar itself unnecessary. You might find that such an arrangement suits your needs, if you have available for a cellar a large and suitably quiet but relatively isolated space.

Your own taste must be your final guide in stocking whatever type of storage space you decide on. Punitive tax laws in many states keep you from enjoying many bottlings of good U.S. wines; in some states it's easier and less costly for dealers to import wines from Europe than from an adjoining state. As a result, many dealers have on their shelves large stocks of European wines—some of them pretty bad—and virtually no bottlings of domestic wines.

If you have a few square feet of wall and floor space in a room near the kitchen, you can build a cabinet that will hold wines which will soon go to the table or be used for cooking. Here, where only a few bottles of several different types of wine are stored, notched shelves are a real convenience.

This worries the domestic vintners very little. Producers of the best varietal wines have more customers than filled bottles to sell them. U.S. wineries producing superior varietals don't need extensive advertising to move their stocks. The boom in U.S. varietals that began in the 1960s is not yet abating, though at the time this is being written expansion of vineyards is gradually allowing production to catch up with demand.

If you're a total stranger to wines and find the term "varietals" confusing, a simplified bit of explanation may be in order. In broadest terms, European wines centuries ago became identified by the name of the regions where they were produced. To keep this simple, let's take the best-known French wine types, Burgundy and Bordeaux, as examples. Each grape variety produces wine that has different characteristics, different tastes. The grape variety planted in most Burgundy vineyards is the Pinot Noir; in Bordeaux, it is the Cabernet Sauvignon. Over the years it became tacitly understood that a Burgundy wine would be predominantly made from Pinot Noir grapes, a wine of Bordeaux from Cabernet Sauvignon.

When U.S. wineries began producing after their Prohibition shutdown, the easiest way to identify their wines was by giving them names of the European regions. Great quantities of

Burgundy wine—made in the United States—flowed to market, and in most cases the Burgundy label was slapped on any bottle of red table wine without regard to the grapes used in the wine's production. For a short while, U.S. wines became a worldwide laughingstock, but time and less haste on the part of the vintners have cured that.

Today, some wine designations, such as Burgundy, Bordeaux, Rhine, and so on, have come to identify wine of a typical character rather than wines from a specific region in France. As U.S. oenology progressed, some vintners began producing wines in which a specific and desirable type of grape was predominantly used. Pinot Noir is a good example. Wines thus produced and identified by grape variety are called varietal wines. Those from the better vineyards are very good wines indeed, commanding premium prices and worth their cost.

Some small vineyards that specialize in varietals limit their sales to the wineries and to a few selected dealers in principal metropolitan areas. However, there are many larger wineries whose products are distributed nationally, and you should have no trouble finding several choices. Such major California vineyards as Almadén, Beaulieu, Beringer, Inglenook, Korbel, Martini, Masson, Sebastiani, and Wente all have nationwide distribution. So do the major New York State varietal producers: Boordy, Konstantin Frank, Gold Seal, Great Western, Taylor, and Widmer.

To get back to that 200-bottle cellar mentioned a few paragraphs back, you might put two-thirds or three-quarters of it into bottlings of such domestic varietals as Pinot Noir, Cabernet Sauvignon, Pinot Chardonnay, Sauvignon Blanc, and Semillon. Match these with bottlings of their French counterparts, red and white Burgundies and Bordeaux. These are the basic table wines that will cover all ordinary service. Before buying cases of any label, though, be sure to get a bottle or two of any wine you contemplate buying in quantity, and select for putting down only those that most appeal to you.

In choosing German-type wines, consider dividing your cellar space between the smooth sweet Rhines and the richer, fruitier Moselles. Italian wines might be represented by the classic Chianti and one or two of the more robust types such as

Barolo and Barbera. While you could quite easily stock a very extensive cellar with domestic wines, remember that there are some European vintages that have no precise U.S. counterparts, just as there are U.S. wines—Zinfandel is a good example—that have no European equivalent.

Many wines should not be laid down in great quantity because they have very short lives in bottle. Rosés, the suddenly popular Lambrusco, the petit Beaujolais, are among them. In general, wines with the lowest alcoholic content have the shortest lives. These should be bought in quantities only large enough to supply your needs for eight months to a year. Most of these lighter wines are already at their peak when delivered to dealers, and deteriorate quite rapidly rather than improving with age.

To use one type of wine as an example, rosé has been promoted as an all-purpose wine but very little has been said about its limited life in storage. If you think that putting down several cases of rosé is the quick and easy answer to creating a cellar, you'd probably find yourself with an oversupply of over-the-hill wine before your stock could be consumed.

Actually, rosé is far from being an all-occasion wine, suitable for serving with any kind of food. Overpromotion of rosé does this wine a great injustice, by claiming for it a characteristic it does not have and failing to stress its very real virtues. As an apéritif, as a midafternoon refresher on a hot day, or served at table with light foods that aren't highly seasoned, a good rosé is very good indeed. Served with a heavy beef roast or a spicy casserole dish, it can be a mistake verging on disaster and a waste of fine, delicately flavored wine.

While such light wines as rosé have a short bottle life, a big Burgundy or its varietal counterpart, a Pinot, will not mature to really prime condition until it has spent four to six years in bottle. After maturity it will live several more years, eight to ten if it's a very big wine, but it then goes into a slow decline and finally dies; the wine loses color and aroma, becomes thin and harsh. Bordeaux wines and the domestic Cabernets take longer than do the Burgundy types to mature; they peak after seven to ten years in the bottle and maintain that plateau for up to twenty years before declining.

White wines, which usually have a lower alcohol level than do reds, mature faster and die quicker. This is true of both the Burgundy and Bordeaux types—with a few rare exceptions among the Bordeaux wines, some of the whites maturing as slowly and living as long as the reds—and is even more applicable to the delicate Rhines and Moselles. Except for the rare and very costly Beerenauslesen and Trockenbeerenauslesen bottlings, the bottle life of Rhines is comparable to that of rosés, and Moselles have a slightly longer span. Give them two to four years to mature, five to peak, and after that they go downhill quite rapidly.

Most wines, red or white, reach dealers when they are only two or three years in the bottle. In both Europe and the United States, vintners must pay taxes on their stored wine stocks, and it becomes prohibitively expensive for them to hold wines in long-term storage and release them only when fully aged. A few vintners in all wine countries do put aside limited quantities of their very finest wines to be held until maturity; a few wine shippers and wholesalers also do this. However, such wines are necessarily very high in price when they finally come to market, and you'll do better by buying young wines and aging them yourself. That's the function a cellar is really intended to perform.

Run-of-the-mill wines, whether domestic or imported, do not mature in bottle at all. This is true of generically labeled imports as well as of domestic jug wines, and some wines bottled in fifths are actually jug-wine quality. All these have been pasteurized, to stop aging. European wines in this category identify themselves on labels only in the broadest regional terms, without pinpointing their precise origin by chateau or Schloss or castello. U.S. jug wines identify the producers, but are labeled only by type.

California jug wines are usually tagged as "Mountain Burgundy" or "Robust Burgundy" or "Hearty Burgundy," or even more simply as "Mountain Red" or "Mountain White." Eastern jug wines will usually be labeled "New York State Burgundy" or "Chablis" or "Rhine." Most of the domestic producers mentioned in an earlier paragraph offer very good jug wines. Some are exceptionally enjoyable: the Mountain Chablis of Almadén,

To re-bottle jug wine into fifths, primarily for convenience in storing and serving, you will need in addition to bottles and corks a funnel, a pair of tongs, and a hand-operated bottling plunger. Sterilize the bottles and let them cool. Wash the corks well and boil them; this softens and swells them so they will slip easily into the bottle and fit tightly. Retread corks are usually quite satisfactory for short-term storage, since boiling expands them to seal the hole made when originally pulled by the corkscrew.

After filling the bottles, slip a cork into the plunger; the cork will be hot, so handle it with tongs.

Seat the bottom of the plunger on the bottleneck, give the
handle a sturdy, steady push, and the job is done. The plunger
is built to seat properly and to stop when the cork is seated. A
bottling plunger like the one pictured will cost from $5 to $7.50,
and by rebottling you can buy jug wine when it's on special sale
and keep a quantity on hand. Since jug wines are almost always
pasteurized, they keep well, but will not improve with age.

Beringer's Los Hermanos Chablis, Masson's Burgundy, and
Italian-Swiss Colony's Zinfandel are all excellent and inexpensive.

For convenience in storing—and in chilling the whites—I
usually decant jug wines into sterilized fifth bottles and close
the bottles with retreaded corks. Whether new or old, corks
must be boiled before they are used, to soften them so they can
be inserted with a small hand-powered bottling-plunger. Boiling swells the corks, and will usually close the hole made by the
corkscrew when drawn. You must, of course, use both a wire-
thread corkscrew and care in opening. However, retreaded
corks will generally seal adequately for the short period jug
wines are stored before being used.

Opening a wine bottle's a lot easier with a good corkscrew. To help you tell bad from good: the straight-pull corkscrew at extreme left is not only unhandy to use, its screw has a solid shaft and shallow threads which tear up corks. Directly above it is a double-screw model of boxwood that has a threaded inner shaft and a wire screw; the inner shaft is operated by its own handle to lift the cork out after the screw is threaded in. Next on the right is a double-lever wing-type corkscrew; these are clumsy to use and this particular one has a solid-shaft screw. The needle extractor on the right operates by pumping compressed air through the hollow needle, which is driven straight through the cork; about four pumps of the handle starts the cork out. At bottom center, the waiter's corkscrew is probably the most versatile of all; it has its own knife for cutting foil, and its wire screw will not damage corks nor pull free from them as do solid-shaft screws.

1. To use the waiter's corkscrew, cut away the foil just below the neck ridge with the corkscrew's built-in knife.

2. Thread the screw into the cork. Always turn the bottle rather than the corkscrew; this makes it easier to keep the screw centered in the cork.

3. Bend the notched lever down until it engages the top of the bottleneck, lift on the handle, and the cork is drawn straight up.

Now you've decided about your cellar; you know whether you want or need one, and approximately what wines you'll keep in it. Let's move on to the occasions when it's your job as host to choose and pour the wines for dinner. The task falls into three parts: pre-dinner, the dinner itself, and a selection of after-dinner beverages.

It's become increasingly popular to serve a chilled white wine instead of liquor with pre-dinner nibbles. If you choose to do this, select one of the dry whites rather than a wine on the sweet side; sweet things before dinner blunt the tastebuds. A lightly chilled dry sherry is also a good pre-dinner choice. Sherry runs a wide gamut of dryness, so you'll want to do some tasting before deciding which label to offer your guests.

Several domestic producers now produce excellent sherries made by the traditional *solera* process. A rule of thumb in making a blind choice is that the paler the sherry, the drier it will be. The drier domestic sherries are usually identified as "Cocktail Sherry," while the imports will be labeled as "Fino," "Vino de Pasto," "Amontillado," "Oloroso," and "Golden" or "Brown," perhaps as "Cream." Fino is the driest, really too dry for those just getting acquainted with sherry; Amontillado is a good all-around choice; and the dark sweet grades from Oloroso on are too sweet and heavy to be suitable for a pre-dinner appetizer. Save them for later.

As for the nibbles to go with your pre-dinner drink, we'll get to them in a later chapter. Wine and food go together everywhere except in a long printed discussion.

Most of the old "inflexible rules" of wine service have long ago gone into the wastebasket. Nobody feels inhibited any more about serving a dry white wine with red meat, or a light red wine with fish or fowl, but from the standpoint of taste affinities, the old rules have a lot going for them. Any of the heavier red wines—a mature Burgundy, a deep-toned Bordeaux, a rich Barolo—would and will smother the flavor of a lightly sauced poached trout or sole. Conversely, a highly seasoned entrée will blanket the delicate fragrance of a Rhine or Moselle. If you feel like breaking the red wine/red meat, white wine/white meat tradition, that's fine. Just be sure when you do that you choose a wine compatible with and complementary to the meal's main course.

Although really formal dinners are vanishing, there's much to be said for the grand style of dining with its traditional wine/food marriages. There are affinities of taste between soups and sherry, fish or shellfish and Chablis, fowl and Rhine or Moselle, beef and Burgundy, lamb and Bordeaux, and desserts and Sauternes. Really, though, the only traditional service rule that you should think twice before breaking is that which calls for white wines to precede reds if both are served at a meal.

Just as long-standing wine/food associations have been pushed aside, so have the rules for using specially shaped glasses for different kinds of wines. There never was much sense to these rules, anyhow; most of them came into being because of regional differences in the glassblower's art—the Burgundy glasshouses favored one shape for wineglasses, those of Bordeaux favored another. When wines began traveling away from their native regions, the glasses that had been associated with them went along as hitchhikers. The only practical tradition in connection with wineglasses was that of serving Rhine and Moselle wines in tinted glasses; in the early days of German wine production, their wines were invariably cloudy, and the tinted glasses hid this flaw. Today, a tinted glass for German wines—or any wine, for that matter—makes no sense at all.

Nor does it figure, in these mobile days, for householders to feel it necessary to keep five or six shapes of wineglasses on hand: one for Burgundy, another for Bordeaux, still another for Rhine, and so on. Having glasses of more than one shape on the table is sensible only when two kinds of wine are being served at the same meal, and then only because it's easier for both host and guest to keep from getting the two confused, as might happen if the same-shaped glass was used for both red and white.

What is important in a wineglass is its shape; the bowl must curve toward the center at its top. This shape traps the wine's aroma and releases it under the drinker's nose, important since what we think of as our sense of taste depends very largely on our sense of smell. As long as your wineglasses do the job of concentrating the aroma and releasing it when the glass is lifted to one's lips, it doesn't matter a bit whether the bowl of the glass is shaped like a bubble or a tulip. However, since the color and

Traditional and magnum wineglasses, shown filled to an appropriate level. From left, traditional round-bowl Burgundy glass; magnum Burgundy; traditional glass (often called a "claret glass") for red Bordeaux; magnum tulip-shaped Bordeaux; standard-size tulip-shaped Bordeaux (both are equally suited to red and white Bordeaux or Burgundy); and Rhine-wine glass. Tallest of the grouping is the magnum tulip-shaped Bordeaux; it stands 9 inches high and if filled to the brim will hold 22 ounces. The glass pictured has in it about 9 ounces of wine, the standard tulip next to it contains about 4 ounces.

clarity of a wine also contribute to your appreciation and enjoyment of it, your wineglasses should be of thin crystal, untinted
and unadorned with ornamentation.

Today's most popular wineglasses are the big magnums.
Soon after these first made their appearance in the late 1950s
we got a few and tried them out. They proved so satisfactory
that we abandoned all the glasses of various shapes and sizes
that had been eating up space in our cabinets. With a few
execptions, we now use only two sizes and shapes of wineglass.
One is in the tulip shape generally associated with Bordeaux
wines; it stands nine inches tall and will hold 22 ounces. The
other has a bubble-shaped bowl, stands seven inches high, and
will hold 18 ounces. In these we serve all table wines.

For sherry, we kept our flutes, which we prefer to the
Spanish *copita* glasses; for other fortified wines, we use a small
tulip-shaped glass. Though they're the very devil to wash and
dry, we retained our hollow-stemmed flutes for Champagne,
chiefly because the wine seems to keep its life longer in them
than it does in saucer-shaped glasses. We also kept our brandy
balloons and some small liqueur glasses. However, even
though the magnum-sized glasses take up more space per glass,
we've gained room in our cabinets by the switch, which cut our
table-wine glass styles from five down to two.

When serving in these big glasses you naturally fill them
only about one-third full. Still, that's a generous seven or eight
ounces of wine as compared to the four ounces that can be
served in average-sized glasses. It's enough to carry most guests
through a full meal without the host finding himself jumping up
and down through dinner to refill emptied glasses. Incidentally,
plan to open one bottle of wine for each four guests at your
dinner table. If you feel opulent, you might consider buying
some of your wines in magnums, which hold the equivalent of
two standard bottles.

There is, incidentally, a slight difference—about two
ounces—between the capacities of European and U.S. wine
bottles. European bottles hold three-quarters of a quart, or 24
ounces; U.S. bottles hold four-fifths of a quart, 25.6 ounces. And
if you're wondering about the big bottle sizes—all but the magnum legendary by now—they are the Jeroboam, which holds

four bottles; the Rehoboam, six bottles; the Methuselah, eight bottles; the Salmanazar, 12 bottles; and the Nebuchadnezzar, 20 bottles. Going in the other direction, there are half-bottles, which hold 12 ounces in Europe and 13 in the U.S.; and splits, which contain seven to eight ounces, depending on the country of origin, and are just about right for one person for one meal.

There's another wine tradition which many shrug off as being nothing more than an unneeded frill, part of the mystique of wine service. This is the need to let wines—especially old wines—breathe for a while before they are served. There is, though, a definite reaction between wine and air. Opening the bottle an hour or so before dinner allows this reaction to take place, and a wine that has been treated to a breathing spell will taste measurably better than one opened and poured at once.

Very old wines that have thrown sediment will need to be opened in advance anyhow. A bottle that shows even a trace of sediment should be stood upright and the sediment allowed to settle to the bottom; it's impossible to open such a bottle without disturbing this perfectly natural deposit that all living wines make in their containers with the passing of time. At least 24 and often 36 hours will be required for the wine to clear. It should then be opened and decanted with a light behind the bottle so you can see when to stop pouring. This moment

A special funnel for use in decanting wine has a slanting spout that guides the flow so the wine will run down the side of the decanter.

arrives when the sediment begins to travel up toward the bottle's neck. There is a special funnel made for decanting that has a generous cup and a slanted spout which guides the flow of wine to the neck of the decanter and prevents over-aeration of the wine. You can do without this little accessory, of course, and tilt a regular funnel to achieve the same purpose.

One final thought before we finish dinner. You're well aware that red wines are customarily served at room temperature, white wines chilled. However, don't make the mistake of serving a red wine that's gotten too warm while waiting to be served on a hot midsummer evening; a temperature of about 60 to 65 degrees is right for most reds. The twin to this mistake is serving an overchilled white wine. Except for Champagne, which should be very cold, white wines are best when served at a temperature of 45 to 50 degrees. Two or three hours in the refrigerator is enough to put them in the best shape for serving. There's now a flexible thermometer gadget that can be slipped around a wine bottle to give you its true temperature, so it's no longer necessary to guess by feeling the bottle.

If you think any of the traditions of wine service are foolish, test their validity for yourself. Taste identical bottles of red wine, one at room temperature, the other chilled; do the same thing for bottles of white. Again using identical bottles, handle one with care and let it rest before opening, and bounce its twin around for a while just before it's uncorked, to see what effect bruising has. And taste identical bottles, one that has been allowed to breathe, the other opened and poured at once. If you test and taste with an open mind, your tastebuds will tell you quickly that there's a lot to be said for traditions.

After-Dinner Drinks

In deciding what to do about after-dinner drinks, there are four ways to go. One is Champagne, the second is Cognac or brandy, the third is liqueurs, the fourth is fortified wines. Like everything else in life, your guide to a choice will have to be your own taste and your own purse.

If you elect to offer Champagne, have both wine and

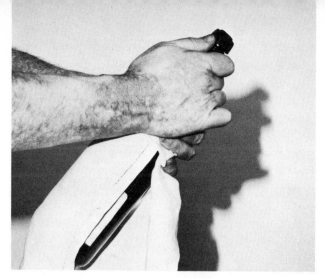

To learn how a Champagne bottle is opened without a froth of wine gushing from it, observe the thumb—not the shadow of a vine-wreathed Bacchus grinning in the background. Press the cork with a thumb, up and away from you, against the bottleneck, until it moves a fraction of an inch. Give the bottle a quarter-turn and repeat; keep turning and pushing until the cork emerges with a satisfying but subdued "pop." The sidewise pressure allows a gradual release of gas and keeps the gas from causing the foam that reduces the time Champagne sparkles after it's been poured.

glasses well chilled. As mentioned earlier, Champagne should be served colder than still wines. Put the bottles in the refrigerator—not the freezer—four to five hours before they will be opened; longer refrigeration will do no harm. An hour or so will chill the glasses enough.

Contrary to some popular beliefs, Champagne should not sound like a cannon being fired when it's opened, nor should the cork hit the ceiling followed by a gushing of froth from the bottle. There is a very easy way to open Champagne properly— really much easier than opening a bottle the wrong way. After stripping off the foil from the neck, untwist and remove the wire cage that keeps the bottle from blowing its cork while the wine is stored. Drape the bottle in a big napkin or small towel; this isn't to catch a sudden gush of wine, but to give your fingers a firm grip on the slippery, moisture-beaded bottle.

Wrap your hands around the bottle's neck, thumbs up, and press the side of the cork with your thumbs. Turn the bottle and press again, with a slight upward pressure. This will bring the cork up about a quarter of an inch from the top of the bottleneck. Turn and press again. By now you should hear a very faint

Three types of Champagne glasses, filled to a suitable serving level. The hollow-stemmed saucer at left and the hollow-stemmed tulip in the center seem to help the wine to hold its bubbles longer than does the saucer at right, but the hollow-stemmed glasses are hard to clean.

hissing when you press, excess gas escaping from the bottle. Another half-turn of the bottle, another application of pressure, pushing the cork more sideways than upward, and remove the cork entirely with one swift twist. It will pop, but won't explode, nor will the wine gush out. You can pour easily, and the Champagne will bubble and foam satisfactorily, and will actually have a longer bubbly life than it would if you'd yanked the cork and let all the gas discharge at once.

One bottle of Champagne serves four scantily. For some reason, most people drink more Champagne than they do still wines. If you want to be a truly munificent host, serve four guests from a magnum of Champagne; this allows two glasses and a small top-off for each guest.

Brandy is another traditional after-dinner beverage. Cognac is a special type of brandy produced in a very small region of France. It is perhaps the finest brandy of them all, though there are now some excellent U.S. brandies, and those from other nations—Spain, Germany, Greece—have very devoted adherents. However, unless you have access to out-standing brandies of superior quality, you'd do well to limit your after-dinner offering to Cognac. It should be served only straight, in big balloon snifters or liqueur glasses. If you have a guest who asks for a mixed brandy, or one on the rocks, don't waste Cognac on him or her; serve a lesser brandy, and reserve your Cognac for those who appreciate its unadorned flavor.

There are 4 ounces of Cognac in the balloon glass at left, not quite 2 ounces in the Dutch brandy next to it. If you buy balloon glasses, be sure the mouth is big enough to make drinking easy; some balloons have such tiny mouths that they're clumsy to drink from. The other three glasses are for liqueurs; each contains about 2 ounces.

From left are two sherry glasses, the flute and the *copita*. Both contain about 4 ounces of wine; the same quantity is in each of the three fortified wineglasses from center to right. All are traditional shapes, all pleasant to sip from.

Cognac is offered by most distillers in several grades, but usually only a producer's top grade, generally identified by the letters "VSOP" on the bottle—"Very Superior Old Pale"— should be considered. Your choice of brands is a subjective thing; only your own tastebuds can tell you whether you prefer the some-what boisterous flavor of Hennessy, the more subtle nuances of Martell or Hine, the assertiveness of Otard, or the fruitiness of Remy Martin. There are some French brandies, notably Courvoisier, which just miss being classified as Cognac because they are not produced in the Cognac area. You might enjoy one of these, or you might enjoy an Armagnac, which in its own right qualifies to stand beside Cognac. Or one of the brandies of Spain, Portugal, Germany, or Greece might be just what your tastebuds have been awaiting. The only way to decide is to try them all.

Liqueurs are available in an almost endless array, if you decide to go this route, and new candidates appear almost daily to vie for attention and acceptance. Most of the newer liqueurs are proprietary bottlings, which means that they are produced by only one firm which in theory owns their formulas. However, today's brisk competition for the liqueur market keeps any formula from being a secret very long; most of the new items are copied almost before they reach the dealers' shelves. The duplicates vary little in taste from the originals.

Only a small select trio of proprietary liqueurs has remained unduplicated over the years. The three are Chartreuse, Benedictine, and Grand Marnier. All have been imitated, but never exactly duplicated, so if you want to enjoy them you must buy the originals.

All other after-dinner potations are available under several different labels, and the only real difference between them is the shape of the bottles in which they come. There is also a big array of generic liqueurs, and all these are offered by several bottlers. Your taste may lead you to prefer one maker's product over that of another, for there is always a slight difference between them. But basically you get the same flavor from such generic liqueurs as Triple Sec, Crème de Menthe, Kirsch or Kirschwasser, Crème de Cacao, Anisette, Curaçao, and so on. The same situation is found among the fruit brandies, all of which are available under the labels of several producers. If there is a true fruit brandy on the market today, its presence has escaped me. At one time, fruit brandies were distilled from the fermented juices of the fruits named on their labels; today, all are fairly mediocre grape brandies flavored with fruit syrup.

Because the array of liqueurs is so huge, it's easy to go wild in buying them. From a practical standpoint you might limit yourself to three or four in order to be sure of pleasing the tastes of all your guests. These might include one of the mint-flavored drinks such as Crème de Menthe, or one of the new mint-chocolate items. Another might be orange-based, Curaçao or Triple Sec, and a third could be either something sharp and brilliant like Kirsch, or bland and chocolatey like Crème de Cacao.

For liqueur service you will need tiny glasses that hold only an ounce or two. Because the flavor of liqueurs is so concentrated, a serving of three-quarters of an ounce is usually adequate. Bottles of liqueurs last a long time because of this, and liqueurs do not deteriorate after being opened. And you get double duty from liqueurs; they're very useful in cooking and in flavoring desserts as a topping.

Fortified wines—Port, Madeira, and Cream or Oloroso sherry—were once the most favored of all after-dinner beverages, with Port holding a slight lead over Madeira and the sherries coming in third. A flood of cheap Ports, both domestic and imported, dropped into the U.S. market in the early 1950s, and gave this wine a bad name from which it is only now recovering. Although the finest Ports once came from the land that gave them their name, the Portuguese Ports no longer stand head and shoulders above their U.S. counterparts. Domestic producers—Paul Masson in particular—offer Ports from the traditional Souza grape that equal all but the very best imports and are superior to run-of-the-mill Portuguese bottlings.

Madeira has already been discussed briefly, as has sherry. The former wine was once a monopoly of the little island of Madeira, but Masson now offers a very satisfactory domestic version. Imported Madeiras continue to offer the only source of this wine in its several degrees of dryness, however. These are Sercial and Rainwater, both pale and dry; Bual, which is golden and slightly sweet; and Malmsey, which is a deep gold and very sweet. The Masson Madeira most closely resembles Bual, a sort of mid-range compromise. For after-dinner service, Bual or Malmsey is recommended.

Sherry, also touched on earlier, makes a very fine after-dinner offering in its sweeter versions, Oloroso or Golden or Cream. It can be served equally correctly at room temperature or lightly chilled. The number of labels under which good sherries are offered seems endless, both in imported and domestic versions. Labels which have always been reliable for me include Gonzalez Byass, Harvey's, Marques de Merito, and Pedro Domecq among the imports, and on the domestic side, Almadén, Paul Masson, Great Western, and Taylor. Many others are equally satisfactory, but all those I've mentioned are nationally distributed and available almost everywhere.

Fortified wines can be served in almost any kind of wineglass that has a total capacity of four to six ounces; since the usual portion is two or three ounces, it would be lost in a bigger glass. There is the traditional *copita* glass and the sherry flute, the modified tulip-shaped glass usually associated with Port, and a wide selection of old-fashioned bell-mouth and modern-decor Scandinavian-designed glasses. All are equally suitable for any fortified wine.

Mixed Drink Formulas

First, your cocktail party shopping list. In addition to liquors, you'll need a few other supplies. These are:

Dry vermouth
Angostura Bitters
Tomato juice
Sweet vermouth
Grenadine
Club soda, other mixers
Orange juice (Fresh-squeezed is best, but frozen concentrate saves a lot of time. Avoid canned "orange drinks"; most contain only three or four ounces of juice, the rest is water.)

Lemons (fresh ones are essential; the peels are used for garnish)

Oranges (some drinks are garnished with thin orange slices)

Stuffed green olives (pimiento or almond-stuffed; avoid anchovy-stuffed because they make drinks taste fishy)

Tiny pickled onions (again, garnish)

Bar cherries (a maraschino-type cherry, pitted, the stems replaced)

Bar syrup (Make this yourself—it takes five minutes and is easier to use than sugar—but your shopping list may need a reminder that sugar is required.)

Cocktail toothpicks

To make bar syrup, dissolve 4 cups sugar in 1 cup water and stir in the white of an egg. Bring to a boil. Skim the froth that rises until no more appears and the syrup is crystal-clear. Cool, pour into a bottle. The syrup keeps for several months without refrigeration, but keep the bottle tightly stoppered or in a time the syrup will crystalize. A spoonful (or other measure) of bar syrup equals one of sugar.

You will also need a few tools: a heavy mixing glass or two—modern bar practice is to stir, not shake drinks—a two-ounce jigger measure, a long-handled stirring spoon, a fork or pick to move olives and cherries and onions from containers to glasses, a bar strainer, a knife, a small cutting board. See the illustration if you're in doubt as to the identity of any of these items.

Prechill everything you'll be using, if this is at all possible. The easiest way to keep things cold in an improvised bar set-up is to get a big ice chest of expanded plastic foam, discard the lid, strew the bottom with ice, and use it to store bottles and garnish containers in. Move these in small quantities from storage to bar or serving-table as needed. Don't forget a couple of buckets on the floor, one for waste liquids, the other for rinsing glasses. And your reserve stock of ice can go under the bar, too, in its own container.

With the ingredients and equipment listed—plus liquor, naturally—you can mix all the most popular cocktail party drinks, using the standard formulas that follow.

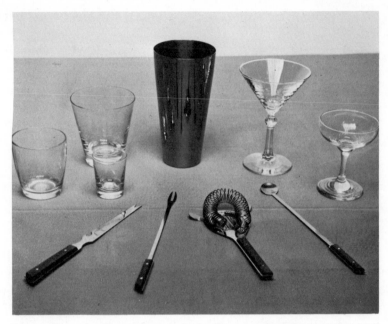

Bar tools you will need include knife, garnish fork, strainer, and stirring spoon, all in the foreground. In the rear from left are standard and double Old Fashioned or bar glasses and jigger glass; mixer is in center; double and standard cocktail glasses are at right.

Martini

1 jigger dry vermouth   3 jiggers gin

Put chunks of ice in the mixing glass, pour in vermouth and gin, stir, strain into cocktail glass, garnish with an olive.

Gibson

½ jigger dry vermouth   4 jiggers gin

Put chunks of ice in a mixing glass, pour in vermouth and gin, stir, strain into cocktail glass, garnish with pickled onion or lemon peel.

(A Gibson, as you see, is a ginnier Martini. The Martini is perhaps the most-abused cocktail in existence. It originated in 1869 on a ferryboat plying between San Francisco and the Suisun Bay port of Martinez; the drink was originally mixed with sweet vermouth and gin in equal parts and was called the "Martinez Cocktail." It was picked up by a barman on one of the British Cunard liners that put in at San Francisco, and appeared on the Cunard bar list as the "Martinez Cocktail" until about 1885, when through either a printer's error or a bit of financial persuasion by a salesman for Martini & Rossi Vermouths its name was changed to "Martini." About 1900, dry vermouth was substituted for sweet and the drink became the "Dry Martini." During the 1920s the ratio of vermouth to gin was changed to 1:3; later, in the 1930s, the Gibson came along as a cocktail made with a 1:4 or 1:5 vermouth-gin ratio. Gin addicts now order "a Martini, easy on the vermouth" because they're probably embarrassed to call for a tot of straight gin. There is no such drink as a "Vodka Martini." Mixing vermouth and vodka does not a Martini make; the flavor of gin combined with vermouth is essential to the Martini's integrity.)

Tom Collins

½ lime   1½ ounces gin
1 tsp bar syrup   Club soda
½ ounce fresh lemon juice

Fill a tall thin glass half-full of cracked ice. Squeeze the lime half over the ice and drop the rind into the glass. Add bar syrup, lemon juice, gin, fill glass with club soda, stir, add a cherry for garnish.

John Collins

Originally made with Holland gin as opposed to the Tom or London Dry gin used in the Tom Collins, a John is now a Tom Collins made with Bourbon.

Whiskey Sour

2 ounces fresh lemon juice	1½ ounces Bourbon
1 tsp bar syrup	2 ounces club soda

Put ice in mixing glass, pour over it the lemon juice, bar syrup, and Bourbon, stir once or twice very briskly, add club soda, stir gently, strain into a Whiskey Sour glass or a wineglass, add a cherry for garnish.

(Though Whiskey Sours rank about seventh on the drink popularity poll, you can make a base in advance by mixing the lemon juice, bar syrup, and whiskey in the proper ratios and putting the mix in a bottle; when the drink is called for, pour 4½ ounces over ice, add soda, stir, and strain. Saves time.)

Old Fashioned (original formula)

1 lump sugar	2 cherries
Dash Angostura Bitters	1½ ounces Bourbon
Strip of lemon peel	Club soda
Strip of orange peel	

In an Old Fashioned glass, crush the sugar cube after dashing the bitters on it; twist the peel strips and drop them in the glass, put in a big chunk of ice, pour the Bourbon over the ice, fill glass with club soda. Don't stir. Add cherries.

But nobody makes an Old Fashioned with lump sugar any more. Use 1 tsp bar syrup, stir the bitters into it, and then proceed as above.

(Some people expect a fruit salad when they ask for an Old Fashioned: a strip of pineapple, a slice of orange, even a strip of cucumber—this last request came from a very new mother who must've been frightened during pregnancy by a Pimm's Cup. Let your conscience be your guide as to how far you want to go down this road to degradation of a basically sound drink.)

Manhattan

Dash of orange bitters   1½ ounces Bourbon
1½ ounces sweet vermouth

Put ice chunks in the mixing glass, dash in the bitters, pour in vermouth and Bourbon, stir quickly, strain into a cocktail glass, garnish with a cherry.

Rob Roy

This is a Manhattan made with Scotch instead of Bourbon.

Tall Presbyterian

1½ ounces Scotch   Strip of lemon peel
Dash of lemon juice   Gingerale

Fill a tall glass about half full of ice chunks. Pour Scotch and lemon juice over the ice, twist the peel strip over the glass and drop it in, fill with gingerale. (Few object if club soda is substituted, but it's nice to stick to original drink formulas.)

Bloody Mary (original recipe)

4 ounces tomato juice   1 ounce fresh lemon juice
1½ ounces vodka   Few drops Angostura Bitters

All ingredients should be prechilled, and so should the glass. Combine tomato juice, vodka, lemon juice, bitters, stir quickly. Don't add ice to dilute the mixture.

(It's easier to mix this popular drink in advance in a pitcher that can be bedded on ice and poured from as needed than it is to make a fresh drink each time. This is the original Bloody Mary formula; it's now changed in many places to a simple mixture of tomato juice and vodka.)

Screwdriver

4 ounces fresh orange juice   ½ ounce fresh lemon juice
1½ ounces vodka

Have all ingredients prechilled, combine and stir.

(This drink first surfaced as the Orange Blossom in the 1920s, and was made then with bathtub gin. Like its kissing cousin the Bloody Mary, it's easier to mix this Prohibition-era retread in a pitcher and keep it on hand to be poured when required.)

Vodka Daisy

2 ounces lemon juice   1½ ounces vodka
1 ounce bar syrup   Club soda
1 ounce grenadine

Fill a tall glass two-thirds full of ice chunks, pour over them the lemon juice, bar syrup, grenadine, and vodka, fill with club soda, stir gently.

(Another Prohibition retread; the Daisy began life along the Mexican border in the 1920s as a Tequila-tamer for palates that couldn't handle the fiery distillation of maguey juice in Mexican style—straight, with lemon and salt before and after.)

Horse's Neck (nonalcoholic)

Rind of a lemon peeled into a   Dash of Angostura Bitters
    single thin strip   Gingerale

Let the lemon peel fall in a spiral to the bottom of a tall glass while holding one end of the strip on the glass rim; fill glass three-quarters full of ice chunks, dash bitters over the ice, fill glass with gingerale.

Shirley Temple (nonalcoholic)

2 ounces grenadine   Gingerale

Fill a tall thin glass three-quarters full of ice chunks, pour in the grenadine, fill glass with gingerale, add a cherry for garnish.

(According to the most reliable apocrypha, the drink was created in New York's "21" during the 1930s when the then-child movie star visited the establishment.)

Punches

Punches are the easiest and simplest mass refreshers to handle, though this should not be taken to suggest that an indiscriminate mixture of any liquids you might have handy can be stirred together and produce a punch of surpassing excellence. Like anything else worth drinking—or eating—a punch should be mixed with a decent regard for the compatibility of its ingredients. In this day of canned and packaged everything, a lot of people who are normally sane and sensible simply buy several cans of the tinted water labeled "fruit drink" or several packets of those chemical powders that produce sweet, virulently colored liquids when added to water, and combine them in a punchbowl. Even when enlightened by the addition of spirits, such mixtures taste like nothing except what they are.

Punches are not difficult to construct, and most of the work of making them can be done in advance. Indeed, it *should* be done in advance, even a day or so before the punch will be served, so the ingredients will have time to consummate a happy marriage in the cold dark privacy of your refrigerator. With a suitable quantity of punch base at hand, the host's job of replenishing a rapidly emptying bowl becomes a simple matter of pouring in the required quantity of base, adding sparkling water or Champagne, and stirring briefly.

There are a couple of essentials connected with the making of a really superior punch. First, when fruit is called for in the formula, use fresh ripe fruits if at all possible. Only fresh fruits have in them the natural acids in proper ratio to natural sugars that give a punch depth and tartness in pleasing balance. Frozen fruits are a second choice, canned fruits a very bad third choice; in both these, natural balances have been altered by the addition of ascorbic acid and sugar. Next, have all ingredients prechilled at the time they are combined in the punch bowl. Finally, use a big block of ice, not several small pieces, in the punch bowl, and as host, ladle the punch over the ice now and then, dipping deeply to the bottom, to keep the flavor alive.

Observing these rules will assure you of serving a punch with a flavor that's memorable, a flavor that will not be unduly diluted by melting ice and result in a weak and watery punch as the day moves on. If you want to be fancy, freeze your own ice block in a big ring mold, a Bundt cake pan, or an angelfood-cake tube-pan, to produce a circular ice ring that matches the punch bowl's curves.

Since man first began distilling the juice of sugarcane, rum has been the mainstay of punches because of its affinity with all kinds of fruits. In punches calling for dark rum, get a high-proof Haitian or Jamaican rum; both are available in 110-, 125-, and 151-proof bottlings as well as the now-usual 90- or 100-proof. While the punch formulas are based on normal-proof rum, you can adjust them for more potent rums by reducing the amount of rum by four ounces for each ten proof-points above 100. And where dark rum is indicated in the formula, don't switch to light rum or you'll ruin the flavor.

Some nonalcoholic punches are included among the formulas, and these are usually based on tea. Neither "instant" nor bagged tea has enough potency to stand its ground and make a proper contribution to flavor when used in a punch. Only Heaven and the processors know what modifications are inflicted on genuine tea in its conversion to "instant," what colorings and chemical "flavor stabilizers" and deliquescents are added to the final product. Whatever these are, they do not produce a tea that tastes like real tea.

A similar mystery surrounds tea bags. Most of them are labeled as "orange pekoe," which is a description of tealeaf size and gives no information whatever as to the type of tea in the bags, its geographical origin, or its quality. Buy a good bulk tea for your punch, one that is honestly labeled and tells you exactly what you're getting. Your best choices are a sturdy Darjeeling from India or an Oolong from Taiwan. Infuse the tea properly, making it double-strength, and your punch will have the kind of character and individuality that your guests will recognize as superior, even if they're unable to explain why.

To make 1 pint of double-strength tea for a punch base, use 8 tablespoons of bulk tea and 2½ cups boiling water. Use a heavy earthenware teapot or lidded bowl in which to steep the tea. Fill it with boiling water in advance of brewing the tea and let it stand until the vessel is very hot, then empty it and immediately put in the tea leaves and pour over them the briskly boiling water. Cover the container and let it stand 15 minutes. Strain 2 cups of the tea into a clean warmed jar and let cool naturally.

Formulas for a half-dozen punches, four alcoholic and two temperance, follow. These should serve for any occasion, summer or winter. There is also a recipe for Sangria, an increasingly popular wine punch. And because the Christmas season is a time for entertaining friends, formulas for an excellent eggnog, for the traditional Tom & Jerry, and for an old-fashioned Wassail Bowl have been added as a sort of postscript.

Schuylkill Fish House Punch

2 quarts 90-proof Jamaican rum	1 quart fresh lemon juice
1 bottle Cognac	1½ cups bar syrup
4 ounces peach brandy	2 quarts cold water

Combine the ingredients in a big crock, still well, chill several hours before pouring over a block of ice in the punch bowl. With one exception—the substitution of bar syrup for loaf sugar, which is no longer readily available—this is the original recipe that dates back to 1732.

Makes about 40 servings. The quantities of ingredients can be halved if a small number of servings is desired.

Rhenish Punch

2 bottles Rhine wine	1 bottle Champagne
½ pint Curaçao	1 quart club soda
¼ pint light rum	Bar syrup or grenadine
½ tsp Angostura Bitters	

Combine the wine, Curaçao, rum, and bitters in a large container and chill several hours, or overnight. Put a big piece of ice in the punch bowl, pour the base over it, add Champagne and club soda; taste and adjust for sweetness with bar syrup or grenadine.

Makes about 20 servings.

St. Cecelia Punch

6 or 8 slices fresh pineapple	½ pint light rum
3 lemons or 5 limes, sliced thinly	1 pint freshly brewed green tea
	1½ cups bar syrup
1 pint Cognac	1 bottle Champagne
1 pint peach brandy	1 quart club soda

Put the pineapple and lemon or lime slices in a bowl, pour the Cognac over them, and marinate overnight. Several hours before serving, drain off the liquid from the fruit and combine it with the peach brandy, rum, tea, and bar syrup. Just before serving, put the ice block in the punch bowl, pour the liquor base over it, then the Champagne and club soda. Add the fruit slices for garnish.

Makes about 30 servings.

Charleston Field Artillery Punch

1 quart brandy
1 pint dark Jamaican rum
1 pint fresh pineapple juice
1 pint fresh orange juice
1 pint double-strength black
    tea

1 cup fresh lemon juice (or lime
    juice)
¼ cup bar syrup
1 bottle Champagne
1quart club soda

Combine the liquors, fruit juices, tea, and bar syrup in a large container and chill several hours or overnight. Put a block of ice in the punch bowl, pour the liquor base over it, and pour the chilled Champagne and club soda over the ice. For garnish, float thin slices of lime or lemon on the punch.

Makes about 30 servings.

Cardinal Punch (nonalcoholic)

3 pounds cranberries
2 lemons
2 cups sugar

1 pint fresh orange juice
1 cup bar syrup
2 quarts gingerale

Wash the cranberries but do not dry them, let them drain and leave some drops of water clinging to their skins. Put cranberries in a saucepan, slice the lemon thickly and add it to the berries, sprinkle over them the sugar. Cook covered over low heat, stirring occasionally, until the cranberries burst and become mushy. Cool, squeeze through a ricer, or pass through a blender and strain through heavy cloth, twisting the cloth into a bag to extract all the juice. Squeeze the reserved lemon and combine the juice with the cranberry juice, orange juice, and bar syrup. Chill several hours or overnight. Put a block of ice in the punch bowl, pour the syrup over it, then pour over it the chilled gingerale. Taste and adjust with more bar syrup or with lemon juice if too sweet. Float a few whole cranberries in the bowl for garnish.

Makes about 20 servings.

(You can bypass preparing your own cranberry juice if you're lazy, but the canned juice you buy will be too attenuated to give the punch its true flavor. If you're going to the trouble of making it at all, do it the right way.)

Ceylon Punch (nonalcoholic)

1 pint double-strength black tea	2 cups grenadine
1 quart fresh orange juice	1 cup fresh minced pineapple
1 cup fresh lime juice	2 tbsp bar syrup
	2½ quarts club soda

Strain all the fruit juices. Combine all ingredients into a large jar and chill several hours or overnight. Put an ice block in the punch bowl, pour the punch base over it, then the chilled club soda. Taste; add more bar syrup if too tart, more lime juice if too sweet.

Makes about 20 servings.

Sangria

3 oranges	2 bottles very dry red wine;
2 lemons	the best is that used in
1 lime	Spain, a harsh wiry
1 cup bar syrup	young Rioja

Slice very thinly 1 orange and 1 lemon and take three or four thin slices from the center of the lime. Set aside the end slices for squeezing. Put the center slices in a bowl; squeeze the reserved oranges and lemon and the discarded ends from the lime and other orange and lemon. Strain the fruit juices and pour over the slices, add bar syrup, cover the container. Chill about 2 hours—longer, if you wish. To serve, put half the fruit slices and half the liquid in which they marinated into a pitcher, pour in 1 bottle wine, stir, and serve in big wine glasses. Discard the fruit, after empty-ing the pitcher, put in the other half of the fruit and syrup, the second bottle of wine, and complete the service. Or, use two pitchers; divide between them the fruit, syrup, and wine.

Makes about 12 servings of 6 ounces each.

Eggnog

12 fresh eggs	¼ pint heavy cream
¾ cup superfine sugar	1 pint milk
1 pint brandy	Nutmeg
½ pint dark Jamaican rum	

Separate the eggs, set aside the whites. Beat the yolks while adding the sugar; beat until all sugar is dissolved. Stir the brandy and rum into the beaten yolks, add slowly while continuing to beat. Put the mixture into a jar, cover tightly, and set aside to stand at least 3 hours while the liquor cooks the egg yolks. About an hour before the eggnog is to be served, beat 1 cup of the egg whites quite stiff. In the punch bowl, blend them with the yolks, cream, and milk. Beat the remaining egg whites until firm but still soft, float them on top of the mixture in the punch bowl, dust the top with freshly grated nutmeg.

Makes 12 to 16 portions; a serving of this rich drink should be 6 ounces.

Tom & Jerry

12 fresh eggs	1½ pints fresh milk
¾ cup bar syrup	Boiling water
12 ounces brandy	Nutmeg
12 ounces dark Jamaican rum	

Separate the eggs, beat the yolks until frothy; beat the whites, adding the bar syrup while beating. Fold yolks and whites together. The other ingredients should be kept in separate containers; this drink is not mixed in quantity, but in individual servings.

To serve: put 2 tbsp egg batter, 1 ounce brandy, 1 ounce rum, and 3 tbsp hot milk into a thick, heavy 8-ounce mug. Fill with boiling water, grate nutmeg over the top.

Makes 12 generous servings.

Wassail Bowl

Peel of ½ lemon   1 cup ale or beer
½ cup bar syrup   1 bottle dry red wine
1 stick cinnamon   Nutmeg
5 whole cloves

In a deep saucepan put 1 pint water and bring to a boil. Add the lemon peel, bar syrup, cinnamon, cloves, and ale, let boil 10 minutes. Strain the liquid into a clean saucepan, add the wine, and keep hot but *do not boil.* Ladle into thick glasses or mugs, dust with freshly grated nutmeg; the drinks should be hot, but not too hot to drink at once.

Makes about 12 servings of 6 ounces each.

You should now be prepared to cope with any occasion where beverages are called for. The omission of coffee is intentional; this fragrant brew will be dealt with in a later chapter. So will the foods that accompany the drinks.

II

Making Appetizers and Buffet Dishes

When you're planning to entertain a fairly large number of people, the moment of truth arrives long before the guests do. That moment comes after you've agreed to take care of the drinks and you're discussing what foods will be served. She agrees that the two of you can handle things as long as you're taking care of the drinks, then adds almost as an afterthought, "and help with the food, too."

Entertaining, complex or simple, is never a solo job. When it's just a matter of close friends dropping in for an informal get-together, one person can do most of the preparatory work, but still needs an assist now and then. When a major blowout's in the offing, though, it's like the looming of a storm at sea; the call is "All hands on deck and turn to."

As is the case with almost everything in life, a bit of planning and some advance preparation save a lot of wasted motion and any number of headaches, so have a pretty definite idea of your objectives before you even begin to work. Lists are invaluable. Make lists in advance, not only shopping lists, but lists of the menu and steps in its preparation, table setting, wines and drinks to be served, what jobs you're going to handle and those for which She will be responsible. If possible, do your listing on a day-by-day, even an hour-by-hour basis. Lists not only save time and headaches, they prevent last-minute hassles and floundering around and eliminate arguments.

Once the target's been established and the lists made up, then work becomes routine. If it's a cocktail party, you can plan to set up a Him and Her production line to prepare canapés and snacks; the same production-line technique can be used to produce frothy goodies for a reception, nibbles to be passed with pre-dinner drinks, whatever else an occasion might demand. While every party, every entertainment, has its own special requirements, there's a pattern common to all entertaining, and once you've established the basic routines in the area of shared work, you can face almost any kind of shindig without the prospect causing your knees to go watery.

There's an easy cop-out to serving a lot of guests. This is to acquire a reputation for one or two house specialties, and to trot out these old familiar standbys on any and all occasions. No matter how great the temptation is to go this easy route, though, it's a temptation wise party planners will shun. A specialty of the house is very handy to have, but variety still spices our lives, and getting stuck in the same old rut can become very, very boring. This is experience speaking, and perhaps shared experiences are our best lessons. Hark, then, to the wherefore.

Quite a number of years ago in the course of my kitchen experiments, I stumbled onto a very, very good pâté mixture. We served it three or four times, then switched to something new, but soon discovered that if this particular pâté didn't appear every time we entertained, our guests seemed to consider its absence as a kind of discrimination. No matter what the menu, several of our guests were certain to express polite disappointment that we didn't serve "that special pâté we enjoyed so much the last time we were here."

Now, the pâté is a good one—you'll have a chance to judge its merits yourself, if you care to, since the recipe's given in the section devoted to such details at the end of this chapter—but after a while I got tired of making it and both of us got somewhat tired of eating it every time we had guests in. Our friends quite naturally didn't stop to think that we'd had the pâté at perhaps a half-dozen other dinners since their last visit, and that for us age had withered and custom staled its charm. It had become a tradition of the house to serve the pâté, though, so I was stuck with it.

This has happened to us with a few main dishes as well. On more than one occasion, when we've invited friends to dinner, they've hinted that they enjoyed a certain entrée we'd served them in the past, which they remembered with pleasure. Knowing that your guests enjoy their dinners is very gratifying to the ego, and an easy out when it comes to party planning, but to scramble a couple of metaphors, it can be a two-edged sword if you fall into the trap of repeating any dish too often. Avoid the snare, then, and don't make a big thing of any specific dish or form of food, not even one for which you might have a special liking. Your enjoyment will fade with repetition; too much of a good thing is a bad thing.

But please don't interpret this as a warning that you shouldn't develop any specialties at all. Both He and She ought to have a small personal repertory of culinary offerings, dishes which repeated preparation has made easy to handle. This will be explored in a later chapter, where some suggestions will be offered that might help you in deciding which way to move in developing your culinary talents. Right now, we're concerned with another problem, how to prepare a reasonably large variety of finger foods and to serve them to a lot of guests with the least fuss and furor.

Finger foods will become your concern in connection with three occasions: cocktail parties, receptions, and preceding dinner parties. Each of these has different requirements, and the easiest way to map out the terrain is to take up one section at a time.

Cocktail-Party Foods

A bowl of salted nuts and a crock of gooey dip ringed with potato chips do not a cocktail party make. This stark simplicity is fine for informal spur-of-the-moment get-togethers with a few close friends, and nobody needs any help in putting together impromptu refreshments of this kind. We're concerned here with taking the trauma out of major bashes, especially those break-the-ice occasions when a lot of your guests will be comparative strangers, people you hope will carry away with them a good opinion of your hospitality. However, as we explore the ways of easing the strains of major entertaining, you might encounter a few ideas that will make informal occasions easier to handle, too.

If your bank balance is obscenely swollen, and you want to stage a large party without personal exertion, you can hire a caterer to provide both food and service. If you live in a reasonably large town, you can probably order manufactured canapés and tidbits from one of the firms specializing in this sort of thing. Before you choose either of these escape routes, though, give a bit of thought to all the pros and cons.

No matter how expertly a catered party is handled, it's apt to have a coolly impersonal flavor that can't be successfully disguised. The same impersonality marks the mass-produced tidbits you buy ready-made; they have a uniformity, a sort of cold perfection, that conveys to your guests the impression that you're entertaining them as a duty rather than to have them share your personal pleasure. If your guests happen to be fairly gregarious types who party frequently, they might even recognize the name of the caterer providing your spread, or that of the shop where the canapés were manufactured.

There's also a more important matter to be considered, that of quality. Caterers and commercial suppliers may use the very best ingredients in their foods, but the very nature of their operations makes it necessary for them to prepare their canapés and other tidbits far in advance and hold them in frozen storage. A lot of the ingredients commonly used in foods of this kind freeze beautifully, but thaw very badly, causing the thawed canapés to wilt quickly and often to become unpleasantly soggy in a matter of minutes. On the other hand, the canapés and tidbits you produce in your own kitchen will be fresh, will bear the stamp of your own individuality, and won't have the dreadful uniformity, the bland blah sameness, of the mass-produced products. Yours might not be as picture-book pretty, but they'll taste better. They'll also cost you a lot less.

Modern living is becoming essentially a do-it-yourself matter, as labor costs soar. In most areas of the country, casual helpers qualified to give you a hand in the kitchen or to serve as extras at parties either aren't available or command fees that strain all but the most generous entertainment budgets. Face the fact that you're going to have to handle both food preparation and service, and take the time to do the planning that will cut both jobs down to their minimums.

This is the point at which we need to do a bit of generalizing about cocktail-party foods. They should be of a type that will provide a bit of ballast for the drinks you'll serve, and they should also have authoritative flavors that won't be overpowered by the potent beverages that will be imbibed with them. Usually, a cocktail party is an afternoon affair, and if it's a successful bash it'll probably overlap into the dinner hour. If the party really takes off, there'll be a percentage of your guests who'll decide to postpone or forego dinner; some may simply forget. These, you'll certainly want to stoke up with foods that are tasteful and substantial enough to make missing dinner a pleasure. Just how luxurious or how spartan your stoking-up is going to be is the first decision you'll face in planning.

To begin at the bottom of the scale, the simplest refreshments you can offer would be a big bowl of seasoned nuts, a tray of relishes such as olives, pickles, and mild-pickle peppers, and a platter heaped with raw vegetables: celery hearts, radishes, cucumbers, tiny cherry tomatoes, and paper-thin slices of Jerusalem artichoke (this bears no resemblance to the spined artichoke; it's a tuber that tastes like a potato when cooked and when eaten raw is very like celeriac). Certainly some low-calorie foods should be included for the benefit of dieters who're already breaking training by taking a drink or so.

If you opt for this kind of layout, be original. Rather than offering salted nuts, season them with herbs; very simple to do. Just oil a baking sheet, spread the nutmeats on it and sprinkle them lightly with finely powdered oregano, basil, or marjoram, then toast them in a very low oven until they are crisp. Instead of putting out sour cream to go with the vegetables, put a bowl of grated Parmesan by them; it's virtually calorie-free, and very compatible with the vegetables listed above.

Rising to the next plateau, you might put out a cheeseboard

If you decide to put out a cheeseboard, don't chop the cheeses into tiny cubes. Let your guests cut their own from bold hunks of natural cheeses. At upper left, Kleine Emmenthaler; upper right, Vermont White Cheddar; lower left, Castello, a noncrumbly veined cheese; lower right, mild Port Salut.

with an assortment of crackers and thin crisp melba toast. Don't cut the cheeses on the board into neat dainty cubes and impale them on toothpicks. Put out big chunks of cheese and a couple of knives, and let your guests cut their own. Your choice of cheeses should, of course, be confined to good natural types; avoid the soapy-tasting process cheeses that have nothing to recommend them but the advertising blurbs of their manufacturers. Process cheeses and their derivatives, the "process cheese food spreads" that come in jars and tubes and aerosol cans, are all more expensive than real cheese in terms of cost per pound. Even worse, they're inferior in units of taste per bite. These products are very like the cotton candy you used to buy from carnival hustlers, all froth and looks that dissolve into nothing when you begin to eat them.

Process cheese contains a small quantity of genuine cheese mixed with neutral, flavorless milk curd, then loaded with chemicals that amplify the flavor of the real cheese and other chemicals to give the mixture color and a semblance of substance. Unfortunately, these additives also give process cheeses a flavor that bears a strong resemblance to laundry soap mixed with glue. The squeeze-tube, jar-packed, and aerosol-can "cheese foods" usually contain only 2 to 3 percent actual cheese; the rest is milk curd and chemicals, and between 45 and 60 percent of their bulk is nothing but water. When put on crackers or toast and allowed to stand a short time, the water in these spurious spreads seeps into the crackers and quickly makes them soggy-wet.

Get good natural cheeses: Cheddar, Swiss, Muenster, Edam, Port Salut, Leicester, Cacciocavallo, Gouda, Gloustershire, Provolone. Try some of the specialty bulk cheeses such as Vermont Sage Cheddar, Kuminost from Scandinavia, with its studding of cuminseeds, Kümmelkäse from Germany with caraway seeds imbedded in it, Pepato from Italy, with cracked peppercorns as its surprising extra ingredient. If you have trouble finding good natural cheeses in your local supermarket, try mail-order houses. During the past few years, we've gotten several dozen cheeses from Cheeselovers International of Freeport, Long Island, and have found them very satisfactory indeed.

Some cheeses should be avoided at a cocktail party, not because they're less tasty than others, but because they're too delicately flavored to be compatible with strong drinks, or because they're soft and crumbly. One of the realities of a cocktail party is that as spirits soar, carelessness does also. Very ripe soft cheeses such as Brie, Camembert, and Bel Paese and crumbly cheeses like Roquefort, Stilton, and Gorgonzola are unwise choices for cheeseboards because small bits of them fall off crackers onto your carpet, where they get stepped on and ground into the pile, forming spots almost impossible to remove.

If you elect to put out a sausage board instead of or in addition to a cheeseboard, you have a wide variety of good flavorful hard sausages, both domestic and imported, from which to select candidates for inclusion. There are the salamis, kosher, Italian, and Danish; smoked sausages from U.S. farms; chorizo and chippolata from Spain; Mettwurst and Bluttwurst from Germany; the good Pennsylvania Dutch summer sausage; and many others. Put out mustard, perhaps one jar of Dijon-type and another, a hot mustard from England or Holland. Heap a platter with breads: rye, black, sourdough. Again, let your guests slice their own, even though they might not be as skilled as you in producing evenly cut paper-thin slices.

Some types of sausage, like some cheeses, should be avoided. Liverwurst, for instance, shares the bad habit of crumbly cheeses in finding its way to carpets. Many soft sausages found on the meat counters today are unfit for human consumption; they are made from such slaughterhouse offal as lungs, tripes, lips, snouts, and other wastes, pulverized and glued together with milk solids—the same milk solids used to make carpenter's glue—and have no real flavor of their own to offer; they're simply a cud to chew on.

Any of the three foregoing suggestions will provide you with a cocktail-party food spread that's easy to plan and to prepare and relatively inexpensive. True, all three are a bit plain-Jane in style, but none of them offers any real kitchen problems.

To dress up a cocktail party with fancier foods is going to involve a bit of labor. Canapés are indicated for a dress-up array, and canapés take time and effort to prepare. Ingredients must be cooked, chopped, minced, ground, grated, or whirled in a blender, then creamed into pliable form and spread on crisps, and finally adorned with some type of garnish. If you choose to go the canapé route and at first glance think the problem of handling all the work will involve a lot of extra effort on your part as well as Hers, cheer up. Even preparing dozens of canapés can be a fast-moving operation if you'll set up a Him and Her production line. It's a method we use to cut labor down to an acceptable minimum.

Begin your planning by selecting the three or four spreads you'll use, and do hold it down to three or four. Break these spreads down into lists of ingredients and processes that require similar operations. Typically, canapé spreads involve ingredients that must be reduced to usable form by the use of knife or food-grinder or blender; those using meats require the extra step of cooking. After the ingredients have gone through the chopping or grinding or blending stage, they must be seasoned and combined with a binder—butter, mayonnaise, cream cheese, or whatever—to make them spreadable. Finally, there's the spreading on crisps and as a last step, garnishing.

All this sounds discouraging, but in practice it really works out quite well and isn't as complicated as it might seem. Let's suppose that you decide to serve four kinds of canapés: one based on liver, one on a red meat such as beef or veal, one on a white meat such as chicken or fish, and one on cheese. Your final job list might look something like this:

	Liver	*Meat*	*Fish*	*Cheese*
Job 1—	Cook	Cook	Cook	—
Job 2—	—	Bone	Bone	—
Job 3—	Chop	Chop	Flake	Grate
Job 4—	Blender	Grinder	Blender	—
Job 5—	Season & combine	Season & combine	Season & combine	Season & combine
Job 6—	Spread	Spread	Spread	Spread
Job 7—	Cut	Cut	Cut	Cut
Job 8—	Garnish	Garnish	Garnish	Garnish

Broken down into its component operations, the job looks nowhere nearly as formidable. Remember, the earlier jobs—cooking, boning, coarse-chopping to prepare ingredients for the grinder or blender—can be done on any kind of schedule, a day or longer in advance of the final preparation. The production line really doesn't begin its functioning until Job 4 is reached, since this is the point at which the preparation must be integrated into one smooth-flowing operation. Even Job 4 and Job 5 can be spread out and the prepared ingredients put into the refrigerator to wait for the last three steps.

If at all possible, Jobs 6, 7, and 8 should be done at the latest moment that will fit into your schedule before the canapés are served. Once the spreads go on their crisp bases, they should be served with a minimum of delay, before the liquids in the spreads soften the bases and spoil their crunchiness. A couple of hours of refrigerated storage will do no harm, but overnight is too long. Nor should the canapés be frozen. The crisp bases will not come back to their original condition; all that you'll do is make your canapés appear sad, wilted, and slightly second-hand. Nobody likes a used-looking canapé.

While crackers or home-baked crusty crisps (like pie crust) are the most satisfactory bases for canapé spreads, you can avoid a lot of work by using plain bread as a base. If you use this labor-saving method, your first job is to find some good, honest bread in long, unsliced loaves. Don't even think of using commercial squoosh-bread for canapé bases; this substance isn't real bread that can be handled in home kitchens, but a chemical sponge manufactured to be sawed into slices by a machine and wrapped by another machine. No knife can slice it unless it is stale.

This isn't blind prejudice speaking, but the voice of unhappy experience. A short while before this book was begun we were faced with the need for a large number of canapés in a hurry, and did not have on hand our usual backlog of home-baked bread. Since the second extension of Gresham's Law (bad products, lavishly advertised, will drive out good ones) had recently brought about the closing of the last small neighborhood bakery in our area, we secured from the big commercial bread factory some unsliced loaves.

Then the troubles started. Our kitchen knives are always kept razor-sharp, but none of them, not even the odd ones with sawtooth and serrated blades, would slice the fluffy stuff. The electric knife—seldom used at our house—was brought out with the hope that its sawing action might be comparable to that of the bakery's slicing machine. It wasn't; it, too, tore the bread into great ugly chunks.

Next, we popped the loaves into a warm oven, thinking to dry them a bit and thus make them firmer, but even after two hours the sponge stayed soft and squooshy, unsliceable. As a last resort, we persuaded our butcher to try slicing them in his electric cutter, and this worked after a fashion, though the few slices that came out untorn were ragged and of uneven thickness. Finally, giving up, we tossed the unsavory stuff into the incinerator and borrowed some home-baked loaves from a friend.

Even when toasted, squoosh-bread dissolves into a pasty mass within a few moments after being spread with any preparation containing a substantial quantity of loose liquid. Fortunately, honest breads are usually not too hard to find. There are still small neighborhood bakeries that turn out good loaves made with the old-fashioned recipe that uses only flour, milk,

Before beginning the final jobs in your canapé production efforts, have everything necessary for them assembled: spreads, bread, garnishes, canapé cutters.

shortening, salt, and yeast. In addition, both Orowheat and Amana distribute good breads nationally. Yes, we tried to find some at our supermarket, but the racks were empty.

Find your loaves of honest bread, then, and slice them thinly, lengthwise, discarding the outer crusts and trimming away the crusts that will remain at sides and ends of the long slices you've cut. Arrange the slices on baking tins without letting them overlap and put them in a very low oven—on the "warming" setting if your oven has one—until the bread is firm but not crisply hard. Turn the slices once during the time it takes them to become firm. Let the bread cool, and you're now ready to go into the last three jobs on your list of canapé-making tasks.

Before starting Job 6, be sure everything you need is assembled and ready: the canapé spreads, the cutters, the bread slices, and the garnishes. How you divide up the work depends on your individual preferences. The easy way is for Her to apply two of the spreads, Him to apply the other two, then after all the slices are spread, He can cut canapés while She puts on the garnish. Jobs 6, 7, and 8 move with incredible swiftness. Within an hour or slightly more He and She can roll about 125 to 150 canapés off the small production line, have them garnished and ready to serve. Each long slice of bread, by the way, yields 5 or 6 canapés, depending on the size of your cutters. The method results in surprisingly little waste; a few odd-shaped bits that can be nibbled on while the team goes about its work.

Unless you've made a couple hundred canapés in preparation for a large cocktail party, you might shrug off or laugh off this meticulous listing of jobs and distribution of labor as being a useless frill. Don't laugh until you've tried the preparation both ways—unplanned and with planning. Then you'll see the virtue of the routinized, job-sharing production line. It's the only way to go.

In the recipes section of this chapter, you'll find a number of canapé spreads and fillings that should fit any occasion. There's also a recipe for the pastry crust which makes a superior canapé base, and one for tiny bite-sized puff-shells that can be filled with a pastry tube—which, by the way, is a handy tool for spreading canapés when making them individually. You can also use these spreads as fillings for sections of celery, hard-cooked egg halves, or tiny cherry tomatoes.

One of the things you'll notice when you reach the recipes is that dips are not among them. This reflects both prejudice and practicality. My own tendency today is to shy away from dips at a party, because the big food factories turn out so many "dip mixes" which are nothing but chemicals that I'm a bit hesitant about eating dips of unknown pedigree. Some of your guests may share this hesitancy, especially if they've read the labels on these "mixes," and might follow my example in giving all dips a wide berth.

From the practical standpoint, dips are the very devil to control at a big party. First, if the dip is firm enough to stay in place on a chip or cracker, it's usually too firm to be dipped into without the cracker crumbling. Then, as the crowd around the dip bowl gets bigger and guests begin to feel a bit exuberant, people not only dip, they drip. Like the bits of crumbly cheeses mentioned earlier, the drippings get stepped on, ground into rugs, carried around the house on shoesoles.

All right. Your Him and Her production line has done its job, you have a mountain of canapés and assorted tidbits assembled. If you're short of trays, and can't borrow from the neighbors or don't like to borrow breakables, improvise by cutting plywood or particle board into rectangles about 18 by 24 inches and covering them with metal foil. Use masking tape to hold the foil in place; regular cellophane tape doesn't stick well enough to do this particular job.

Arrange a variety of canapés on each tray; don't put all of one kind on one tray. You want your guests to move, to circulate, but not to race from one serving tray to another in search of variety. Try to avoid refrigerating the canapés after they're made, but if refrigeration is absolutely necessary, cover the trays with cloth that's very, very lightly moistened. Avoid using plastic film, which forms condensation on its inner service and will make your canapés soggy. Take the trays out of the refrigerator just long enough in advance of serving for them to lose their gelid chill; they ought to be just a trifle cooler than room temperature.

Earlier, the recommendation was made that you avoid combining the food and beverage service areas at a large cocktail party. Carry that recommendation one step further. Arrange two or three food-service areas, depending on the size of your room and its layout. Have each area supplied with an assortment of all the foods you're offering. When one tray or bowl is badly depleted, return it to the kitchen and replace it with one that's completely filled; shuffle the contents of depleted trays together to keep full ones available. Put the trays on any piece of furniture that will accommodate them—small tables, bookcases, wherever they are best located from the standpoint of keeping food-service areas apart.

Dividing food-service areas and separating them from the bar has several virtues. It encourages your guests to circulate, keeps them from packing into one spot and hanging there like salmon waiting below a waterfall to go upstream to spawn. No cocktail party is a success unless the guests are kept in pretty constant motion, and no cocktail party guest is so totally lacking in curiosity that he or she won't visit all the service areas in turn to find out what kind of foods each one is offering. And, by setting up several areas and using prefilled trays, you make the host's job of keeping ahead of the refreshments a lot easier.

Reception Foods

Receptions tend to be stylized, somewhat in the nature of a ballet. They are more formal and of much shorter duration than cocktail parties, and also call for a much lighter touch in refreshments. Always consider the hour and timing of your reception when you plan the menu. Generally, these aren't events at which guests are prone to linger, as they do at cocktail parties. Most of the guests drop in for a polite few moments and go on their way. Keep in mind that if your reception is in midmorning, your guests will be going from it to lunch; if the affair is in midafternoon, your guests will be sitting down to dinner shortly after they leave. Guests at an evening affair will very probably be only a short time away from rising from their dinner tables.

Let the refreshments, then, reflect the timing. For morning and afternoon affairs, keep food on the interesting side, light and intriguing rather than filling: meringues, watercress sandwiches made almost as thin as paper. Avoid excessively sweet foods at any reception from which guests are apt to go on to a meal. Sugar kills appetites. If the reception is an evening affair, sweets can be offered more freely, as many of the guests will have finished dinner and the reception sweets will be their dessert.

It's also good gustatory practice to let the kind of punch you're offering set the keynote for the solid refreshments. Play counterpoint. If the punch is on the sweet side, try offering tidbits of nutbreads sliced thinly and cut with canapé-cutters into decorative shapes, or thin rectangles of melba toast spread sparingly with a compound butter or an almost-invisible film of ripe Camembert. With a tartly assertive punch, go to spicy cookies such as cardamom and Pfeffernuesse.

Besides punch, there is one other traditional reception beverage: Champagne. Quite often, Champagne is a key ingredient of your punch, so there's really no way to escape it. Not that anybody really wants to escape Champagne, except for the fact that it's usually associated with foods as costly as the wine. Caviar, for instance, was for centuries virtually an obligatory accompaniment to Champagne, but those days have perhaps gone forever.

Genuine caviar has zoomed from being merely expensive into the prohibitively costly category. Each grain represents the price of a semiprecious stone of equivalent size. There are plenty of phony caviars around, made from the roes of lumpfish, whitefish, and even salmon roe, which brings around $1.50 per half-cup when sold as bait to fishermen and is priced at $3.50 to $4.00 per half-cup when sold as caviar. Naturally, you'd no more think of offering these ersatz caviars to your guests than you would of eating them yourself. All those I've tasted have ranged from being oversalted and coarsely unpleasant to repellently rank and fishy.

There are many other delicacies that can be put in the place once reserved for caviar. You won't really miss the sturgeon's second most famous product, and will be well advised to pass it by unless you're interested in contributing to our overseas trade deficit and making a vulgar and ostentatious display of wealth by serving the genuine article.

Instead, make thin, thin sandwiches using fillings not ordinarily encountered: minced watercress in Sauce Chantilly; chopped cucumbers sustained in Maltaise Sauce; or simply spread these on crisp toast triangles. Serve shrimp paste on squares of ultra-thin black bread; fill bite-sized pastry shells with a delicate mousse of crabmeat or chicken or lobster. Or make what the chefs of old called *bouchées*, "little mouthfuls," by cooking small puff-paste balls and filling them with a spicy forcemeat.

All these go as well with punch as they do with Champagne, and recipes for all of them will be found in the usual place near the chapter's end. Remember, you're not really expected to feed guests substantially at a reception. All you need to offer is a modest array of nonfilling delicacies to go with the punch, and the word "delicacies" is used in its strictest dictionary definition: *"delicate:* fragile, pleasing because of its fineness."

By putting to use the techniques of the Him and Her production line outlined in earlier paragraphs, and preparing some of the delicacies that appear in the recipe section, you can be sure your reception will be handled without undue strain, and will be remembered for the excellence of its refreshments rather than for their spartan simplicity.

Pre-Dinner Nibbles

Because they lend themselves to the production line and fall into the same general category as the finger foods served at cocktail parties and receptions, this seems as good a place as any to look at the tray of nibbles that's usually passed with drinks preceding a dinner party. Again, we exclude the casual kickshaws that are usually offered at casual, spur-of-the-moment meals shared by a few close friends.

Any foods passed with pre-dinner drinks ought to be a prelude to the meal that will follow, not a meal in themselves. Somewhere along the way we've lost sight of the fact that what we today quite erroneously call "hors d'oeuvres" have little or no relationship to the hors d'oeuvres that were originated by the master chefs whose menus ushered in the two centuries of *haute cuisine* that began around 1730 and ended shortly after World War I with the retirement of Auguste Escoffier in 1921.

Escoffier, better than any of the masters who preceded and followed him, understood the human palate. Nearly a century ago, he began advocating the omission from all dinner menus of the kind of appetizers that even in his day had come to be called hors d'oeuvres, and confining their service only to luncheons, which usually feature less elaborate entrées. In his writings, this culinary genius pointed out more than once that hors d'oeuvres should be what the words literally mean, a sample "from the work"; in other words, a suggestion of the dinner that is to come, a hint of its theme.

Dinners rarely have themes any more, at least not themes that can be translated into terms of an introductory offering. But this is beside the point; the point is that in offering pre-dinner nibbles you should avoid filling foods, foods that lie heavy in the stomach and inhibit the appetite, or that stultify the taste-buds and bring your guests to the dinner table too sated to enjoy the dinner you and She have shared in preparing.

This means omitting from your hors d'oeuvre tray all foods that are excessively salty—nuts, potato chips, and so on—as well as foods that are excessively sweet. Sugar and salt have one thing in common, even though they occupy opposite poles of the taste spectrum. Both smother the tastebuds, shock them with raw flavor, and both have the same effect that a heavy, rich dish would: they take the edge off appetites. So, in addition to crossing off your nibbles list items that fall within the extreme range of saltiness or sweetness, you should also avoid canapés spread with rich cheese, creamy spreads, and heavy oily mixtures.

While it might not be your cup of tea, we have for quite some time been setting out a huge tray of *crudités* for guests to nibble on while enjoying drinks before dinner. Modern farming practices and refrigerated shipping make the necessary raw vegetables for our tray available the year around. On the tray are tiny raw mushrooms—or large mushrooms thinly sliced if we can find no small fresh buttons—baby carrots, celery hearts, icicle and red radishes, cucumber fingers that have been soaked in salted water and drained, slivers of raw Jerusalem artichoke, even very thin slices of small raw turnips.

With them we set out a bowl of unsalted butter—you can wash the salt from any butter by kneading it in water, changing the water several times, and squeezing the desalted butter to remove excess water when the washing's finished—and a bowl of Maltaise Sauce. Usually we add another dressing made by beating two egg whites with a tablespoon of white wine vinegar or lemon juice and folding them into about a half-cup of our homemade mayonnaise. We may substitute for one of these seasonings a bowl of sour cream into which powdered dillweed has been beaten.

Crudités do very well as pre-dinner nibbles for several reasons. They go with any kind of drinks, and they appeal to those who are dieting or watching waistlines, which in this era includes most of the adult population. We usually serve them on occasions when the dinner menu does not include a salad course; as often as not we omit salads in favor of a hot soup in the winter or a cold soup on hot midsummer days.

Equally as satisfactory for pre-dinner nibbles are small shrimps, shelled and deveined, accompanied by a pot of melted herbed butter. If you have no soup on the dinner menu, Seviche is a good pre-dinner nibble; make it with scallops, clams, and raw fresh or frozen fish. Small batter-fried oysters may precede a light dinner; serve with them a choice of sauces, one based on tomatoes and the other the genuine Sauce Tartare, not the clammy versions offered in most restaurants or sold bottled. These sauces go equally well with shrimp, cracked crab, or other seafoods.

Not to belabor the matter, any of the foregoing fill the requirements for nibbles to go with drinks; all of them go well with any beverages. All stimulate instead of killing appetites, and none of them will bring your guests to the table too well fed to enjoy dinner. And, as a bonus, none of them present major problems of preparation to a host and hostess already jointly engaged in putting together an elaborate meal.

Buffet Service

Serving meals buffet-style first rose to popularity as part of the trend to more casual and relaxed entertaining; the practice became ubiquitous as the number of individuals willing to do such casual labor as kitchen helping and serving at table dwindled. Buffet service is now locked in to our daily entertaining plans; it is accepted everywhere, in private homes and public dining places. Who remembers the era when the only first-class restaurants that served buffet-style were those featuring smörgåsbord?

There's certainly nothing intrinsically wrong with buffet service, but there's often a great deal wrong with the manner in which the dining arrangements have been planned and the kinds of foods offered at a buffet-style meal.

Take the arrangements first. There's a theory that buffet service allows you to accommodate a larger number of guests than would be possible at a sit-down meal. Like a number of theories, this one doesn't work out in practice. Carried to extremes, it results in a jam of guests sardined into inadequate space, attempting to eat while reclining in an engulfing lounge chair, teetering on a flimsy folding chair, or perched precariously on an ottoman. Nor is it especially soothing to try cutting a piece of meat on a plate that slips back and forth on knees cramped together, or while bending forward from the equivalent of yoga's lotus position to reach a plate resting on the floor. These are not ideal conditions under which to enjoy dining.

Do, then, seat your guests at tables. Even improvised tables are better than juggling plates in easy chairs or cushions on the floor. There are all sorts of folding, temporary table extenders available; some are designed to fit atop card tables, others to increase the capacity of regular dining tables. In planning seating arrangements, group your guests in numbers as large as your space will allow; have your sit-downs arranged so that some diners aren't isolated in lonely groups of two or three—or, sadly, by themselves—in far corners of a room.

Out of respect for your guests' convenience—and for the sake of your floors—place the tables as close to the serving area as you can, in spots easy to get to. Don't ask your guests to juggle their loaded plates along a narrow hallway, or to pick their path through an obstacle course of chairs, divans, and other furniture. Above all, allow adequate elbow room in your seating arrangements, so that adjacent diners won't find themselves forced to intertwine arms and lean forward and backward in unison when eating, as though they were performing some new kind of seated folk dance. Dining intimately is enjoyable, but it becomes ridiculous when one of your guests lifts a bite on his fork and it reaches the mouth of the person seated next to him.

Have tables set in advance with silver, napkins, bread and butter, and the glasses for whatever beverages you're offering. A good way to control the buffet line is to serve the salad or soup course at the table; this allows you to control the seating arrangements, for when the guests rise to serve themselves from the buffet they will return to their established places. And since no two people eat at the same pace, you'll have an orderly trickle passing along the buffet line instead of a crowd waiting hungrily in a long line.

Arranging the service in this fashion serves another purpose: It allows you to set up the buffet at the last minute, and also allows you to clear away used salad or soup plates a few at at time. It also reduces the number of items the diners will have to juggle while enroute back to their seats, and spaces out conveniently the job of beverage service.

One of the pleasant ways to take the stigma of impersonality from a meal served buffet-style is for the host to fill the guests' glasses after they have gone through the line and are seated. There are few things more annoying than trying to carry a filled glass or cup from buffet to table, and few things more expressive of hospitality than the act of the host or hostess in filling a guest's glass or cup. Circulating with the beverages—

To set up a temporary buffet serving table, use that same ironing board and plywood that provided you with a temporary bar; have the table far enough from the walls to allow a line to pass down each side at the same time.

whether wine or pink lemonade, coffee or tea—gives the host an opportunity for a few words with each guest, or even a chance to join briefly in table conversation.

As for the buffet itself, fall back on the disguised ironing board that was used as a bar for your cocktail party. Change the false front a bit this time, though. Drape both sides and ends with folds of cloth and adjust the height to one that will make it easy for your guests to serve themselves. By moving your improvised buffet away from the wall, you can pass guests along it on both sides, which keeps jam-ups from developing and makes for quicker serving. Even if your home has a pass-through from kitchen to dining room, don't try to use it as a serving area. Not only is it less convenient, but it gives your dinner an institutionalized atmosphere. Use the pass-through for soiled china, but don't try to serve from it or through it.

There are some pitfalls to be avoided when planning your menu. One is trying to be too lavish, offering a spread that resembles the serving counter of a busy cafeteria where foods are arrayed in a seemingly endless line. This kind of thing is necessary in commercial establishments, where crowds of people with widely varying tastes come to buy their meals. It's out of place in a home, where guests have come to share a meal reflecting your taste in selecting and skill in preparing foods.

When confronted with an array of foods offering a choice of

three meats, a half-dozen vegetables, and other miscellaneous items, few guests will have the courage to pass up a dish of which they may be only marginally fond. Through a perfectly natural psychological quirk, they feel obliged to try something of everything, out of deference to the host and hostess. The result of a too-elaborate buffet offering invariably is overloaded plates and overstuffed guests, who make a beeline for the antacid tablets the instant they get home.

Some of the buffet dinners at which I've been a guest have reminded me of menus encountered in cookbooks of the eighteenth and nineteenth centuries. These were the days when *haute cuisine* was flowering into its fullest bloom, and the menus were incredible. If you'd like to share one vicariously, a typical dinner menu follows.

Plover's eggs and caviar began the meal, followed by melon to clear the tastebuds for the soups—two soups, one thick, the other a consommé. Trout poached in wine came next, then oysters and mussels on the half shell; after these, a sauced chicken accompanied by grilled mushrooms. Next, a leg of lamb with green peas and potatoes, then another taste-clearing course, snails, with which a sparkling punch was served. After the punch, roast duck appeared, asparagus came with it, then a tossed green salad followed. The meal finally drew to a close with assorted pastries and a set-piece dessert, a Baked Alaska. The wines included sherry with the soup, Rhine with the trout, Chablis with the shellfish and chicken, Bordeaux with the lamb, Burgundy with the duck, and Champagne with the sweets, and coffee with Cognac at last ended the repast.

Nobody eats on this scale today, of course, not even at state dinners in the world's great capitals, and even the most ambitious buffet dinners that I've experienced certainly haven't matched the foregoing. But many of them have been much too elaborate for enjoyment; they've offered such a plethora of foods that the guests who shared them tasted and sampled rather than dining.

So, don't expose your buffet dinner guests to a bewildering array; concentrate on a main meat course and a couple of vegetables that are complementary to the meat chosen. Remember, too, that your guests will be carrying their own plates to the table, and avoid soupy, runny foods. Serve sauces, yes, or gravies, but serve them in bowls already on the table. There are all kinds of small utensils designed to keep sauces and gravies warm, and there are also plug-in trays that can be used on your buffet to keep the main dishes at the correct temperature.

As for the composition of your menu, there are few hard and fast lines that can be drawn between foods suitable for buffets and those you'd serve at a sit-down dinner. The method of a meal's service needn't be a menu index, as long as the choices take into consideration the difference between meals at which foods are served from offered platters or passed across a table and those at which guests serve themselves and carry their own plates to the spot where they will sit down.

Aside from these obvious no-nos, which your common-sense would have led you to deduce anyhow, let your own good taste and judgment—and your budget—be your guide. If budget is the main criterion, let me pass on to you a very economical way of serving a crowd. It was given me by one of my professional chef friends, Wes Sours, and is an excellent answer for those occasions when you must serve a large number with a full meal. Buy a large turkey and bone it restaurant-style—as illustrated in the accompanying series of pictures. They will show you how the boning is done to reduce a turkey to four large pieces of boneless meat that are very simple to carve into uniform portions of white and dark meats.

Cook the turkey pieces on a baking sheet, or in a shallow pan, or on top of the dressing for which a recipe is given in Chapter IV. Boned and cooked in this style, a 20-pound bird will serve 50 people. You can, of course, scale down the size of your turkey in ratio to the number of guests you'll be serving. The method illustrated is an easy and economical way to serve a large number of people good food at a very low cost.

In the recipe section on the following pages you'll find other answers to your planning and serving meals. It contains pâtés, canapé spreads (which are also suitable for sandwiches), light finger-foods for receptions or pre-dinner nibbles, some soups for your dinners, and a number of entrées and side dishes that lend themselves especially to buffet service and are also suitable for a sit-down dinner.

BONING A TURKEY

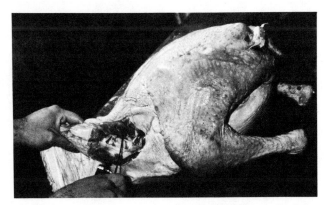

1. Perhaps the most economical way to serve a large number of guests is to buy a big turkey—20 pounds or more—and bone it restaurant-style. First, remove the tail. Next, as shown above, make a deep cut back of the wings, bend the wings forward to expose the tendon in the shoulder joint, sever it, and then cut straight down to separate wings from carcass. Take both wings off. They will be put aside for some other meal; they could be boned, but not so as to make large neat slices.

2. Cut off the flap of neck skin by making a V-shaped cut that follows the contour of the breastbones.

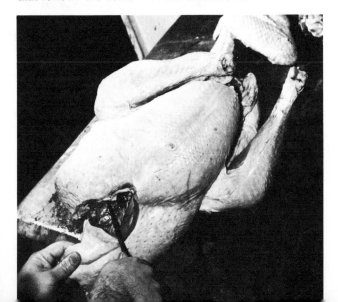

3. With the bird on its back, pull the legs away from the body and cut deeply into the side in front of the thighs to get the greatest amount of meat when you remove them. Then cut downward into the carcass with the knife blade angling toward the back, to expose the hip socket. Cut the tendon in the socket.

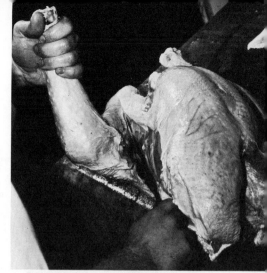

4. After severing the hip-socket tendon, roll the turkey on its side to make it easy to finish removing the leg.

5. For the greatest amount of meat, let your knife follow the hip bone; angle it to connect with the cut you made in front of the leg. Then take off the other leg.

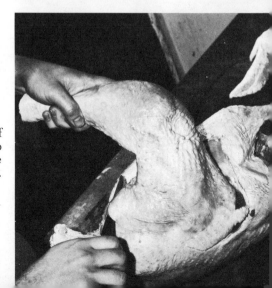

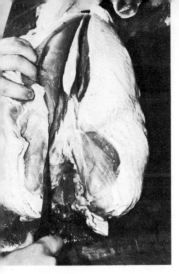

6. Get the bird on its back again and make cuts on both sides of and parallel to the breast-bone; the cuts should start at the V of the neck and extend the full length of the breast. Pull the flesh away from the breastbone as shown, and while your left hand lifts the strip of flesh with steady pressure, your right hand guides the knife along the rib bones.

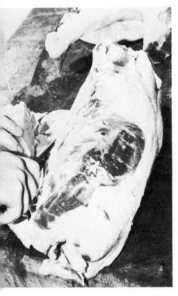

7. Keep your knife close to the bones and move it in short, almost scraping cuts as you follow the ribs around to the back.

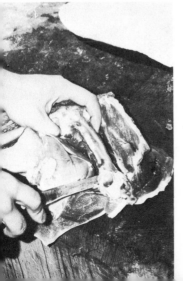

8. Bone out the legs. First, cut down to the bone from inside the thigh, across the leg-joint, and down to the tip of the drumstick. Then, pull up an end of one of the bones and free it from the flesh by undercutting it. Skip the joint for the time being when you reach it, and finish freeing the two bones.

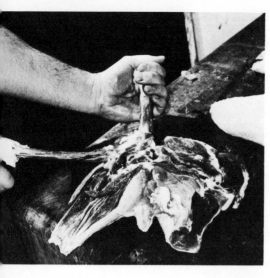

9. Free the joint by lifting and turning the leg bones so you can cut around the joint itself.

10. When the boning is finished—and with practice it can be done in ten minutes or less—you have four big pieces of boneless meat that contain over 85 percent of a turkey's edible flesh. Cook them as described in the text; the four pieces shown, sliced across the grain of the meat, will yield 40 to 50 portions, each containing white and dark meat.

Pâtés and Canapés

Pâté Maison en Terrine

1 calf's tongue, ¾ pound
6 cloves
2 pods very hot chili pepper
1 pound calf or chicken livers
¾ pound pork
1 onion, 2-inch diameter
2 shallots
¾ cup dry vermouth
2 tbsp butter

3 tbsp flour
1 cup milk
1 cup heavy cream
3 eggs
2 tsp salt
1 tsp freshly ground black pepper
½ tsp powdered allspice
½ to ¾ pound fresh pork fat

Put the tongue, cloves, and chili peppers into a saucepan, cover with cold water, bring to a boil, reduce to simmer, skim froth from the surface until no more appears, cover the pan, and simmer until the tongue is tender, about 45 minutes. Set aside to cool in the cooking water. Put the liver, pork, onion, and shallots through the meat grinder, using the coarsest blade. Strain the liver and discard the juices. Combine liver, pork, onion, shallots, pour the vermouth over them, set aside, stirring occasionally.

Melt the butter over low heat and stir in the flour, taking care not to let it brown; stir until a smooth paste forms, slowly add the milk, then the cream, while stirring; do not let the mixture thicken. Beat the eggs with the salt, pepper, and allspice; combine eggs, the milk mixture, and the meat mixture, stirring into a thick purée. Drain the tongue, skin it, and slice lengthwise into long strips about ¼ inch thick. Set aside 4 long choice center strips. (Use the remaining tongue for sandwiches or grind for a canapé spread.)

Cut the pork fat into long thin slices and line a rectangular terrine or loaf pan with the slices. Pour in ⅓ of the purée, arrange 2 tongue slices on the surface, add ⅓ more of the purée, the remaining 2 tongue slices, the rest of the purée, cover the top with slices of pork fat, and put the lid on the terrine; if it has no lid, cover it tightly with foil.

Put the pâté pan into a larger baking dish and pour in hot water until it reaches about halfway up the sides of the pâté pan.

Bake in a preheated 350-degree oven 1½ hours. Remove and let cool and set, put a weight on top of the pâté, and chill overnight in the refrigerator, leaving the weight in place. Turn the pâté out on a small platter; slice thinly to serve.

This pâté yields about 12 slices when cooked in a 4-by-4-by-9-inch terrine, and keeps for 2 to 3 weeks in the refrigerator.

Pâté en Croûte

For the crust:

4 cups flour	½ tsp salt
⅔ cup butter	2 egg yolks
⅔ cup lard or solid shortening	

Work butter and lard into the flour, then work in salt and egg yolks, to form a stiff dough. If too stiff, add water by teaspoonfuls until the dough reaches the right consistency. When mixed, roll the dough in small pieces on the mixing board into cylinders or balls, then form into one big ball. Wrap in moist cloth and chill 2 hours before using.

(This is a basic dough; in addition to using it for a pâté crust, it can be baked in muffin tins or small individual pans into tart shells or rolled out and cut into shapes, then baked on a baking tin for canapé bases.)

For the pâté:

3 tbsp butter	2 tsp salt
½ pound liver (calf or chicken)	½ tsp freshly ground pepper
2 cloves garlic	¼ cup Cognac
3 shallots or ½ small onion	1½ tsp powdered marjoram
2 eggs	Large pinch freshly grated nutmeg
1 pound ground pork	Large pinch ground cloves
1 pound ground veal (chicken, duck, turkey, goose, rabbit, or venison can be used instead)	

Heat the butter, sauté the liver gently together with the minced or mashed garlic and shallots; when the liver is tender, mash it into a smooth paste with a fork, together with the butter left in the pan. Beat the egg, combine it with the liver, then combine all remaining ingredients. There is a special oval spring-form pan used for cooking pâté in a crust, but if you do not have one, a regular loaf pan will do equally well. Oil it thoroughly, line with the rolled-out dough, reserving enough dough to cover the pan later. Cook with the pan covered with foil in a preheated 325-degree oven for 2 hours, remove foil cover and put on the dough top, pressing it well against the edges of the pan, return to the oven for 10 to 15 minutes, until the top crust browns. The pâté can be served hot or removed from the pan, chilled, and served cold.

Pâté Gola

1 pound chicken livers
2 tbsp flour
6 tbsp butter
3 tbsp minced shallots
⅓ cup Port

1 tsp salt
¼ tsp freshly ground white
   pepper
Large pinch freshly grated
   nutmeg

Trim the livers of fat and white tissues, cut them in halves, dredge in flour, and sauté very gently in the butter, together with the shallots. When the livers are very tender, mash with a wooden spoon into a fine paste, incorporating the butter from the pan and the bits of shallot. Blend in the remaining ingredients. Oil a loaf pan or mold and line it with waxed paper, pack the liver mixture into it firmly, chill overnight, turn out and slice to serve.

Chicken Liver Canapé Spread

½ cup butter
½ pound chicken livers
½ cup grated onion
4-ounce package cream
   cheese

2 tbsp brandy
½ tsp paprika
1 tsp salt
Large dash cayenne

Melt the butter over low heat, clean and halve the livers, sauté them gently, adding the onion about midway of cooking. Mash the livers or put them through the blender with the butter left in the pan; have the cream cheese at room temperature, and blend into it the liver purée and remaining ingredients. Pack into a small crock and chill 2 to 4 hours before using as a canapé spread.

Meat Canapé Spread

½ pound cooked veal, beef,   8 stuffed olives or pitted ripe
   pork, ham, chicken, etc.   olives
¾ cup celery   1½ to 2 tbsp homemade
¼ cup walnut meats   mayonnaise

Grind together the meat and celery; mince together until very fine the walnut meats and olives; combine the ground meat and the nut-olive mixture with enough mayonnaise to bind into a smooth paste. Chill lightly before spreading.

Mushroom Canapé Spread

½ pound small fresh   1 cup heavy cream
   mushrooms   ⅓ cup dry white wine
1 cup homemade   ⅛ tsp cayenne
   mayonnaise   ¼ tsp onion juice

Wash the mushrooms and parboil them 10 minutes in lightly salted water, drain well. Remove the stems, take two or three thin slices from the center of each cap, reserve the slices, and mince the remainder of the caps and the stems. Combine the minced mushrooms with the mayonnaise, whip the cream, adding to it the wine and seasonings, combine the mushroom mixture with the whipped cream, refrigerate until firm. Spread the canapés, topping each with one of the reserved mushroom slices.

Shrimp Canapé Spread

¾ pound shrimp
4-ounce can midget shrimp
¼ pound butter
⅓ cup homemade
    mayonnaise

5 or 6 drops Tabasco
Large pinch dry crumbled
    tarragon

Clean and devein the large shrimp, and pound them in a mortar or heavy mixing bowl together with the butter, mayonnaise, Tabasco, and tarragon into a smooth paste. Spread canapés, top each one with a well-drained midget shrimp. (If you can find any of these tiny morsels fresh, by all means use them instead of the canned variety.)

Egg Canapé Spread

4 hardcooked eggs, grated
1 cup drained cottage
    cheese
2 tbsp drained pimientos
1 tbsp homemade
    mayonnaise

¾ cup minced green pepper
½ cup grated sweet onion
½ tsp salt

Combine all ingredients into a smooth paste, spread canapés, garnish with a slice of stuffed olive or a pair of capers.

Finger Foods

Mayonnaise (blender method)

1 egg
½ tsp sugar
¾ tsp salt

½ tsp Dijon-type mustard
3 tbsp fresh lemon juice
1 cup peanut oil

Break the egg into the blender, add sugar, salt, mustard, lemon juice, and ⅓ cup oil. Cover the blender, blend at LOW speed about 5 seconds, switch to HIGH speed, remove cover and pour in the remaining oil in a steady stream. Blend 5 to 7 seconds after the last of the oil has been added. The mayonnaise will be thin; it will firm up when chilled, but will never get as gluey as commercial mayonnaise.

Makes about 1 pint.

Sauce Chantilly

Blend 1 cup homemade mayonnaise with ⅔ cup whipped cream.

Hollandaise Sauce (blender method)

4 egg yolks	2½ tbsp fresh lemon juice
½ tsp white wine vinegar	Dash cayenne
½ tsp salt	½ pound melted butter

Put egg yolks, vinegar, salt, lemon juice, and cayenne into the blender. Have the melted butter ready; it should not have been allowed to brown while melting and should be hot when added to the blender. Start the blender at LOW speed, blend about 5 seconds, uncover, and pour in the butter in a small steady stream. Turn off the blender the moment the sauce begins to thicken, which will be 15 to 20 seconds after the last of the butter has been added. DO NOT substitute margarine for butter; most of today's margarines contain additives that will keep them from blending with acid liquids such as vinegar and lemon juice.

Makes 1 scant pint.

Maltaise Sauce

To 1 cup Hollandaise, add 3 tbsp fresh orange juice and 1 tsp grated orange rind, stir to blend.

Cucumber Sandwiches

6 large cucumbers	½ cup cream cheese
2 tbsp salt	3 or 4 drops Tabasco
1 cup homemade	
mayonnaise	

Peel the cucumbers, quarter them lengthwise, and remove the soft inner core and seeds. Put the cucumber strips in a shallow bowl, sprinkle them with the salt, let stand 45 minutes. Wash the strips in cold water, drain and blot dry, then mince the cucumber and combine it with the remaining ingredients. Chill lightly to allow it to get firm. Make into sandwiches, open-face or closed, cut into strips or triangles, using very thin slices of crisped bread. Garnish open-faced sandwiches with slices of pitted black olives, strips of pimiento, or a sprinkling of paprika.

Makes about 20 triangle sandwiches or 30 strip sandwiches.

Watercress Sandwiches

⅓ to ½ pound watercress	1 cup cream cheese
1½ cups Maltaise Sauce	½ tsp salt

Wash the cress, pull the leaves and fine stems off the coarse bottom stalks. Chop the leaves and fine stems coarsely, mince the coarse stalks, and pound them in a mortar to form a fine smooth paste; do not drain off the juice. Combine all ingredients and work until smooth.

Makes about 15 triangle sandwiches or 20 strip sandwiches.

Boreks

8-ounce package cream	1 tsp Worcestershire Sauce
cheese	3 drops Tabasco
2 tbsp grated Parmesan	1 recipe pâté crust

Soften the cream cheese, combine it with the Parmesan and seasonings, set aside to let the flavors marry. Roll out the dough into a square; it should be about ⅛ inch thick. Cut dough into 2-inch squares. Spread the cheese mixture on each square, leaving about ½ inch margin along one edge. Roll toward the margin, moisten the unspread strip with water, press to seal to the roll. Space the rolls seam-side-down on a lightly oiled baking sheet, bake in a preheated 350-degree oven 15 minutes, or until nicely browned. If a glazed crust is desired, brush the rolls with milk or lightly beaten egg white before baking.

Makes 18 to 20.

Sesame Seed Crisps

1 recipe pâté crust	½ cup grated sweet onion
¾ cup dairy sour cream	¼ tsp salt
2 tbsp melted butter	½ to ¾ cup sesame seeds
1 egg, beaten lightly	

Oil a baking tin, roll the dough into a rectangle that will cover it, put dough in place on baking tin. Combine sour cream, butter, egg, onion, and salt, blend thoroughly, spread over dough. Cover surface of dough with sesame seeds. Bake in a preheated 350-degree oven 15 to 20 minutes, until the pastry dough is firm. Cut into squares or strips while still hot.

Makes about 40 1½-inch squares.

Crab Cups

1 pound crabmeat, well picked	4 egg whites
3 capers	1 cup heavy cream
3 or 4 drops Tabasco	2 tsp unflavored gelatin
1 tsp salt	1 recipe pâté crust
½ tsp freshly ground white pepper	

Be sure all inedible parts are removed from the crabmeat, then put it in a heavy mixing bowl with the capers, Tabasco, salt, and pepper, and work into a smooth paste with a wooden spoon. Beat 2 egg whites and combine them with the crab, then chill the mixture in the refrigerator for 45 minutes. Whip the cream lightly, beat the remaining 2 egg whites until quite stiff. Dissolve the gelatin in a tablespoon of cold water, beat the cream and gelatin into crabmeat, then gently fold in the beaten eggwhites. Return to the refrigerator to chill until firm.

Roll out the pâté crust dough to ⅛-inch thickness, and with it line tartshells or the cups of small-sized (1¼-inch) muffin tins. Bake in a preheated 350-degree oven 15 minutes, until nicely browned. Cool on a rack, then fill the shells with the crabmeat mixture, using a pastry tube or spoon. Garnish with a dab of mayonnaise or half a pitted black olive.

Makes about 20 filled 1¼-inch muffin-cups.

Chicken Bouchées

Substitute cooked white meat of chicken for crabmeat in the preceding recipe and make up the following dough:

¼ cup butter	½ cup sifted flour
⅛ tsp salt	2 eggs

Put ½ cup water in a saucepan, add butter and salt, bring to a boil. Remove from heat, add the flour—all of it at once—and beat briskly with a wooden spoon. Return the pan to low heat and continue beating until the mixture forms a ball and comes away from the sides of the pan. Remove from heat, beat in the eggs one at a time, beating briskly as each is added until the dough is smooth. Beat until the dough begins to form strands. Have the oven preheated to 400 degrees. Drop the dough by level tea-spoonfuls on an ungreased baking sheet, bake until the dough puffs and becomes a rich tan—about 20 to 25 minutes. Let the puffs cool on a rack where no cold air will strike them. When cool, open a small slit in the top and fill with the chicken mixture.

Makes about 40 puffs.

(These puffs can also be filled with the crab cup mixture or with any of the canapé spreads listed earlier in this chapter.)

Chicken-Almond Puffs

1 cup flour
¼ tsp salt
½ cup butter
1 cup chicken stock
4 eggs

½ cup cooked chicken white
   meat
2 tbsp chopped toasted almonds
¾ tsp paprika

Sift the flour, measure and discard excess, add salt and sift again. Put butter and stock in a saucepan over low heat until butter melts. Add flour—all at once—and stir briskly until mixture forms a ball and pulls away from the sides of the pan. Remove from heat, beat in the eggs one at a time; continue beating until a thick, smooth dough is formed. Mince the chicken meat and stir into the dough together with the almonds and paprika. Have oven preheated to 450 degrees. Drop dough by level teaspoonfuls on a lightly greased baking sheet, bake 10 minutes, reduce heat to 350 degrees, and bake 5 to 10 minutes more, until nicely browned.
Makes about 50 puffs; serve them hot or cold.

Marinated Mushrooms

¾ pound small (no bigger
   than 1-inch diameter)
   fresh mushrooms or 8-
   ounce can mushrooms

¼ cup olive oil
¼ cup dry red wine
2 tbsp pimiento
⅛ tsp pepper

If fresh mushrooms are used, wash them well and remove stems; if canned mushrooms, drain them well. Stir together the remaining ingredients, pour over the mushrooms in a bowl, cover, marinate at least 24 hours. Drain before serving, spear each mushroom cap with a cocktail pick, transfer them to a tray or large platter.
Makes about 30 servings.

Cookies and Sweets

Tuiles

3 egg whites
¼ cup confectioner's sugar
⅓ cup sifted flour
¼ tsp salt

1 tsp vanilla extract
1 tsp Cognac
3 tbsp melted butter
⅔ cup chopped almonds

Beat egg whites until they form soft peaks, add sugar while beating, then add salted flour a little at a time while beating until the egg whites will hold stiff peaks. Whip vanilla and Cognac into the butter, add almonds, and fold this mixture into the beaten whites. Drop batter by heaping teaspoonfuls onto a lightly oiled baking sheet, bake 10 to 12 minutes in a preheated 350-degree oven. Have several bottles handy, lying on their sides, and when the cookies come from the oven drape them over the bottles while still warm; they will settle and cool into the curved form of the roofing tiles that give them their name.

Makes about 20 cookies.

Meringues

12 egg whites
1 pound superfine sugar
1 cup boiling water

1 tsp fresh lemon juice
Flavoring and decorations as
    desired (see below)

Have the egg whites at room temperature. Dissolve the sugar in the boiling water and let cool until lukewarm. When cool, stir in the lemon juice. Beat the egg whites and as they begin to stiffen add the dissolved sugar in a thin steady stream while continuing to beat. Beat until the whites hold sharp peaks. Dust a lightly oiled baking sheet with flour, drop the batter on by heaping teaspoonfuls. Flavor by sprinkling the tops with granulated sugar that has been moistened with a liqueur: Kirsch, Crème de Cacao, Eau de

Framboise, etc., or with grenadine. Bake in a preheated 300-degree oven about 25 to 30 minutes, until firm and delicately brown.

Makes about 36 cookies.

Krabeli

2 eggs	¾ tsp grated lemon peel
1 cup sugar	1½ cups flour
1½ tsp anise seed	¼ tsp baking powder

Beat eggs until they begin to foam, add sugar, beat until eggs turn a light lemon shade. Add anise seed and lemon peel, stir together. Blend flour and baking powder, stir briskly into the egg mixture to form a firm batter; you may need a bit more or less flour, as flours vary. Chill dough 1 hour, then turn out about a quarter of the dough at a time on a lightly floured mixing board and roll into cylinders about ½ inch in diameter. Cut into 3-inch lengths, put on well-oiled baking sheet, curving the dough into a semicircle. Bake in a preheated 350-degree oven 10 to 12 minutes, until lightly browned. Slide at once from baking sheet onto cooling rack.

Makes about 36 cookies.

Pfeffernuesse

2 eggs	⅓ tsp freshly grated ginger
1 cup sugar	Grated rind of 1 lemon
¼ cup ground almonds	3 cups sifted flour
¼ tsp ground cloves	3 tbsp dark Jamaican rum
1 tsp cinnamon	Confectioner's sugar
¼ tsp freshly ground pepper	

Beat eggs, adding sugar, until eggs are frothy, continue to beat while adding all remaining ingredients *except* rum and confectioner's sugar. Turn out the dough on a lightly floured board and knead until smooth. Form into a roll about 1¼ to 1½ inches in diameter, chill lightly, then cut into ½-inch slices. Put slices on an oiled baking sheet, let stand overnight. Next day, turn over each slice, bake in a preheated 300-degree oven 20 to 25 minutes until lightly browned. While still warm, sprinkle with rum, roll in confectioner's sugar; when cool, store in a tightly closed container. Pfeffernuesse should be made as far in advance of serving as practical; they improve with age.

Makes about 24 to 30 cookies.

Soups

Seviche (also called Escabeche and Souse)

3 cups raw scallops (about 10)
3 cups raw shelled shrimp
3 cups raw minced fish (any kind)
3 tbsp very light pale rum
3 cups fresh lemon or lime juice

3 cups tomato juice (fresh, if possible)
1 large (3-inch diameter) sweet onion
½ sweet green (bell) pepper
3 drops Tabasco
Salt to taste

At least 8 hours before serving time, quarter the scallops, cut the shrimp in halves lengthwise, and put them with the fish in a deep bowl; add the rum and lemon juice, stir well, let marinate 6 to 7 hours, stirring occasionally. (Actually, the rum and citrus juices are cooking the raw seafood during this time.) About an hour before serving, drain the seafood, return 1 cup of the marinade to the bowl. Add the tomato juice, mince and add the onion and pepper, add the Tabasco, taste and adjust seasoning with salt. Chill, stirring occasionally, until time to serve; ladle into consommé cups or small soup bowls. Seviche should be neither too liquid nor too cold, nor should it be harshly hot with pepper flavor.

Serves 8 to 10.

Solferino Soup

4 leeks trimmed of all green tops	1 cup minced fresh tomatoes; measure after peeling, draining, and removing seeds
1 medium-sized carrot, peeled or scraped	
½ cup minced sweet onion	2 cups cooked mashed potatoes
½ cup butter	2½ cups chicken or veal stock
	1 cup chopped string beans

Chop the leeks and carrot coarsely and sauté them and the onion in half the butter. When the leeks are soft, add the remaining butter, the tomatoes, potatoes, stock, and beans and cook covered for 20 minutes, stirring every 5 minutes to prevent sticking. If the soup gets too thick, add a bit more stock. When all ingredients are soft, pass the soup through a blender or press through a sieve or ricer and return to the pan to reheat; again, if it becomes too thick, adjust by adding more stock.

Makes 8 cups of soup.

(When serving this soup, I use a trick given me by Maxime Gérome, the owner-proprietor of Chez Maxime's restaurant in Reno. After ladling the soup into small ovenproof bowls, cut a nice slice of mild cheese—Gruyère, Baby Swiss, or Muenster—that will just fit the top of the bowl, float the cheese on the soup and put in the oven under the broiler until the cheese bubbles. This is a nice way to serve any soup, as the bowls can be put on the table and the cheese covering will keep the soup piping hot while the diners are being seated.)

Plum Soup

25 to 30 plums, pitted and halved	1 cup graham-cracker crumbs
1 cup Rhine wine	1 tsp (approximately) powdered ginger
⅓ cup Port	Lemon juice to taste (see below)
1½ cups heavy cream	

Measure the pitted plums; you need 10 cups. Over low heat, stew the plums in the wine until they are very soft. Pass them through a ricer or blender, reserving all liquid and pulp, including the pan liquid. Combine all the remaining ingredients *except* the lemon juice, then stir briskly. Add lemon juice until the soup is tart rather than sweet—you will need 2 to 2½ tbsp, but be guided by your taste rather than the measure. Stir well, chill lightly.

Serves 8 to 10.

Dishes Suggested for Buffet Service

Swiss Steak

2½ pounds round or rump steak, about ¾ inch thick	1 clove garlic
	2 tbsp peanut oil
	2 cups canned tomatoes
⅓ cup flour	¾ tsp dry crumbled oregano
1 tsp salt	1 tbsp minced fresh parsley
¼ tsp freshly ground pepper	

Remove any bones from the steak, trim fat or skin from edges. Pound lightly with the serrated face of a meat mallet or the rim of a thick saucer. Combine flour, salt, and pepper, rub generously on both sides of the meat, and pound lightly to incorporate into the surface. Sauté the garlic clove in the oil until brown, remove and discard garlic. Cut the steak into 8 serving-size pieces, brown both sides of each piece in the oil. Chop the tomatoes and pour them over the meat, together with the juices from the can. Add the oregano. Cook over medium-high heat 10 minutes, cover the pan, and reduce heat to low; cook 1 to 1¼ hours, until the meat tests tender to a fork. Drain the meat from the pan to a heated platter, sprinkle with parsley. Pour the gravy into sauceboats; let your guests serve themselves with meat, then add gravy from the boats on the tables.

Serves 8.

Beef Pot Pie

2 pounds boneless chuck
½ cup flour
1 teaspoon salt
½ tsp freshly ground pepper
3 tbsp peanut oil

2 cups beef or veal stock
2 cups fresh or frozen peas
1½ cups peeled cubed carrots
1 cup milk
½ recipe pâté crust

Trim fat and connective tissues from the meat and cut it in ½-inch cubes. Combine flour, salt, and pepper and dredge beef cubes thoroughly. Bring oil to high heat in a casserole dish and brown the beef cubes, stirring to color all sides evenly. Add the stock, peas, carrots, milk. Cover the casserole and cook in a preheated 300-degree oven for 1½ hours. Stir once or twice. If more liquid is needed, add a bit of stock. Roll out the dough thickly—¼ inch or so—in shape and size to cover the casserole. Uncover, put the crust on the casserole, slit it in two or three places to allow steam to escape, brush with cold water or milk to glaze. Return to oven, cook 15 to 20 minutes, until the crust is nicely browned.
Serves 8 to 10.

Deviled Pork Chops

8 to 10 center-cut pork chops
⅓ cup peanut oil
1½ tsp salt
½ tsp cayenne

2 tsp Worcestershire Sauce
⅛ tsp Tabasco
½ tsp dry mustard
1 tbsp brown sugar

Trim excess fat from the chops; they should have a rim of fat only about ¼ to ⅛ inch wide. Use about half the oil in a heavy ovenproof pan and brown the chops moderately on both sides. Combine the remaining oil with the rest of the ingredients, pour over the chops, and cook covered in a preheated 350-degree oven for 45 minutes; turn once at midpoint in cooking. Remove cover from pan, baste the chops well in the pan liquid, cook 15 to 20 minutes more, turning once, or until they are a deep brown and test tender to a fork. Remove chops to a heated platter, skim loose fat from the small amount of pan juice, strain the remaining juice and pour over the chops.

Serves 8 to 10.

Spiced Meatballs

2 pounds ground beef	1 tbsp chopped fresh mint leaves
1 cup soft fine breadcrumbs	1 tsp crushed anise seed
1 cup grated onion	2 eggs, beaten lightly
¾ cup dry red wine	Flour
1½ tsp salt	1 tbsp peanut oil

Break the beef into small chunks in a large mixing bowl. In a small bowl combine the breadcrumbs, onion, wine, salt, mint, anise, stir well to blend, then work the mixture well into the meat. When combined, work in the eggs. Spread flour over a mixing board, flour your hands well, and form the beef mixture into small meatballs, no larger than ¾ to 1 inch in diameter. Chill for about 1 hour. Oil a shallow baking pan and distribute the meatballs in it; there should be space between them, but it will do no harm to arrange them in the pan 2 or 3 layers deep. Cook uncovered in a preheated 325-degree oven for 45 minutes to 1 hour, until meatballs are brown and firm.

Makes about 60 meatballs.

(Made very small, about ½ inch in diameter, these make good cocktail-party nibbles.)

Chicken Kiev

8 large whole chicken breasts	Flour
¼ pound butter	1 egg, beaten lightly
1 tbsp Kirsch	1 cup very fine dry breadcrumbs
1 tsp freshly ground white pepper	

Several hours in advance of cooking, skin the chicken breasts, and place 1 breast at a time between sheets of waxed paper, then pound gently with the smooth face of a meat mallet or the flat of a cleaver to flatten them. Put the breasts in the refrigerator to chill. Combine all but 2 tbsp of the butter with the Kirsch and pepper, form the mixture into 8 rectangles of equal size, about $\frac{1}{4}$ inch thick, and put on waxed paper or foil and freeze until hard. When ready to cook, put a piece of the butter on each breast, fold the meat over and secure the edges with small skewers or cocktail picks. Rub each breast with flour, dip in the egg, then roll in the breadcrumbs. Melt the reserved butter in a heavy skillet over medium-high heat, brown each breast on both sides, transfer to a shallow baking pan and cook uncovered in a preheated 400-degree oven for 15 to 20 minutes. Remove the skewers just before serving.

Serves 8.

Tomatoes Parmigiana

4 large (4-inch diameter) firm-ripe tomatoes	1 tbsp grated Parmesan
$\frac{3}{4}$ cup grated sweet onion	$\frac{1}{2}$ cup melted butter
$\frac{1}{2}$ cup minced parsley	1 tsp salt
2 cups cooked chopped spinach	$\frac{1}{8}$ tsp cayenne
$\frac{3}{4}$ cup ricotta or cottage cheese	$\frac{1}{2}$ cup fine dry breadcrumbs

Plunge the tomatoes into very hot water, then very cold water and peel. Cut in halves, remove seeds, juice, and inner dividing pulp. Combine onion, parsley, spinach, ricotta, and half the Parmesan, the butter, salt, and cayenne, and divide this mixture between the tomato shells, filling them rounded-full. Mix the reserved Parmesan with the breadcrumbs and cover the tops. Put the tomato halves in a shallow, lightly oiled baking pan, cook under the broiler at medium-low heat for 10 to 12 minutes, until the filling is hot and the tops nicely browned.

Serves 8.

Broccoli Calabrese

2 to 3 pounds broccoli
½ pound pasta (any of the
    small shapes, stars,
    shells, or fine macaroni,
    ditalini)
½ cup olive or peanut oil

2 cloves garlic
⅓ cup pine nuts (pignoli or
    piñons)
⅓ cup currants or dark raisins
2 tsp salt

Wash the broccoli, cut off flowerets, cut small stems (up to ¼-inch diameter) into short sections, discard large coarse stems. Wash the broccoli a second time, but do not drain. Put into a saucepan with a close-fitting cover, cook over very low heat 10 to 12 minutes, shaking the pan occasionally. Remove pan, put broccoli in a colander, hoid briefly under cold running water, set aside to drain. Bring 4 cups water to a rolling boil, add 1 tsp salt, put in the pasta a bit at a time, stir, cook 12 to 15 minutes, checking during the final 5 minutes by cutting a piece in half; when no flour line appears in the center, the pasta is cooked. Drain pan, fill at once with cold water, drain again, putting pasta in a colander or strainer. Heat oil in a large skillet, put in the garlic, cook until it is brown, remove and discard. Add the nuts, cook 3 to 5 minutes, stirring. Add currants, salt, broccoli, pasta, stir well, cook 3 to 5 minutes, only long enough to heat.
    Serves 8.

Stuffed Mushrooms

16 large (2–3-inch diameter)
    fresh, field mushrooms
8 slices Canadian bacon
½ cup minced sweet onion
1 tbsp flour

1 cup fine dry breadcrumbs
½ tsp powdered allspice
3 eggs
2 tbsp milk
½ tsp salt

Wash the mushrooms, parboil 4 to 5 minutes, drain, remove and mince the stems, reserving the caps. Sauté the bacon until crisp, drain the skillet, reserving the drippings; in the fat clinging to the skillet, sauté the onions until they begin to turn color, then drain them on a paper towel. Crumble or chop the bacon, combine it in the skillet with the minced mushroom stems, sprinkle with the flour and stir 3 or 4 minutes over low heat. Add the breadcrumbs and allspice. Beat the eggs with the milk, pour over the mixture in the skillet, and cook, stirring, until the eggs set up. Add salt. Rub the mushroom caps with some of the bacon dripping, put them bottom up on a lightly oiled baking sheet, divide the bacon-bread-crumb mixture between the caps, mounding it up. Put the stuffed mushrooms under the broiler at medium heat for 5 minutes, just enough to reheat both mushrooms and stuffing.

Serves 8.

Hong Kong Pockets

3 cups bean sprouts, drained	1 tsp salt
1 cup finely slivered green pepper	½ tsp powdered allspice
	1 recipe pâté crust
1 cup minced Chinese cabbage	1 egg white, beaten lightly
1 cup grated Monterey Jack cheese	

Combine the bean sprouts, green pepper, Chinese cabbage, cheese, salt, and allspice. Roll out the pâté dough into a square about ¼ inch thick, cut into 3-inch squares. Divide the vegetable-cheese mixture between the squares, moisten the edges of the dough with water, and fold into triangles; press the edges with a fork to seal. Put the triangles on a lightly oiled baking sheet, brush with beaten egg white, cook in a preheated 375-degree oven for 20 to 25 minutes, until the crust is richly browned.

Serves 8 to 10.

Fried Cauliflower

2 heads fresh young cauliflower, about ¾ pound each	¼ tsp freshly ground pepper
	1 tbsp grated Parmesan
	3 eggs, well beaten
1 cup flour	Fat for deep frying
1 tsp salt	

Remove most of the green leaves from the stalks of the cauliflower, wash heads under running water, then plunge them into boiling water and simmer 3 to 4 minutes. Drain. Break up the heads, reserving the small flowerets—about finger to thumb size—for frying. Save the stalks and greens for a salad or a casserole dish. Combine flour, salt, pepper, and Parmesan. Roll the cauliflower flowerets in this mixture, dip in the beaten egg, and fry in deep fat until delicately browned. Drain on paper towels before serving.

Serves 8 to 10.

While the recipes for entrées and vegetables in the foregoing have been chosen with an eye to their suitability for buffet service—none of them is runny or slippery—they'd go equally well at a sit-down dinner. Conversely, the meat entrées you'll encounter further along are as suitable for buffet service as for more formal dining. And, in the next chapter's recipe section, you will find a representative selection of salads suitable for any occasion.

By the way, if you didn't identify the special pâté mentioned at the beginning of the chapter, it's the first one in the recipe section, Pâté Maison en Terrine.

III

Making Festive Salads, Chafing-Dish Specialties, Desserts, and Coffee

To begin with, let's agree that His participation in culinary preparations for a fairly elaborate dinner or other entertainment needn't be and perhaps shouldn't be limited to lending a hand at specific tasks which She requests and itemizes. Every man who doesn't have a totally incurable dislike for kitchen-puttering ought to be ready and able to supplement Her work in getting ready to receive guests and feed them.

Which parts you decide to accept as your responsibility will depend to some extent on how deeply you've swallowed the legend, perpetuated by generations of women, that cooking is hard work and involves endless hours of sweating over a hot stove. This may have been true at one time, when kitchen ranges not only lacked automatic temperature controls, but had to be stoked by hand with wood or coal. It certainly isn't true today, even when you're cooking from scratch without the use of so-called "convenience" foods.

Few cooking processes require undivided attention for hour after hour. Most dishes are prepared in two or three periods of actual work. The first period involves getting the ingredients assembled and ready, the second is spent composing the dish and putting it to cook, and the shorter third period arrives when cooking is completed and the dish is made ready to serve. Between these three busy times there are usually long stretches when the cook has nothing at all to do. If you're the cook, you'll find that you can spend these in-between times lolling in an easy chair with your feet propped up on a hassock, watching football on tv or reading a book or working chess problems or puttering in the workshop, or enjoying whatever form of indoor recreation you favor.

If you want to prove this to your own satisfaction, take a few minutes and analyze a half-dozen typical recipes. Incidentally, if you haven't yet learned how to read and interpret and analyze a recipe, it's a knack you'll find very useful to acquire. There's nothing difficult about it. Only a few abbreviations are used, and you may have to learn a bit of cooking nomenclature, but most of the phrases simply extend into the kitchen words that are in common everyday use. The most common abbreviations are the measurements: "C" for cup, "tbsp" for tablespoon, "tsp" for teaspoon. Some recipes give measurements in pounds or ounces, and these may sometimes have to be translated into cups and spoonfuls.

There'll also be times when it will be necessary to substitute an ingredient that's on hand for one missing from the kitchen cabinet. In almost every case where substituting is required, alternates are available. If you know what they are— or know where to look to find out what they are—a lot of hassling and perhaps a special trip to the store will be avoided. Often it's necessary to double a recipe, and while this is generally a pretty straightforward procedure, there are some pitfalls to avoid, especially when it comes to doubling quantities of seasonings. A good rule of thumb is to double the quantity, then use two-thirds of that amount and taste; you can always add more to adjust the final flavor of a dish, but you can't remove seasonings once they're added and the dish is cooked.

To help your translation of measurements, a conversion table is included that changes kitchen measurements from cups and spoonfuls into ounces or pounds and also into grams, the metric equivalent. And the most common substitutions are also given in this appendix.

Your contribution to the preparation of a dinner menu,

then, might take any of several forms. You might offer to cook an entrée or some of the side dishes. You could assume the job of making the salad, or preparing a spectacular dessert, or something unusual in the way of an after-dinner coffee. Going a step further, you might acquire skill at chafing-dish cooking, and on some occasions prepare part of the dinner right at the table. All these are possibilities worth exploring, so let's explore.

Salads

Perhaps the greatest contribution you could make to a dinner would be to assume full responsibility for the salad, and this is one of the several functions traditionally carried out by the host. There are other reasons than work-sharing for you to take a special interest in salad making. Although women have become more knowledgeable about salads in recent years, a lot of them still suffer from the woman's-magazine syndrome. This is a serious but not fatal affliction acquired from reading "home service" magazines in which the text is prostituted to serve the interests of the advertisers rather than the readers. For the past two decades, both ads and text of a majority of these magazines have devoted a great deal of effort to convincing their women readers that a salad is a gooey mess of colored sweetened gelatin in which miscellaneous canned fruits—and often nut-meats and marshmallows as well—have been imbedded.

Actually, these gelatinous contrivances are desserts, and nobody with any gastronomic sanity wants both to begin and to end a meal with dessert. As has already been noted, sweets before dinner kill tastebuds and appetites. Cold sweets eaten on an empty stomach also put that organ into such a state of shock that it's unable to perform its digestive functions properly. About nine-tenths of all gastrointestinal upsets can be traced to the fad—inspired by the sweetened gelatin makers and abetted by the women's magazines—of serving these unsavory concoctions in place of an honest salad. The other 10 percent of stomach problems, if you're interested, can probably be attributed to the barbaric habit of swilling inordinate quantities of icewater and oversweet iced tea during a meal; this, too, keeps a stomach in a condition of shock.

Ensure that your dinners include a proper salad. The easiest way to do this is to become your household's salad chef. Investigate the kinds of lettuce and other salad greens that are available seasonally or regularly in your area's markets. It takes at least three kinds of greens to make a good salad, and there are few neighborhoods today where your choice is limited to only three.

Romaine (properly, cos lettuce) is available almost everywhere the year round, and is perhaps your happiest choice for a salad's basic green. Add to the romaine a smaller quantity of redleaf (also called Australian) lettuce, and for a third, choose from butter, looseleaf, or Boston. Or, you might choose endive or escarole for your third green, though these pungent greens must be used sparingly. Don't let yourself be tempted by the cheapness and ready availability of iceberg lettuce. This is a pale, watery substitute for the more desirable varieties; it is favored by growers because it's easy to grow and withstands shipment, and favored by grocers and restaurant operators because it has high salvage value in that the rotting outer leaves can be peeled off and discarded for several days. Its commercial virtues do not make iceberg lettuce a superior green; avoid it if possible, but when it's the only green available, make the best of it.

Other greens that go well in a salad include Chinese cabbage (bok choy), which is closer to lettuce than cabbage; leaves of tender young spinach; and the already-mentioned endive and escarole. If you relish their piquant tang, use watercress and parsley in moderation. A variety of greens makes a very good salad indeed, but if you want to expand your choice is very wide. A tossed salad might include, in addition to its lettuces, slivers of tomato, green or sweet red pepper, mushroom buttoms or big mushroom caps sliced thinly, shreds of onions or leeks, capers, cucumber, raw zucchini, radishes, celery, or Jerusalem artichoke.

If a salad is to be served within a relatively short time after the greens are prepared, they can be cut instead of torn. Many salad recipes stipulate tearing the leaves because cutting creates bruises that within two or three hours after the cutting causes the cut edges to darken and grow soft. If you are preparing greens for a salad that will not be served for several hours, tear them; if not, you'll find cutting them saves a great deal of time.

There is also an infinite variety of dressings with which to point up the flavors of your salad ingredients. These range from a simple vinaigrette through several variations of mayonnaise to the more exotic dressings such as Russian with its cheerful orange glow, Parisian with its nutlike cheesy flavor, Green Goddess, and a host of others. There are also herbs to be considered; in addition to the more commonplace ones like rosemary, marjoram, chives, and thyme, you might enjoy experimenting with some of the more pungent and less widely used herbs such as fennel, coriander, and sorrel.

While the simple but subtle salad composed of several kinds of greens tossed in a freshly made dressing has no peer, if your meal is on the light side you can quickly make your salad quite substantial. To the greens add slivers of spicy salami or prosciutto; or coarse gratings of an assertive cheese, Mimolette or Bierkäse or sharp Cheddar. Alternatively, you could combine with the greens some flaked fish, chunks of crabmeat, shrimp, or shredded lobster. There are also meal-sized salads: Chef's, Caesar, Shrimp, and Crab Louis.

Composing the salad dressing at the table is another pleasant task assigned by tradition to the host. No matter how excellent the salad ingredients may be, their virtue is sacrificed if the dressing is inferior. The only way to be sure of a good salad dressing, in today's world of phony foods, is to mix your own. Salad dressings and dressing "mixes" are high on the list of spurious "foods" turned out by the modern food factories.

Components of a chafing dish are blazer pan, lid, water jacket, stand, and heat source. Visible through the stand's top is the old jellied-fuel burner; in the right foreground, the much more efficient butane-fueled burner. Ronson makes the one shown; it uses standard lighter refills.

Assembled, from the bottom up, are stand, butane burner, water jacket, blazer pan, lid.

Beware of any bottled dressing or any packet of foil or plastic that purports to contain ingredients which, if mixed with liquid, will produce a salad dressing.

Read the labels. You'll find the bottled products hold more water than anything, in which several chemicals are held in emulsification by several other chemicals. The packets of "mix" usually contain a few flakes of desiccated onion and parsley and some powdered protein made from hydrolized carrots; the rest is all pure chemicals. Make your own salad dressings, then, using good oil, wine vinegars, and lemon juice, and real herbs. Recipes for some dressings and for composing a few of the more substantial salads are in the recipe section that closes this chapter.

Chafing-Dish Cookery

Chafing-dish cookery has been a masculine avocation for decades, going back to the Silly 60s of the 1800s, and becoming a very big part of that century's Naughty 90s, when suave men-about-town leered in anticipation at ladies from the chorus over a chafing dish at intimate after-theater suppers for two. The art dipped in popularity for a while, but it's returned to become very much a part of the modern cooking scene.

Let's first consider the components and the thermal dynamics of the chafing dish. The components, as the illustration shows, number only five: stand, water jacket, blazer, lid, and a heat source. The stand is designed to hold the two pans, water jacket and blazer, separately, or with the blazer resting on and in the filled water jacket. In this mode, the chafing dish is precisely the same utensil as a double boiler used in the kitchen. It is unexcelled for delicate dishes such as scrambled eggs; for cheese-based dishes that must not be subjected to high heat, such as a Welsh Rabbit; and for producing fine sauces. When quick cooking is required, as in sautéeing, the water jacket is set aside and the blazer used directly over the heat.

Many newcomers to chafing-dish cookery, who begin without first checking out the utensil's operation, find cooking difficult, even disappointing. This is because the manufacturers of chafing dishes generally cling to an outmoded heat source, and provide only a small container in which jellied naphtha is burned. A few provide spirit lamps, which burn wood alcohol and furnish a more controllable and reliable flame. However, the most efficient heat source is one of the small refillable butane burners, which lights at once, is readily adjusted, and provides about three hours of smokeless flame with each filling. If you become serious about chafing-dish cooking, by all means invest in one of these butane burners.

Should you get involved in chafing-dish cookery, you'll also find you can put more than one dish to good use. There are three sizes: large, which come in 2½- or 3-quart capacity; smaller ones holding about 1½ quarts; and tiny ones holding only 6 or 7 ounces. The large dish lets you produce a sizable quantity of food; the smaller size is ideal for sauce making and for holding a large amount of a delicate sauce at an even temperature for a long time; the tiny ones are handy for holding melted butter or syrups and for heating liquors used in preparing dishes that are flamed.

A chafing dish is a remarkably versatile utensil. With the water jacket it not only cooks delicately, but keeps dishes warm without becoming too hot. Remove the water jacket and it can be used as a wok for stir-frying, as a sauté pan, and for such dramatic effects as dishes flamed during their last stages of preparation. Chafing-dish cookery is something that appeals to most men, and it's a style of food preparation that you, too, might find compatible. There are recipes at the end of the chapter with which you can experiment.

While on the subject of at-table cooking, we might as well take a passing glance at the poor relation of the chafing dish, the fondue pot. After skyrocketing to fad popularity in a burst of overnight publicity, fondue-pot cooking dived into near-obliv-

Three sizes will give you more scope if you get serious about chafing-dish cookery. Bottom left, 8-ounce; center, 2½-quart, right, 1½-quart. The smallest size isn't really practical for cooking, but fine for holding melted butter or keeping a sauce warm.

ion, but is returning to occupy a small but permanent niche in the cooking spectrum. A fondue pot isn't something you'd bring out at a formal dinner, to be sure. For informal occasions, it's a good utensil to have around. Its use is no longer limited to making cheese sauces into which cubes of bread are dunked— you can do this in a chafing dish, if you wish—but has now been extended with the electric fondue pot to preparing tempura in the Japanese style.

Tempura involves impaling bits of meat and vegetables on skewers or forks, dipping them into a thin batter, then deep-frying them quickly. If you buy a new fondue pot, by all means get the electric type, or get one with a stand high enough to allow you to use the butane burner mentioned earlier as its heat source. Tempura—and many other foods—can be cooked in electric skillets as well as in chafing dishes and fondue pots at the table, but while these utensils become more attractive year

If you get a fondue pot, buy a big one, electrically heated.

after year, they still haven't gained acceptance for use at any but the most informal occasions, the kind of impromptu affairs limited to a few very close friends.

To some extent, this applies to all at-table cooking, though chafing dishes have been around a long time and bring to the table a sort of nostalgic glamor that gives them quite wide acceptance. But the fondue pot and the electric skillet are still pretty much confined to after-theater gatherings, late suppers following a sports event, after-ski parties, Sunday brunches, and such other casual occasions.

To an even greater extent, this limitation also applies to hibachi cooking. I find it difficult to enthuse over indoor use of the hibachi for two reasons. The first is that it's very messy to use a hibachi indoors; it seems invariably to spatter table, floor, and chairs with grease. The second and perhaps more cogent objection is that it's often dangerous to use a charcoal-fueled hibachi in a U.S.-built house. In the Orient, where hibachi cooking originated, houses are not often tightly constructed, but tend to be drafty. In American houses, with weatherstripped doors and windows, the fumes from a charcoal hibachi can bring death from asphyxiation. Electric hibachis are quite safe to use indoors, if you don't mind cleaning up after them. My feeling is that if you're going to cook with electricity, there are cleaner ways to do so than at the table in an hibachi.

Desserts

Now, let's jump to the end of a meal to look at another area. Your offer to help in the kitchen might result in something as simple as the preparation of an unusual dessert and a special after-dinner coffee. If these do turn out to be your share of the entertainment-preparation chores, count yourself lucky. There's such a wide choice, from spartan to spectacular, that you'll never be stumped for a climax that will suit any occasion.

Even during a period of universal dieting and waistline-awareness, desserts hold their place and their popularity. Most people, men and women alike, will cut down on meals rather than forego dessert. And keep in mind that the most lasting impression a guest carries away from the dinner table is generally that made by the dessert. The meal itself might fall short of being stupendous, but if the dessert's satisfying and delicious, everybody at the table is likely to label it a success. Many an otherwise routine dinner has been salvaged by an outstanding dessert and something special in the line of after-dinner coffee.

Desserts needn't be elaborate to be outstanding. We have several quite simple toppings that we serve over plain vanilla ice cream, and these draw more praise and seem to be remembered longer than our occasional Baked Alaska. The most successful of these toppings is made with overripe bananas and dark Jamaican rum, and takes all of ten seconds to whip up. We've discovered that the key to its flavor is using bananas that are black of skin with flesh soft to the stage of mushiness. When made with firm bananas the blend is blah. To make it, simply peel the bananas into the blender, allowing one-half banana per serving, then add a jigger of rum for each three bananas. Switch on the blender to HIGH for five seconds, and spoon the resulting golden creamy mixture over the ice cream.

Next in popularity is a topping made by heating a cup of undiluted condensed milk with a half-cup of peanut butter and stirring until smooth. This one has a secret, too: use nothing but natural peanut butter, the kind that is made only from peanuts and salt and hasn't been "texturized" by the addition of lard or hydrogenated cottonseed oil or homogenized to make it smooth and creamy. Combine the milk and peanut butter in the top of a double boiler and stir until the two blend; it should simmer about three minutes without boiling. Spoon the sauce over vanilla ice cream while it's still hot.

Running about neck and neck with the peanut-butter topping, but a poor third to the one made with bananas and rum, is a concoction of apples and Port. The apples aren't peeled, just cored to remove seeds and stems, and quartered. Then they're put into the blender with a quarter-teaspoon of honey and a teaspoon of good Port per apple. The blender is whirled at HIGH for about ten seconds—long enough to reduce the apple skins to fine slivers—and spooned on the ice cream. The tiny unidentifiable shreds of skin add both color and a toothy texture to the topping; it's not as good when the apples are peeled.

Serving these toppings—not all at the same meal, of course—will go a long way to convince you that a dessert needn't be all gussied up to make a good impression or to taste good. In fact, an overelaborate dessert after a big meal can be just a bit too much, sometimes. Nor are such simple desserts limited to ice-cream toppings. A plain egg custard sauced with caramel or a fruit poached in syrup can be just as much a conversation piece, and a compote of fruits marinated with a subtle liqueur or fruits flamed at the table in a chafing dish can add a special touch to a meal without adding to kitchen chores.

To compose a fruit compote, select by both color and flavor: apples, peaches, bananas, and pitted cherries; or, pears, apricots, plums, and white grapes. Don't overkill. Three fruits and a bright berry are plenty. Marinate in your favorite liqueur. Triple Sec, Curaçao, Grand Marnier, and Kirsch blend compatibly with any combination of fruits you choose. So will Cognac. If you use bananas, add them at the last minute or they'll get dark and mushy; otherwise, marinate your fruits in the liqueur you're using for about 2 hours and serve lightly chilled but never icy-cold.

No recipe is going to help you make up a compote, because fruits vary in sugar content from one geographical area to the next, from one season or period of the year to another, and generic liqueurs will vary slightly according to brand. You'll just have to taste and test, adding a bit of bar syrup or honey if the dish isn't sweet enough, a bit of lemon juice if it's oversweet. But do add the liqueur with a light touch; its presence should be sensed, never consciously tasted.

During strawberry season, pass big bowls of fresh berries and provide each guest with two small coasters, one containing a little Rhine wine, the other holding sugar. Then hold the berries by the stem, dip them first into the wine, then the sugar, and eat them out of hand. Don't stem the berries; this seems to rob the diners of some earthy, atavistic pleasure. But do provide extra napkins—paper—when you serve this.

Chafing dishes are very much in their place at the table at even the most formal dinner when it comes to producing dessert spectaculars. A flamed dessert certainly fits into the "spectacular" category, and flamed fruits are among the easiest of all desserts to prepare. If you want to add a fillip of showmanship, do as some restaurants do—dim the lights before you light the liqueur in the chafing dish and let the colorful flames of Cognac or other brandy illuminate the scene for a few moments.

These two spirits, by the way, aren't the only ones that can be used to flame foods. Bourbon, gin, vodka, Scotch, and rum can all be used. So can a galaxy of liqueurs, though the most useful are Kirsch, Triple Sec, Grand Marnier, and slivovitz. All these come from the bottle at 84 to 90 proof, and not only ignite readily but are based on ingredients that harmonize with virtually all fruit flavors. Cordials and liqueurs in the 60- to 80-proof range don't light easily, and need to be reinforced with a dash of brandy or 100-proof vodka or an orange or almond extract. It's really a good idea to use one of these high-proof boosters when using Cognac, which is in the 84- to 86-proof range.

One important thing to remember: any liquor or liqueur used in flaming must be preheated. There are several small utensils suitable for this job: a tiny chafing dish, a butter warmer, or a sauce warmer. Measure the spirits you'll be using for flaming and have them warmed by the time you need them, and you'll never have a flameless failure.

Recipes for flamed desserts—including the all-time favorite, Crêpes Suzette—will be found toward the end of this chapter. Also among the recipes you'll find one given me by a good British friend who converted me into a lifelong aficionado of the most sinfully rich dessert of all, English Trifle. A trifle, if you'll excuse the Irish bull, is nothing to be trifled with, and should be served only after a very light meal, because it's a dessert in which overindulgence isn't merely easy, but almost inevitable.

Also suitable after a light meal is a dessert of fruit and cheese. Tradition favors apple wedges as an accompaniment to cheese, but crisp chilled pears go equally well; so do most varieties of grapes. We've already touched the subject of cheeses, but the list of varieties is almost inexhaustible. Try apples or pears with the sharper kinds—Roquefort, Gorgonzola, Stilton—but remember these fruits go as well with creamy cheeses like Brie, Camembert, and Liederkranz. Grapes and apricots are more at home with the mild cheeses such as Port Salut and Havarti, and with Cheddars, Swisses, and Edams. Be sure the fruits are chilled to crispness and the cheese is at room temperature.

Or, omit fruit entirely and simply pass some of the more unusual varieties of cheese with unsalted crackers. There is the La Grappe from France, cured by burial in grape seeds left from the wine presses; its close cousin, Fromage du Marc, which is cured the same way but in addition is anointed with several sprinklings of Cognac or Marc while curing. Other seldom-seen cheeses that might be offered are the Cheddarlike Mimolette, bright orange in color; Rambol Poivre, a white cheese formed into small cylinders and cured in a nest of peppercorns; Blue Castello; Boursault; and Chantilly.

You could take a large Edam or Gouda, remove a slice from the top, scoop out its insides, and blend them with a few spoonfuls of Cognac or brandy and a drop or two of Tabasco. The blending must be done by taste, as no two cheeses are quite the same, nor are any two kinds of Cognac. When blended, return the seasoned cheese to the red shell, and let it age a few days before offering it to your guests as an after-dinner touch more interesting than many sweets.

After-Dinner Coffee

Finally, there's the matter of after-dinner coffee, and a bit of propagandizing seems called for at this point. Whether you serve coffee unadorned, or gussied up with some of the trimmings that distinguish such dessert coffees as Brûlot and Petit Brûlot, Epicé, Mazagran, Capuccino, Flamand, or Charente, let it fit the famous requirements for good coffee: black as night, strong as true love, hot as Hell.

This automatically rules out of consideration any "instant" coffee, and most of the packaged coffees. If you live in the area around New Orleans, you can find a number of chicory-laced coffees that are very potent indeed. The best-known and most widely distributed vacuum-packed brand that makes a really strong coffee is the Italian Medaglia d'Oro. But if you want the very best coffee that can be brewed, you'll have to grind your own. Judging by the reappearance of coffee beans on grocer's shelves where they've been absent for ten or fifteen years, and by the number of electric coffee grinders appearing on the market, home grinding of coffee is returning in a big way. For some of us, it never left.

Using freshly ground coffee is a habit that once acquired, you don't give up easily. If you'd like to put it to the test, beans are available very widely now, and you can get them by mail order if no stores in your area have caught up with this new demand. Coffee grinders are plentiful. Salton makes one, so does Kitchen Aid; these are big machines, around $30 in price. Smaller electric grinders are made in Europe by Peugeot and Molineaux and sell in the U.S. for around $12. There are plenty of hand grinders on the market, replicas of antiques, that run in price from around $8 to $20. If you're very lucky, you might find a working antique grinder, but be prepared to pay up to $50 for one of these. That's the last offer we refused for our wall-mounted Arcade grinder for which we paid $6 in the early 1950s, and which we still use regularly in spite of having a pair of electric models.

One of the most astonishing culinary discoveries you'll make is that if coffee is ground immediately before brewing, it doesn't matter much what brand or blend you use—you won't get a bad cup in a barrelful. Over the years we've bought coffee beans from about a dozen different retailers and restaurant-supply houses (these latter are an unfailing source of supply if the food stores fail you) and on occasions we've experimented with blending our own. It appears the secret's not in blending as much as it is in grinding the beans just before brewing the coffee, though if we want an unusually rich special-occasion coffee, we add about a half-dozen beans of XXXX grade Columbian coffee to the grinder.

Coffee, like pepper, carries its virtue in a highly volatile oil that is locked into the unbroken bean. Within minutes after grinding this oil begins to evaporate, and the longer coffee is exposed to air after it's ground the greater the loss of this essential flavor factor. You can store coffee beans forever—or so it seems—without having them lose flavor. But even vacuum-packed coffee begins to deteriorate the moment that first gush of air whishes into the can when the vacuum seal is broken.

Our coffee is brewed in a big drip-pot, using the method the French call *refiltré,* which simply means that the moment the boiling water has passed through the grounds once, the contents of the pot are poured into a pitcher and emptied into the top of the drip pot for a second run. This time the liquid goes through in half the time the first filtering required, and seems to extract just a bit of extra essence from the heated grounds. The brew is neither bitter nor overly strong, just richly rounded in flavor, as good coffee ought to be.

Now, to help you make up your mind what you'll be willing to volunteer to do in helping with the dinner, recipes follow for salads and salad dressings, chafing-dish specialties, a few desserts, and some special after-dinner coffees.

Salads

Vinaigrette Dressing

1½ tbsp lemon juice (or use 1 tbsp white wine vinegar)
Large pinch salt
Small pinch freshly ground pepper

¼ tsp prepared Dijon-type mustard
⅓ cup olive oil or peanut oil

Procedure 1—if mixing in a bowl: use a small wire whisk, blend lemon juice and seasonings, then slowly add oil while beating briskly. Put in greens and toss with mixing forks.

Procedure 2—if mixing in a jar: put in all ingredients, shake very briskly for 2 to 3 minutes, pour over salad greens, toss.

Quantities given will dress a green salad to serve 8. Remember, it isn't necessary that the greens be thickly coated—in fact, they shouldn't be; a thin film of dressing is all that's required.

Vinaigrette Dressing is the original "French" dressing, not the oily orange stuff sold in jars bearing that name.

Russian Dressing

1 cup homemade
   mayonnaise
1 tbsp drained bottled chili
   sauce
1 tbsp minced celery

1 tbsp minced drained pimiento
1 tbsp minced sweet green
   pepper
1 tbsp minced fresh parsley

Combine all ingredients by stirring briskly.
Makes 1½ cups.

Homemade Sour Cream

2 cups whipping cream   2 tbsp buttermilk

Pour cream and buttermilk into a sterile glass jar. Cover tightly; if possible, use a jar with a screw-top lid and boil both jar and lid before using. Let jar stand in warm place until mixture thickens; this will be about 24 hours in warm weather, 48 hours in cool. When thickening occurs, shake jar briskly, let stand an hour or so, chill in refrigerator. For a smoother texture, beat very lightly with a wire whisk after the cream has chilled. You will need sour cream for several salad dressings, so make your own—it's better.

Parisian Dressing

¾ cup light cream
1 tbsp homemade sour
   cream
1 tsp prepared Dijon-type
   mustard

3 tbsp fresh lemon juice
Dash of salt
Large pinch freshly ground
   pepper

Combine all ingredients in bowl with small whisk. Pour over salad greens to coat lightly, toss with mixing forks.
Makes 1 cup plus.

Blue Cheese Dressing

⅓ cup blue cheese
½ clove garlic
1 tbsp grated sweet onion
½ cup homemade
    mayonnaise

½ cup homemade sour cream
1 tbsp fresh lemon juice
1 tbsp white wine vinegar
Dash freshly ground white pepper

Crumble the cheese, mince the garlic; combine all ingredients in mixing bowl. Blend with a small whisk; or pass through blender, 3 to 4 seconds at HIGH speed; or use electric mixer, blend at LOW speed until smooth.
Makes 1½ cups.

Green Goddess Dressing

1 cup homemade
    mayonnaise
1 cup homemade sour cream
½ cup fresh minced parsley
¼ cup fresh minced chives
1 tbsp fresh minced tarragon

2 tbsp minced drained anchovy
    fillets
1 tbsp fresh lemon juice
3 tbsp white wine vinegar
½ tsp salt
Small pinch cayenne

(This is the original recipe from the Palace Hotel in San Francisco, where the dressing originated in the 1930s.) Combine all ingredients, using either a whisk, mixer, or blender. If a blender is used, the ingredients need not be minced in advance of mixing.
Makes about 2½ cups.

Tossed Green Salad

Your choice of at least three greens:
Romaine (cos lettuce)
Leaf lettuce
Australian lettuce (redleaf)
Butter lettuce (Boston)

Savoy cabbage
Escarole
Endive
Spinach (only very young leaves)

Wash greens and blot dry; a watery salad is an abomination. Greens should be cool but not ice-cold. Tear or cut greens into salad bowl; add the dressing (unless it was mixed in the bowl) and toss to coat greens lightly.

Chef's Salad

Slivers of boiled ham	Slivers of roast beef
Slivers of sharp Cheddar cheese	Dressing—Mayonnaise, Vinaigrette, etc.
Any two kinds of lettuce, the leaves torn or cut	Hardcooked egg, quartered

Put all ingredients except egg in salad bowl, add dressing, toss, garnish with egg quarters. Ingredient quantities depend on number served.

Crab Louis

For the dressing:

2 cups flaked crabmeat	¾ cup bottled chili sauce
2 cups homemade mayonnaise	1 tbsp grated onion
1 cup whipped cream	1 tbsp minced parsley
	Dash cayenne

For the salad:

2 cups well-picked crabmeat in large chunks	Lettuce leaves
4 cups shredded lettuce	4 hardcooked eggs

(This is the original Crab Louis recipe, created by and named for the chef at the Portland Athletic Club in the late 1920s. It is equally good with shrimp instead of crab.) Combine all dressing ingredients, blend well. On each serving plate, make a cup of lettuce leaves. Divide the shredded lettuce between the plates, mounding it up in the leaf cups. Divide the large pieces of crabmeat between the plates, putting about half of each portion on the mounded lettuce. Divide the dressing between the plates, pouring over the salad; put the remaining big pieces of crabmeat on the plates atop the dressed lettuce mounds; garnish each salad with two egg quarters.

Serves 8.

Chicken or Turkey Salad

4 cups coarsely shredded chicken or turkey meat, about ⅔ light and ⅓ dark meat
1 cup minced celery hearts
1 tbsp minced tarragon

1 cup chopped tomatoes, drained
2 tbsp minced chives
1 cup homemade mayonnaise
Lettuce leaves
Hardcooked egg slices

Toss all ingredients except lettuce leaves and egg slices in the mayonnaise, arrange in lettuce-leaf cups on salad plates, top with egg slices.

Serves 8.

Chafing-Dish Specialties

Scrambled Eggs

1 dozen eggs
¾ cup light cream
¾ tsp salt

⅛ tsp freshly ground white pepper
1 tbsp butter

Fill the water jacket with boiling water, turn flame high; boiling must be maintained. Put blazer into water jacket. In a bowl, stir (not beat) all ingredients except the butter. Put butter in chafing dish and as soon as it has melted pour in the eggs. Let cook 5 minutes, then with a wooden spoon pull the eggs from the sides of the pan toward the center. Work slowly in long strokes all around the pan. Uncooked egg will flow into the path of your spoon and twice around the pan should see the eggs cooked, fluffy but solid, tasting "eggy." Serve over toast points.

Serves 8.

Scrambled Egg Variations

Have a plate of crisp bacon bits at hand and stir them into the eggs when mixing them to scramble.

Mince the tops of tender young scallions and sauté them in the butter for a few minutes before putting the eggs in the chafing dish.

Put about ⅔ cup of chopped soft cheese, such as Monterey Jack or Muenster, into the pan and let soften for about 3 minutes before pouring in the eggs.

Add 2 tbsp well-drained capers to the eggs while stirring them.

Batter-Fried Oysters

For the batter:
1 cup flour
½ tsp salt
Small dash freshly ground
    pepper

⅔ cup milk
2 eggs, well-beaten

For the oysters:
4 dozen oysters, drained and
    rolled in cloth to dry
Flour

½ cup butter
½ cup peanut oil

To make batter, combine flour, salt, pepper; beat milk into eggs, add to flour mixture, stirring to blend.

Put the blazer on directly over the heat source, bring butter and peanut oil to bubbling heat. Roll each oyster in flour, dip in batter, drop in fat. Add slowly so the temperature of the fat stays constant. Cook until brown on one side, turn, and when evenly browned remove to drain briefly on paper towel before serving.

Sauce Tartare:

1 cup homemade
    mayonnaise
2 hardcooked egg yolks
1 tsp minced chives
1 tbsp minced parsley

1 tsp grated sweet onion
2 minced shallots
½ tsp minced capers
1 tbsp minced gherkins

Mash egg yolks and work them into the mayonnaise until smooth; blend in the remaining ingredients.
Serves 8.

Pasta e Scampi

2 pounds raw shrimp
⅓ cup fresh lemon juice
¾ tsp salt

4 tbsp butter or peanut oil
2 cups cooked fine spaghetti
1½ tsp chopped fresh dill

Shell and devein the shrimp, cover with lemon juice and salt, marinate 2 hours before cooking. Stir occasionally. Drain shrimp. Have the pasta cooked; use one of the fine spaghettis such as spaghettini, or pasta shapes such as shells or stars. Put the blazer on over direct heat, put in 3 tbsp of the fat, sauté the shrimps until they are pink and tender. Add the remaining fat and the pasta, sprinkle with the dill, stir until heated thoroughly, serve.
Serves 8.

Shrimp Sevillano

2 pounds raw shrimp
1 pound raw mushrooms
2 tbsp olive or peanut oil
1 cup grated sweet onion

1 clove garlic, minced
3 tbsp well-drained pimientos
½ cup dry white wine

In advance, shell and devein the shrimp, halve them length-wise; wash and parboil the mushrooms for 5 minutes, drain, cut them into quarters; chop the pimientos coarsely. Put on the blazer over direct heat, sauté the shrimp and mushrooms in the oil about 5 to 7 minutes, add the onion and garlic; cook 5 minutes with

frequent stirring. Add pimientos and wine, let the dish simmer 5 minutes, spoon over toast points or boiled rice.
Serves 8.

Steak Diane (also called Steak au Poivre)

8 slices beef tenderloin cut ½
    inch thick
2 tsp white peppercorns

2 tbsp peanut oil
2 tbsp butter
1 cup heavy cream

Using the smooth face of a meat mallet or a cleaver's side, pound the tenderloin slices until they are ⅛ inch thick. On waxed paper, crush the peppercorns into small pieces. Press the steaks into the peppercorns firmly so the pepper adheres to the meat. Put between waxed-paper sheets until ready to cook. At the table, put the blazer on over direct heat, get the oil and butter hot. Have a heated platter ready. Sauté the steaks quickly, two or three at a time; cook no longer than 3 minutes per side, transfer to platter. When all the steaks are cooked, pour the cream into the blazer, let it get hot, pour over the steaks, serve at once.
Serves 8.

Oyster Stew

1 quart oysters with their
    liquor
1 cup milk
1 cup light cream
Dash Angostura Bitters

6 to 8 drops Tabasco
½ tsp paprika
⅓ cup butter
Oyster crackers

Put the water jacket on, fill with boiling water, set the blazer in place. Put oysters, milk, and cream in the blazer, let the milk simmer 5 minutes without boiling. Stir in the Angostura and Tabasco, let simmer briefly. Ladle into bowls, dust with paprika, put a blob of butter on each to melt, as well as floating a few oyster crackers on each bowl. Have bowls of oyster crackers around the table.

Serves 8, but unless you have a large-size chafing dish you may have to cook two batches and serve small initial portions and seconds.

Crab Imperiale

3 egg yolks	2 tbsp slivered mushrooms
⅓ cup very dry sherry	¾ tsp dry mustard
½ cup butter	Large pinch freshly ground
½ cup cream	white pepper
½ cup milk	2 pounds picked crabmeat

Fill the water jacket half full of boiling water, over moderate heat. Put blazer into water jacket. Stir the egg yolks together in the blazer, using a wooden spoon, and slowly add the sherry while stirring. Add the butter by spoonfuls, continuing to stir. When the mixture thickens begin pouring in the combined cream and milk, stirring, until smooth. Add all remaining ingredients, stir occasionally while they simmer—about 5 to 7 minutes. Serve over toast points, or have tartshells made of homemade pâté crust and fill them with the crab mixture.
Serves 8.

Cantonese Fry

1½ pounds beef chuck cut into thin strips about 2 inches long	2 tbsp peanut oil
	1 cup bean sprouts (canned)
	1 cup bamboo shoots (canned)
½ cup soy sauce	½ cup chopped scallions
½ cup very dry sherry	1 tsp cornstarch
1 clove garlic	¼ tsp powdered ginger

In advance, marinate the beef strips in the soy sauce (and get a good soy sauce, such as Kikkoman, not a watered-down domestic version) and sherry, adding the garlic clove, mashed. Let stand about an hour, turning the meat strips occasionally. When ready to cook, drain the beef, reserving the marinade. Use the blazer over direct heat, medium-high. Heat the peanut oil, add the ingredients in batches, stirring constantly. Cook each batch about 2 minutes, remove to a warmed platter, cook another, until all ingredients are cooked. Dissolve the cornstarch in 3 tbsp of the reserved marinade, put it in the pan, stir in the ginger, cook until it thickens, pour over platter. Serve with steamed rice or noodles.

Serves 8.

Welsh Rabbit

1 cup flat beer or ale, warm	¼ tsp grated Sap Sago cheese
1 tsp dry mustard	1 egg yolk
3 drops Tabasco	Toast
¾ pound sharp natural Cheddar	Paprika

Fill the water jacket with boiling water, put over medium heat, the blazer inside the jacket. Combine beer (let stand overnight to get flat), mustard, Tabasco, Cheddar, Sap Sago (this cheese acts as a flavor amplifier for other cheeses; if you don't have it, don't worry about it, but your Welsh Rabbit will be better if it's used), and egg yolk. Cook, stirring, until the cheese melts and a smooth mixture forms. Spoon over toast points, dust with paprika for garnish.

Serves 8.

Welsh Monkey

1 pound medium-sharp Cheddar	¾ cup fine dry breadcrumbs
1¼ cups milk	1 egg, beaten lightly
½ tsp dry mustard	Toast points
1 tsp Worcestershire Sauce	Paprika

Fill water jacket with boiling water, over medium heat, put the blazer in the jacket. Dice or grate the cheese. Bring milk to the boiling point, stir in the cheese and seasonings. When the cheese begins to blend with the milk, begin adding the breadcrumbs by tablespoonfuls, stirring; when all the crumbs have been absorbed, quickly beat in the egg. Serve over toast points, dust with paprika for garnish.

Serves 8.

Fondues

There are as many recipes for fondues as there are cheeses. A basic recipe follows; feel free to change it by substituting any hard or semi-hard cheese that you choose. Suitable cheeses include Cheddar, Swiss, Kleine Emmenthaler, Mimolette, Gouda, Bierkäse, Provolone, Dunlop, Jarlsberg, Gruyère, and some 20 to 30 others. There must be some kind of liquor, liqueur, or wine in the fondue to emulsify the cheese; Kirsch is the traditional one, but Rhine wine, vodka, Schnapps, and even Scotch whisky can be used. If you have or can find a cone of Sap Sago, add about ½ tsp, to amplify the flavor of the basic cheese, and your fondue will be much improved.

Basic Fondue

1 clove garlic
1 ounce Kirsch or ¾ cup
   Rhine wine
3 cups natural cheese,
   grated

1 tbsp flour
3 or 4 drops Tabasco
Bread cubes
½ tsp Sap Sago, grated

Rub the fondue pot with garlic, discard any remaining garlic. Heat the liqueur or wine and begin adding the cheese in small amounts, alternating with sprinklings of flour—about ½ tsp per addition of flour. Stir until the cheese thickens and bubbles, add the Tabasco and Sap Sago if the latter is used. Reduce heat to keep the cheese fluid but hot. Dip bread cubes in the pot, using long forks. As the pot is depleted, more cheese can be added. Dust the cheese lightly with flour, stir another jigger of Kirsch in, and add the cheese in small quantities, stirring to combine it with what is in the pot.

Serves 8.

Tempura

This is not a recipe; rather, it's a style of cooking akin to fondue. Indeed, many recipes for Tempura-style cooking are labeled as "Beef Fondue" or something of that sort. Usually, but not invariably, the bits of food cooked in the Tempura pot are first dipped in batter. You will also need bowls of Tempura Sauce in which to dunk the foods after they are cooked.

Tempura Batter

1½ cups sifted flour
4 tbsp cornstarch
1½ tsp salt
1⅔ cups water

2 eggs, separated, the yolks stirred, the whites beaten stiff

Combine flour, cornstarch, and salt in a mixing bowl. Make a depression in the center of the flour, pour in half the water and the egg yolks. Stir while slowly adding the remaining water. Just before the batter is to be used, fold into it the beaten egg whites. You should have a bowl of Tempura batter for every three or four guests.

Tempura Sauce

½ cup chicken or veal stock
½ cup Kikkoman soy sauce
½ cup sake or dry sherry

1 tsp freshly grated ginger
½ tsp freshly grated black radish

Combine all ingredients; place small bowls within convenient reach of each cooking station.

Typical foods for Tempura might include:

Shrimp	Chicken	Beef
Scallops	Turkey	Veal
Green pepper	Eggplant	Kidney, veal or lamb
Onion rings	Bamboo shoots	Button mushrooms
Scallions	Water chestnuts	Green beans

All foods should be cut into small pieces of reasonably uniform size: the shrimp halved or quartered, scallops quartered, chicken, beef, turkey, veal, and kidneys cubed, and so on. Peanut oil is best for the frying; cooking can be done in a fondue pot, chafing dish, wok, or electric skillet. One utensil should be provided for each four or five people, and there should be plates of all foods as well as bowls of batter and sauce at each cooking station. Bamboo skewers are the most satisfactory but fondue forks can be used. The method of cooking is for each person to spear a bit or two of food, dip it in batter, cook it quickly in the hot fat, dunk it in sauce, and eat it with fingers.

Desserts

Recipes for ice-cream toppings and fruit compotes are given earlier in this chapter. Here are a few more desserts.

Sherry Custard

4 egg yolks, beaten lightly   3 tbsp Cream or Oloroso sherry
1 cup light cream   ¼ cup sugar
¾ cup milk   Dash salt

In a saucepan over low heat, combine the liquids and stir to blend; add sugar and salt after about 5 minutes cooking time and continue to stir until mixture thickens. When a metal spoon inserted in the custard brings up a coating on being removed, take pan from heat and put at once in icewater to cool. This is a rather thin custard. It can be served in sherbet bowls, with a spoonful of grenadine poured on it for color, or used as a topping for fruits or sauce for a slice of sponge cake.
Makes about 2 cups.

Fruits Flambé

Almost all fruits can be served flamed. There are some special affinities: bananas and rum, cherries and Kirsch, strawberries and Curaçao or Grand Marnier, peaches or apricots and Triple Sec, plums and slivovitz; any fruit and Cognac or brandy. Cook at the table in the chafing dish.

4 cups fruit	¾ cup liqueur or Cognac
1 cup bar syrup	2 tbsp 100-proof vodka

Use the blazer over the water jacket, the jacket filled with boiling water, the heat medium-high. Put in the fruit, combine half the liqueur with the bar syrup, and pour over the fruit. Cook 8 to 10 minutes, until the fruit begins to soften. Combine the remaining liqueur with the vodka and heat it in a small vessel while the fruit poaches. Touch a match to the heated liqueur-vodka mixture, pour slowly over the fruit in the chafing dish. Serve when the flames die away, spooning some of the syrup over each portion.
Serves 8.

Typical of a flamed fruit dessert is Bananas Flambé. The bananas are poached in a mild rum-flavored syrup, then doused with lighted rum. When the blaze dies down, they're ready to serve.

Crêpes

Crêpes Suzette are the best-known, but there are other versions as delicious. The method for preparing all of them is about the same, and the same recipe for the cakes is used in all.

6 eggs	2 tbsp cold water
4 tbsp flour, sifted twice	⅛ tsp salt
½ cup scalded milk	

Beat eggs until frothy, beat in the flour a little at a time, and when the mixture is smooth and lump-free, beat in the milk, water, and salt. (Scald milk by putting it over low heat in a saucepan until bubbles begin to form where milk and pan meet; do not boil. Remove from heat, strain, cool.) The batter should be quite thin. Drop about 1 tbsp batter in a lightly buttered 6-inch skillet over medium-low heat, tilt and turn the pan quickly until the batter covers the bottom. Cook until the top surface is firm, turn and brown the uncooked side very lightly. Crêpes should never be darker than a golden tan. Put them on a plate between pieces of waxed paper; they can be prepared several hours in advance. The recipe yields about 24 crêpes.

The most famous flamed chafing-dish dessert is Crêpes Suzette. The thin pancakes, cooked in advance, are steeped in a liqueur-flavored syrup while being folded in the chafing dish.

Next, the crêpes are sprinkled with orange-flavored sugar.

Finally, Cognac, heated in a separate vessel, is lighted and cascaded into a large spoon, and sprinkled over the crêpes; the flaming liquor ignites the syrup briefly, and blue flames flicker over the dish. When they die down, the crêpes are served.

Crêpes Suzette

24 crêpes	2 tbsp 100-proof vodka
½ cup butter	½ cup granulated sugar
1 tbsp grenadine	8 drops vanilla extract
⅓ cup Curaçao	3 drops fresh lemon juice
⅓ cup Kirsch or Cognac	2 drops orange extract

Have the crêpes stacked on a plate to the left of the chafing dish, the vessel for warming the liqueurs to the right. Put boiling water in the water jacket, place the blazer in the jacket. Melt the butter, stirring in the grenadine, half the Curaçao, and half the Kirsch or Cognac. Combine the remaining Curaçao and Kirsch with the vodka, put in the small vessel to heat. Sprinkle the sugar with the vanilla extract, lemon juice, and orange extract, stir. By now the butter will have melted and combined with the grenadine and liqueurs. Put a crêpe in the chafing dish and fold into quarters (crêpes can also be rolled, but folding is easier and faster, and the folded crêpes can be arranged in overlapping tiers around one side of the chafing dish, increasing its capacity). Follow this procedure until all the crêpes—or as many as the chafing dish will accommodate—have been folded. Arrange them in the blazer to cover its bottom. Sprinkle with the seasoned sugar. Touch a match to the heated liqueurs in the small vessel and slowly trickle the flaming spirits over the crêpes; the liqueurs in the pan sauce will take flame. Let the flames die, serve at once. If you make a second batch, add fresh liqueurs to the sauce and refill the small vessel.

Serves 8.

Crêpes Helena

Follow the recipe and procedures given for Crêpes Suzette, but instead of the blend of liqueurs, use Grand Marnier.

Crêpes Fraises

In advance, marinate sliced fresh strawberries in a mixture of
⅓ bar syrup and ⅔ Triple Sec. Fill the rolled or folded crêpes with
a spoonful of the berries, use the marinade in the sauce rather
than the grenadine/Curaçao/Kirsch mixture used in Crêpes Suzette; flame with Cognac, top the crêpes with whipped cream when
they are served.

Crêpes Anana

Bake 4 bananas in their skins for 10 minutes in a 375-degree
oven; peel, beat the flesh with 2 tbsp dark Jamaican rum, and use
this as a filling for the crêpes. Use rum in the sauce and for
flaming, dust the crêpes with confectioners' sugar before serving.

Traditional English Trifle

To make a good trifle you must have a good, firm sponge
cake, which mixes won't yield. Bake your own, a day or two in
advance of the time the trifle is to be served.

For the cake:

5 eggs, separated	¼ tsp salt
1 cup sugar	1 cup flour
1 tbsp fresh lemon juice	
Grated rind of ½ lemon	

Beat egg whites until stiff but not dry, add ½ cup sugar to
them as you beat. Add lemon juice and rind to the yolks, beat
them until they are thick and light yellow, then beat into them the
remaining ½ cup sugar. Fold the egg yolks into the whites. Add
salt to flour, sift four times, cut the flour into the eggs. Put a small
amount of flour into a tube pan, tilt and roll the pan until its interior
is covered, discard excess flour. Pour in the batter, cut through it
several times to break up air bubbles. Bake in a preheated 325-
degree oven for 50 minutes to 1 hour; test by thrusting a straw or

thin skewer into the cake; if it comes out clean, the cake is done. Let the cake rest 5 minutes in the pan, then invert pan over a wire rack until the cake slips free. Cool before using.

For the trifle:

The sponge cake   1 cup apricot or peach jam
½ cup Cognac or 1 cup   ¾ pint whipping cream
   Cream sherry

Cut the cake into three circles of equal thickness; the easiest way is to pass a thin strong string through it. Put the bottom section of the cake in a deep bowl; the bowl should be as nearly the same diameter of the cake as possible. Sprinkle ⅓ of the liquor or sherry on the botton section of the cake, and spread the cake with ½ the jam. Top with the center section, sprinkle it with liquor, spread with the remaining jam. Put on the top section, sprinkle with the remaining liquor, spread with the whipped cream. Let stand 15 to 20 minutes, but no longer than an hour, before serving in moderately thick slices.

Serves 8 to 10, even 12 if you cut thin slices.

Dessert Coffees

Café Brûlot

Rind of ½ orange   5 ounces Cognac
Rind of ¼ lemon   Pot (12 cups) strong black
2 sticks cinnamon bark   coffee
10 cloves
8 lumps sugar

Cut all white pith from the rinds in advance and slice them into ¼-inch strips. Put the blazer pan of the chafing dish over direct heat, twist the peel strips over the pan, drop them in, quickly add the cinnamon, cloves, and sugar, pour in 3 ounces Cognac and wait about 15 seconds, then light it. Begin adding the coffee with a ladle, working quickly but carefully so the flames are not drowned. As soon as the coffee has been added, pour the reserved Cognac into the hot ladle, light it, and lower the ladle into the coffee to let the flaming liquor float off on its surface. Serve by ladling into demitasse cups.

Petit Brûlot

1 whole orange	4 lumps sugar
½ bay leaf	2 ounces Cognac
2 sticks cinnamon bark	Pot of strong black hot coffee

In advance, score the orange all around about two-thirds of the way up from one end. Remove the rind from the one-third section and using the smooth handle of a teaspoon carefully work the remaining rind free by sliding the handle between rind and fruit; leave the top ½ inch or so of rind attached to the orange, and pull the rind up to form a cup, as shown in the picture. Cut off the bottom third of the orange to make a pedestal base, stand the fruit in the middle of the chafing dish blazer, cup at the top. Put the bay leaf, cinnamon, and sugar in the cup made by the orange rind. Put the blazer on over direct heat, pour in the hot coffee. Warm the Cognac and slowly pour the flaming liquor into the peel-cup, letting it run over into the coffee. When all the Cognac has been poured, begin ladling coffee from the pan into the peel-cup. Do this until all the flames die down, then ladle the coffee into demitasse cups and serve at once.

Special after-dinner coffees can be prepared in your chafing dish. This is Café Petit Brûlot, made by peeling back the skin of an orange to hold sugar cubes, a stick of cinnamon and a bay leaf, placing the orange in the chafing dish, and filling the dish with coffee. Warmed Cognac, lighted, is poured into the orange-peel cup.

Café Diablo (also called Diabolique)

1 stick cinnamon bark	12 lumps sugar
1 tsp whole cloves	½ cup Cognac
2 tsp coriander seeds	Pot (12 cups) strong hot black
1 tbsp whole coffee beans	coffee
Grated rind of 1 orange	

Have the blazer pan over direct heat. Put cinnamon, cloves, coriander, coffee beans, orange rind, and sugar in the pan, pour half the Cognac over them and light as soon as it warms—about 10–15 seconds. Stir once and pour the coffee in quickly. Put the reserved Cognac in a ladle, light it, pour the flaming liquor into the coffee with the ladle held about 8 inches above the pan. As soon as the flames die, ladle into demitasse cups and serve.

Café Capuccino (also called Mazagran)

Half-fill large coffee cups with dry red wine, add ½ tsp sugar, fill with strong hot black coffee.

While the liquor in the orange-peel cup blazes, hot coffee from the dish is ladled over it; the flames run down and play above the surface of the coffee, bringing with them the flavors from the orange cup.

Café Flamand

4 egg whites, beaten stiff   Sugar
2 cups heavy cream   Strong hot black coffee

Into the bottom of each cup, put a blob of egg white, a dash of cream, a scant teaspoon of sugar. Fill with coffee.

Café Royale (also called Café Gloria)

Use thick-walled demitasse cups. Into each cup put a lump of sugar, half-fill with strong hot black coffee, carefully pour ½ liqueur glass of Cognac over the coffee, set aflame. Stir to extinguish the flames. This can be made in the chafing dish, but somehow it doesn't taste the same as when made in the cup.

Espresso Menzogna

For espresso, a special pressure-brewing pot is needed; if you have one, fine, if not, use double-strength coffee or beef up regular coffee by adding chicory to the grounds when brewing.

3 egg whites   ½ cup whipping cream
3 tbsp confectioners' sugar   Espresso coffee

Beat the eggs with the sugar, whip the cream, fold into the egg whites. Pour coffee into demitasse cups, top each cup with a blob of the foam.

Certainly from the suggestions given in this chapter you can find a means of helping Her cope with a flood of guests—though you still might find that She expects more assistance, especially in the kitchen. Further ideas will be found in later chapters.

IV

Preparing, Cooking, and Carving Main Dishes

When she asks you to "fix the meat," don't frown. No matter how much of a job "fixing the meat" might seem, it's to your advantage in two ways. First, the more you handle meat, doing such jobs as boning roasts and disjointing fowl, the more you learn about bone structure—which makes carving a lot easier. Second, easy carving begins with the cooking. No matter how sharp the blade of your carving knife, if the meat's not properly cooked, carving's going to be an unhappy job.

Actually, both jobs, helping fix the meat and carving, begin with Her knives. Their care is one chore you should reserve for yourself, whether or not She asks you to. The respect for good cutlery that seems to be born in most men is seldom part of the natural endowment of females. My own observations in many kitchens convince me that almost no woman pays any attention to the kitchen knives she uses—more accurately, tries to use—every day.

As a result of having watched quite a large number of women struggle valiantly with dull knives, hacking and sawing until their tempers are shot, their nerves frayed, and their patience exhausted, I've evolved a theory that this kind of battle, carried on two or three times a day, day after day, leads to

the accumulation of subconscious frustrations. These frustrations are carried by such women to the dinner table and
unloaded on their husbands in minor outbursts of bad temper,
and for the most part the husbands are genuinely puzzled to
account for the snappishness they so frequently encounter.

Don't dismiss this theory lightly, with a grin or chuckle. It's
totally illogical to think that a woman, who uses her kitchen
knives much more frequently than does her spouse, should fail
to understand that knives become dull with continuous use and
must have their edges renewed by sharpening. Even if this is
illogical, it happens to be true. And no woman—or man either,
for that matter—who must battle dull knives while cooking
dinner is going to be at her sparkling best while the meal's
being eaten.

If you aren't already doing so, assume at once the job of
caring for Her knives. Begin by going to the kitchen and
inspecting those in current use. You'll probably find a miscellaneous assortment, some old, some new, some bought, some
received as gifts or as box-top premiums, none of them really
very good. Most of the knives will be of the type to which
women seem fatally attracted; they will have blades of shiny
soft "stainless" steel, and pretty plastic handles. Chances are
100-to-1 that they'll all be jumbled into a drawer together with
cooking forks and spoons, spatulas, and other utensils. The
drawer will quite probably contain some jar lids, beer-can
openers, and similar hard miscellaneous articles guaranteed to
abrade or nick a knife edge. The feminine mystique applied to
knives includes using them as screwdrivers, paint scrapers,
letter and box openers, levers to pry off tops from jelly jars, and
similar ruinous and unsuitable tasks.

Since you're married to Her, it's a safe assumption that you
love Her and would like to make your shared life more harmo-
nious. Buy Her, then, a set of really good kitchen knives and a
rack on which to keep them, one that will protect their edges
and points. Preferences in racks vary, but my own is for one of
the magnetic bars that hold a number of knives flat, and can be
mounted at the end of a kitchen cabinet where the knives will
be out of harm's way, readily visible, and easily accessible.

How many knives a kitchen needs depends a lot on how

much cooking is done in it. Four is about an absolute minimum. These would include a chef's knife with its tapering triangular blade, 8 to 10 inches long, for chopping; a standard butcher knife with a blade about 8 inches long; a 6- or 7-inch utility knife, the kind often called a "bull cook knife"; and a small vegetable or paring knife with a 3- or 4-inch blade. Over the centuries the shapes of knife blades have evolved into different styles designed to do different jobs superlatively well. The chef's knife is perfect for mincing and chopping and in a pinch will do duty for carving. A butcher knife has a blade shaped precisely for making deep cuts in big hunks of raw meat, and for slicing such outsized objects as melons. The utility knife is fitted with a sort of compromise blade that lets it do a lot of jobs well, but its blade is too thick and clumsy for precise carving and too short to replace the butcher knife. The vegetable knife

Though a kitchen can get along with four knives, we find the complete array pictured here saves a lot of work. From left: 6-inch cleaver; 12-inch chef's; 11-inch butcher; 8-inch boning; 10-inch carver; 7-inch butcher; 8-inch chef's; 6-inch boning/carving; 6-inch utility (the "bull cook" knife); 4-inch vegetable; 3-inch paring. A magnetic bar holds the knives at the end of a cabinet where they're always at hand. If knives are kept in drawers, their edges are apt to get nicked and dulled.

or paring knife is short, trim, and easy to handle in such tasks as peeling, coring, and cutting up fruits and vegetables.

If you want to go beyond the basic blades, a long thin roast slicer with an almost-straight blade is probably the next most useful. This is my favorite for carving both in the kitchen and at the table. Our kitchen rack also holds a boning knife with an extra-long, very flexible blade; a mid-sized vegetable knife; a small utility knife that's just right for carving chickens and steaks and boning chuck roasts; and an oversized chef's knife and butcher knife to handle big cuts and quantity mincing for which the shorter blades are inadequate. Any fish I fillet are done with the knives from my fishing kit, but if the job happens to be done at home, I'll reach for my carving blade.

When you select kitchen knives, choose the unpretty kind with blades of carbon steel and wooden handles that are riveted firmly in place. Such knives don't rust, in spite of the implied claims of the makers of stainless-steel cutlery. As carbon-steel knives are used, the action of food acids forms a virtually rustproof patina on their blades. They're not dishwasher-proof, but good knives ought never to go in the dishwasher and be rattled around against crockery and glassware that will nick or dull their edges. Just rinse knives under hot running water and wipe dry. While the methods of tempering stainless steels have advanced greatly in recent years, I've yet to see a stainless-steel blade that will hold a keen edge as long as will high-carbon steel. You will, of course, avoid knives with serrated and saw-tooth blades; they will not hold an edge longer than a few days, even if they're not used.

In spite of the advertisements for knives made from "a new miracle steel that never needs sharpening," such miracle metals simply don't exist. So, when you buy Her knives, get a sharpening steel as well, and persuade Her to use it. Incidentally, don't get one of the sharpeners made of abrasive material formed into the shape of a steel. These things ruin knives almost as quickly as do the whirring attachments found on most electric can openers, which will draw the temper from a blade while putting on a wire edge that cuts satisfactorily for a short while, then bends to uselessness.

You may find it a bit difficult to persuade Her to use a

This is the usual method of using a sharpening steel—the tip up, the knife-edge drawn along opposite sides in alternate downward strokes.

Most women find it easier to use the steel tip-down, resting on a counter-top or table. The knife, of course, is still drawn downward in alternate strokes along opposite sides.

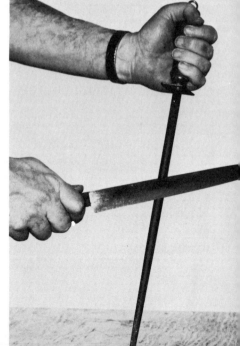

sharpening steel. During the years I've been writing and talking about cooking, my remarks about the need for good kitchen cutlery have led to invitations from quite a few women to teach them the use and care of knives. I've yet to meet one who didn't flinch from using a sharpening steel in the conventional style—that is, with the tip held upwards. So universal has this hesitation been that I'm convinced it's rooted in some hidden phallic fear which psychiatrists might find worthwhile to probe, especially since most women quickly learn to use the steel when its conventional position is reversed. When I've suggested that they rest the tip of the steel on a table or countertop and draw the knife across it, they readily learn the proper way to use this important adjunct to knife care. Though a steel used in this position isn't as efficient as it is with the top upward, it's better than no steel at all.

When whetted on a steel three or four times a week, a knife having a carbon-steel blade needs to be sharpened on the oilstone only about twice a year. If you have a workshop and use edged tools regularly, you'll certainly have an oilstone and perhaps an Arkansas stone around. If you aren't equipped to handle any kind of sharpening, then add an oilstone to Her kitchen equipment for the semi-annual knife whetting. Knife-sharpening procedures are shown in the accompanying illustrations.

A word of caution might be in order at this point. Once you're moved to buy knives for Her kitchen, you run the risk of getting snared in the Kitchen Gadget Trap. Many men of strong and sterling character, men who would not think of falling for the wiles of a female charmer, are seduced each year by the ten thousand gadgets that are offered in homewares stores. They become compulsive gadget-buyers, and on occasion get hooked so deeply that after having bought all the gizmos and whatchamacallits that could conceivably be useful, they plunge deeper and deeper and start buying duplicates of cute kitchen gadgets that might possibly be used one every two or three years.

This is an addiction that is not easily broken. Eventually those hooked on it bring home so many small kitchen tools that Her cabinets and catchall drawers are overcrowded, so cluttered with nonessentials that She's unable to find the tools

SHARPENING KNIVES

1. Use a medium-grit whetstone for sharpening kitchen knives and keep it well wet down with oil. Begin sharpening with the blade's tip. Hold the knife at an angle of 18 to 20 degrees in relation to the stone, and slide the blade forward with light, even pressure, letting the forward motion follow the curve of the blade's tip.

2. Maintain pressure as the straight section of the blade comes into contact with the stone; keep pushing the blade straight forward until the entire length of its straight portion is on the whetstone.

3. Change the movement now to an oscillating rotary motion; keep the pressure constant along the length of the blade. Depending on the condition of the edge, four to six passes from the tip through the sharpening sequence should hone one side of the blade.

4. Turn the blade and begin at the beginning, with the tip, to whet the untouched edge. The movement of knife on stone and the angle of the blade are the same when sharpening each edge.

5. Sharpening the right-hand side of the edge puts your hands in an awkward position, but with a little practice you can keep the same gentle, even pressure you kept on the left-hand edge.

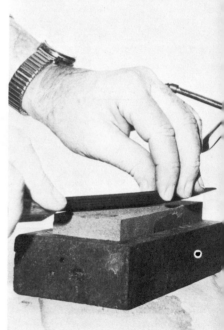

6. This closeup shows the angle at which you'll work with most kitchen knives, which have relatively thick blades. These knives must have an edge with a fairly wide V. A narrow-V edge is too delicate for most kitchen cutting; it will not stay keen as long and chips more easily than a wide-V edge.

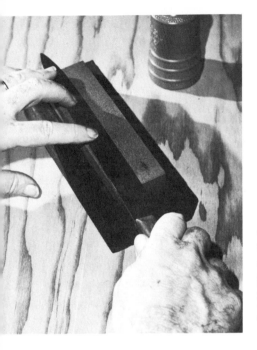

7. On knives with thin, flexible blades, like a carver, the V of the edge is virtually an extension of the sides of the blade; the edge should have no noticeable taper. Such knives should be held at a flatter angle, 8 to 10 degrees, when they are sharpened.

She's accustomed to using regularly. She complains, and the complaint triggers a second addictive stage, which causes Him to begin rearranging the kitchen storage areas. On cold Sunday afternoons when normal husbands are watching football on TV on sunny summer Saturdays when orthodox husbands are out playing golf, during evenings when unaddicted husbands would be playing poker, the addict is fitting dividers into the drawers of Her kitchen cabinets, perhaps even building new drawers so that he can buy more gadgets to fill them.

Now, the cold hard fact is that out of every 10,000 kitchen gadgets available, 9,999 are totally unnecessary. Most of them are designed to do only one specific job, and while they do this job with superb efficiency, they have absolutely no other function. Most of the small jobs they do can be performed about as easily with a knife or fork or some other multipurpose tool. Keep your generous instincts in firm control, and confine your buying to a new set of knives and the necessary sharpening equipment.

One of the bonuses you'll get from equipping Her kitchen with knives that actually cut is that when you're called to lend a hand by doing some boning, disjointing, chopping, or mincing, to say nothing of carving, you'll have knives that you'll find a pleasure to work with. Looked at this way, it's simply a matter of self-defense to invest in a set of good knives, just as self-defense dictates that you learn to be skillful in other kitchen chores you might be called on to handle.

Even aside from the times when extra-large meals must be cooked or special preparations undertaken for entertaining guests, there are jobs preliminary to many kitchen operations that you might undertake. Unless they play golf or tennis regularly, most women don't develop the wrist and forearm muscles that enable them to make light work of boning a roast or flaying a breast of lamb or veal in preparing a roll roast or pocket roast. There are also a number of jobs more easily done by four hands than by two. Stuffing and trussing a big turkey, for example, is very hard work for one, but a fast job if two do it.

Keep in mind that when you have most preparatory jobs such as boning done by the butcher, you pay for them at the rate of several cents per pound of the meat involved. Even such a simple job as disjointing a chicken at home will reduce the price of the bird by as much as one-third. Food budget dollars stretch a lot further when you're able to do at home the things for which a butcher must make an extra charge.

To help you handle these home kitchen tasks, step-by-step illustrations of the most common ones accompany this chapter. These pictures and the text that is associated with them, together with the good knives you've bought for Her kitchen, should equip you to handle almost any job of preparing the most usual cuts for cooking. Remember, though, cutting through raw meat requires a knife with a keen edge. Be sure the knives you use are sharp when you begin, and keep them that way by using the steel from time to time while you work. Don't be afraid to stop in the middle of an operation to whisk your knife over the steel.

After the meat cuts or the fowl you've prepared are ready to be cooked, you'll still be expected to carve them. As remarked earlier, easy carving starts with the cooking, so invoke the rule

DISJOINTING A BIRD

1. Whether you're disjointing a chicken, a sparrow, or an ostrich, the cuts made are almost identical. All birds have much the same bone structure; the difference is one of size. Begin at the tail. Cut it off.

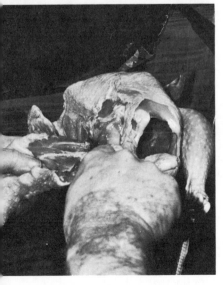

2. Pull the legs away from the body and cut downward, angling the blade inward toward the body, to reach the socket that connects thighbones and hip. When you can see the joint, slip the knife tip into it and cut the tendons. This will cause the joint to open, and you can continue with your downward cut to sever the thigh from the body.

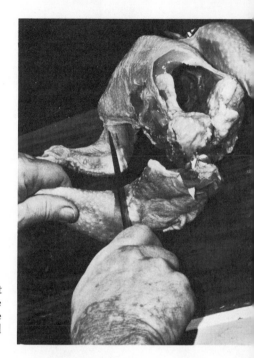

3. Hold the drumstick firmly and cut down into the joint to part it from the thigh; if you're not sure where the joint is, press the flesh of the leg until you locate it.

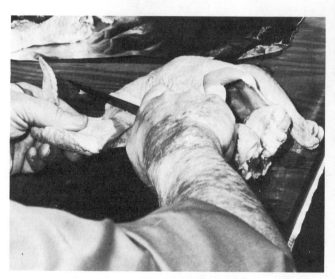

4. Pull the wing away from the body and cut at the base of the breast to reach the "shoulder" joint. It's deeper in the body than you think. When the joint is exposed, sever it just as you did the hip-thigh joint, then continue cutting downward to part wing from body.

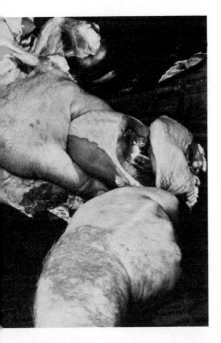

5. Hold the bird's body firmly in your left hand. Start a cut at the forward point of the breast, where the breastbone begins. Cut straight down until you feel the knife touch bone, then angle the blade to the right and let it follow the bone down. You will be cutting against the breastbone, and the forward section of breast you're taking off contains the wishbone.

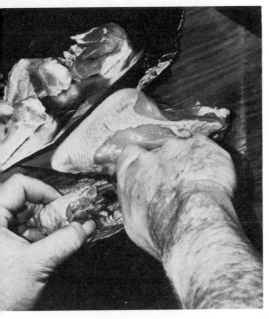

6. Grasp the hip joint between the thumb and forefingers of your left hand and make a cut that slants to the right, following the bottom edge of the breast. Cut until you feel the knife touch the bird's backbone.

7. Put aside the knife, take the breast in one hand, hips in the other, and bend the carcass back until the backbone snaps. Then, cut through the cords of the backbone and through the thin layer of flesh on the back.

8. Hold the breast section with the breastbone down and cut along the backbone, through the ribs, to separate the back and breast. Always keep your knife sharp by honing it on the steel now and then while you work; the bones of a chicken are soft, but the sharper the knife, the easier the job of cutting through them.

9. At the neck end of the cut you've just made, the V-shaped bone that ends on each side of the body in the shoulder socket must be cut from the backbone; cut one side away at a time.

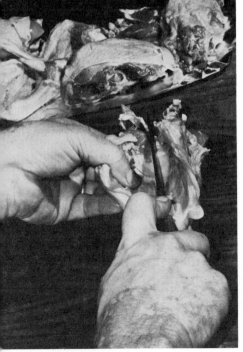

10. Rest the breastbone on the cutting board and halve the breast section lengthwise. The cut is made on one side of the breastbone. A similar cut beside the spine separates the back section into two pieces. You've now disjointed the chicken and have 12 serving pieces: two drumsticks, two thighs, two wings, two breast halves, the wishbone piece, and the hip section.

BONING A WHOLE BIRD

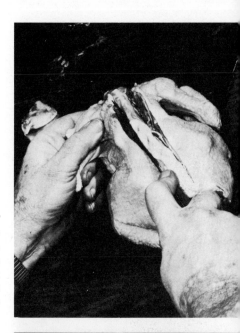

1. Boning a chicken, or any other bird, so that it can be served whole isn't a hard job. Begin by resting the bird on its breast to make your first cuts, parallel incisions that run the entire length of the carcass on each side of the spine.

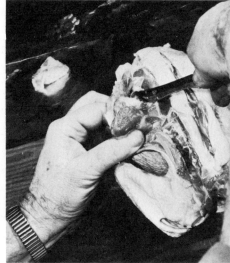

2. Pull the flesh of one of the cuts away from the backbone, cutting with short scraping strokes along the rib bones while lifting the flesh to keep your working area exposed. Free the flesh from the ribs the entire length of the body.

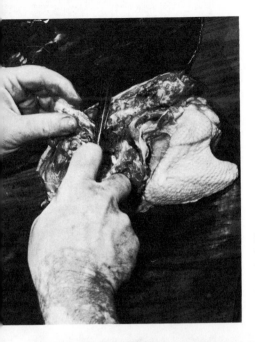

3. When you reach the hip socket that holds the thighbone, bend the thighbone and cut the tendon in the socket with the tip of your knife. Then, with scraping cuts, work down around the bone until you free it from flesh.

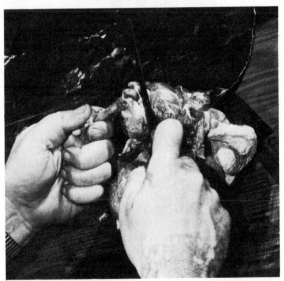

4. Pull the thighbone up when you get to the joint between it and the drumstick, bend the joint and force your knife tip into it to break the joint. Leave the drumstick bone in the carcass.

5. Move to the front of the body now and cut and scrape away the flesh toward the breast and neck until you see the "shoulder" joint that holds the upper wingbone. Bend the wing down, using your knife tip as you did on other joints, to cut the tendon inside the joint. Scrape and cut along the upper wingbone to free it of flesh, cut the bone free at the center wing joint, and leave the wingtip bones in the carcass.

6. Breast meat, which is very soft and tender, starts below the wing joint. Scrape rather than slice as you work around the rib cage, pulling the flesh up and away from the knife. Cut up along the breastbone and down to the ribs on the unboned side. Then, turn the carcass end-for-end and bone out the second side just as you did the first.

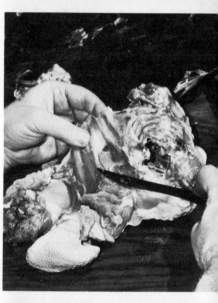

7. When the job's finished, the only bones remaining in the carcass will be those in the wingtips and drumsticks. The bird is stuffed, the back closed by sewing or with skewers, and the chicken patted into its original shape. When cooked, it can be carved straight across the body, like a roll roast or meatloaf.

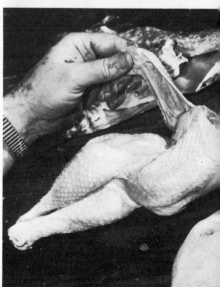

BONING, STUFFING, AND ROLL-ING BREAST OF VEAL OR LAMB

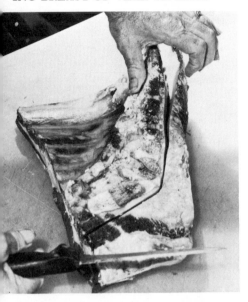

1. To prepare a breast of veal or lamb for a pocket roast or roll roast, it must be boned. The boning takes five minutes; the procedure is the same for both veal and lamb. Start with the breast bone side up on the carving board and make an L-shaped cut about ¾ inch deep along the edge of the ribs and chine (backbone) that outlines their location.

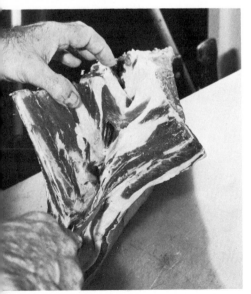

2. Stand the roast on edge with the tips of the ribs at the top. Slice into the meat along the edge, cutting along the rib bones.

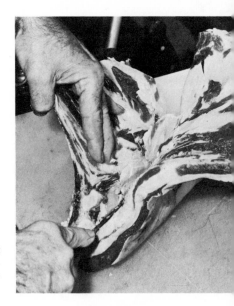

3. When you get to the chine, cut along its length and connect your cutting with the first cut made to free the bones.

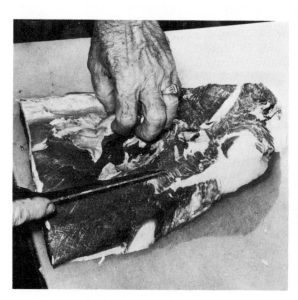

4. Trim off suet and white connective tissue from both sides of the roast. This is really a job of shaving the surface of the meat, so keep your knife razor-sharp by honing it on the steel.

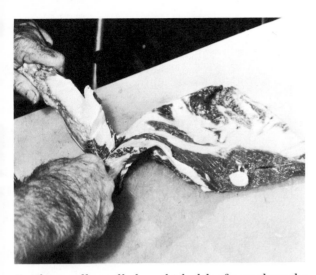

5. There will usually be a thick slab of suet along the chine. This should be taken off completely.

6. Starting with the thickest edge, roll the roast into a cylinder and tie it at 3-to-4-inch intervals with heavy cord. The roast can be cooked as it now is, or can be stuffed before it is rolled, as shown in the illustrations following.

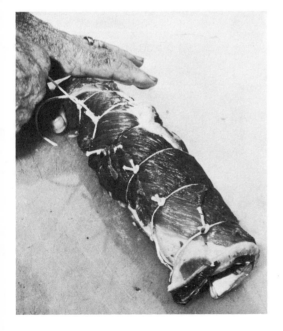

7. Since both veal and lamb are dry meats, a stuffing adds moisture and flavor to them. Spread the roast out flat and apply the stuffing in an even layer, like buttering a slice of bread.

8. Starting at the thickest edge, roll the meat and stuffing up as you would a jellyroll.

9. When rolled, the roast can be secured with cords, as already shown, or with long skewers, as above.

STUFFING AND TRUSSING A TURKEY

1. Stuffing and trussing a turkey is much easier for two pairs of hands than one. One person holds the bird balanced on its breast, above, while the other puts stuffing into the breast cavity.

2. A long skewer holds the flap of neck skin that's pulled smoothly across the back. The skewer also helps hold the bird on an even keel in the roasting pan and serves as a lashing post for the trussing cord. Start trussing by looping one end of the cord around a wing just above the joint, carry it across the back and loop it around the other wing, pass it up and loop it around the wingtip, bring it across the back and secure the second wingtip, then loop it several times around the skewer and secure with half-hitches. Never never carry a trussing cord over a fowl's breast; the cord will cut into the flesh as the bird swells during cooking and spoil the finest part of the meat.

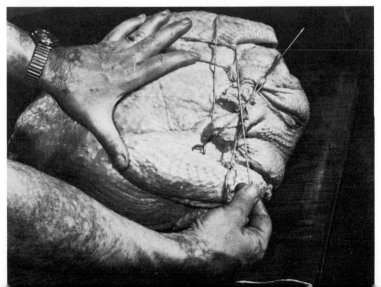

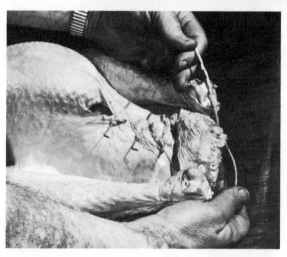

3. Now, the turkey is placed on its back. Stuffing is much easier with two pairs of hands. One person holds the body slanted up toward the tail and grasps the drumsticks and skin around the body cavity, while the second puts in the stuffing.

4. Pack stuffing loosely; it will expand during cooking. Close the cleaning cut with skewers and a lacing of cord, as shown above. The same cord goes around the tailpiece and pulls it up to close the body cavity, and is then looped around the tips of the drumsticks, pulling them together and down. Skewers and cords are removed from the body cavity and legs before the turkey goes to the table for carving; those in the back can stay until the carcass is cleaned up. To open the cavities so the stuffing can be served, the carver cuts away the flap of skin along the bottom line of ribs after the legs have been removed.

BONING A LEG

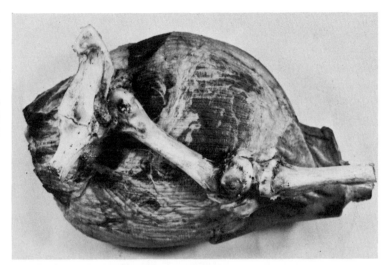

This picture of a ham with a bone laid on it shows how the legbones of all domestic animals lie inside their flesh. There will be some variations between animals—and even between hams—in the angle of the hipbone, at left. In some legs this bone may cross at right angles to the central legbone in a perfect T; in others, it will slant either to left or right. However, once the position of the bones in an animal's leg is understood, removing the bones is a simple job. First a cut is made above the bone line, then the slit is pulled apart to give the boning knife working room, and the knife is drawn along the bones. The cut is spread wider as the boning knife moves along, and the bones are lifted to give access to the joint. The only difference between boning a turkey leg and a ham or leg of veal or lamb is the size of the bones removed.

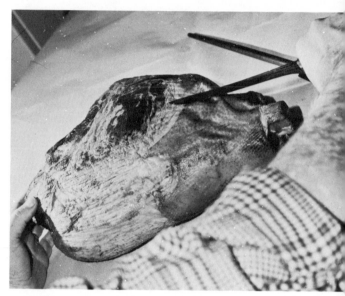

1. Preparing some leg cuts for cooking requires removing an outer covering of one kind or another. In veal legs, a layer of tissue and fat covers the flesh; in lamb it is a membrane called the "fell"; in hams and fresh pork legs it is skin and fat. The procedure in all cases is the same. A first cut is made on the inner side of the leg, above the bone, a cut only deep enough to part the tissues that are to be removed, more of a scoring cut than a slice.

2. In a ham, the scoring cut parts the skin. A corner of the skin is lifted, and the knife moves between skin and flesh, cutting through the layer of fat. The knife should be held roughly parallel to the meat's surface and should scrape rather than slice along the skin's bottom side.

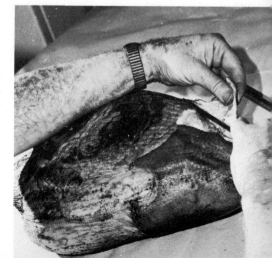

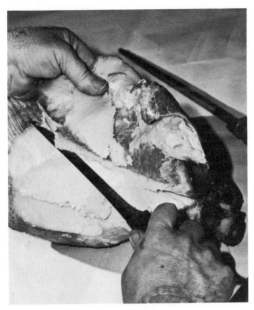

3. When the skin on both sides of the scoring cut has been freed, the ham is turned over and the skin taken off the top, or outside surface.

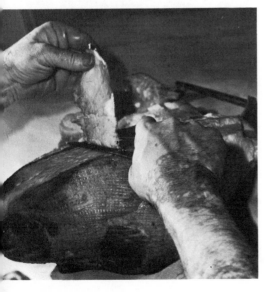

4. After the skin has been removed, excess fat is shaved from the entire ham, leaving only a layer about a quarter-inch thick.

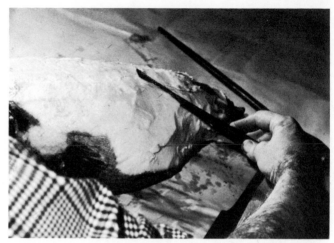

5. Scoring the fat's surface follows the shaving operation; make shallow cuts in a diamond-shaped pattern.

6. Final step is to stud the surface with cloves. Some cooks like to rub brown sugar or a mixture of sugar and molasses into the fat before the cloves are stuck in.

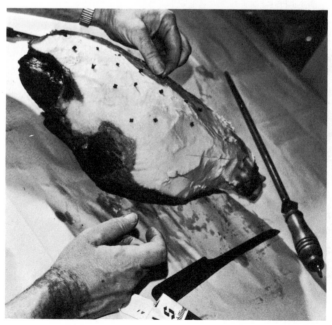

of self-defense to justify taking a hand in the actual cooking of any major cut of meat or any fowl you'll be carving later on. At the risk of being unduly repetitious, a roast that comes from the oven with an impenetrable inch-thick crust or a fowl that reaches the table with a skin as unyielding as a top-grade leather shoe sole is going to defeat even the expert's carving knife. And it will do you no good to take the coward's way out and bone every cut of meat, every bird, before it's cooked, because boning won't reduce the toughness of a crust on an overdone roast or soften the leathery skin of a badly cooked fowl.

Actually, boning meats before cooking is not something I look on with joy. There are essences of flavor contained in the bones and marrow of all animals and birds that should be transmitted to the meat during cooking. This is universally true. It explains why the ready-prepared boned roasts that you buy at the self-service meat counters or the frozen-foods bin of super-markets usually taste so pale and thin. This is one reason (among several others) why canned hams, which are chemically cured and then boned before being sealed in their cans for cooking, taste like pale pink blotting paper, no matter how skillfully they're prepared for serving.

Unless you're going to cook a boned cut of meat or a boned fowl using a recipe that compensates for the loss of flavor resulting from the removal of its bones, don't pre-bone any meat. Even if you do compensate by stuffing a savory mixture into the space left by the bone, it's a good idea to include in the pan the biggest bones that were taken out. They will add immeasurably to the flavor of both the meat and the pan juices, which will usually be the base for a gravy or sauce.

Most of the meats cooked today are either broiled, braised, or roasted. Technically, what we call roasting is baking; that is, the meat is cooked by convection heat in an enclosed space, the oven, while roasting is accomplished by revolving the meat on a spit over or in front of a stationary heat source. Broiling is confined in usefulness to thin cuts of red meats such as steaks and chops, and to small fowl such as chickens. Braising is usually the method selected for cooking the tougher beef cuts, brisket and shanks, and in cooking the breast cuts from dry meats like lamb and veal. Fish when cooked whole are generally either poached or baked. We're not going to be greatly concerned here with the different kinds of surface cooking: deep-fat frying, pay frying, and sautéeing.

There's really no excuse for a roast to come out of the oven with a thick, hard, charred crust encasing it like armor plate. Even if meat is cooked to be well done, it can still remain tender outside as well as inside. If you have a meat thermometer the job of timing is simply a matter of looking at it two or three times and adjusting the oven temperature, but even without a thermometer it's easy to cook meat properly.

Beef roasts should be seared for a brief period of preliminary cooking at relatively high oven temperature—375 to 400 degrees for 45 minutes to an hour. Then the oven temperature is reduced to 250 and the roast cooked 15 minutes per pound. This produces rare roast beef; for medium, cook 20 minutes per pound, for well done, 25 minutes. When using a meat thermometer, cook at 375 degrees for 45 minutes, reduce temperature to 250 degrees, and cook until the thermometer reads 150 for rare, 160 for medium-rare, 180 for well done.

Leg, rack, and loin cuts of lamb and veal should be seared at 325 degrees, then cooked 15 minutes per pound at 225 degrees for best results; leg and rack of lamp are timed at 12 minutes per pound if you like these on the rare side. Meat thermometer readings for these meats are 160 degrees for medium, 180 for well done, and the same oven settings used for searing and final cooking. Breast cuts and rolled or stuffed roasts are timed at 12 minutes per pound after searing.

Pork should always be cooked thoroughly. Sear it at 375 degrees, cooking about 1 hour, then reduce the temperature to 250 degrees and cook 30 minutes per pound. When using the meat thermometer, it should read 185 degrees before the meat is considered cooked. When using the thermometer on any meat, it should be inserted in the thickest part of the cut and should not touch or rest on a bone.

Because in our kitchen chickens and turkeys are always cooked by the self-basting method, meat thermometers are never used with them. These thermometers are of very little use in cooking chicken, because the birds are so small that their bodies do not have any area fleshy enough to allow for a proper reading. Use the old-fashioned way of piercing a chicken's thigh joint with a knife. Judge the bird ready when only clear juices, with no tinge of pink, flow when the knife is withdrawn. If you want to use a meat thermometer on a turkey, push it into the thickest part of the thigh and cook the bird at 250 degrees until the thermometer reads 185 degrees.

Just how good the pop-up indicators are on frozen turkeys is something on which I cannot comment, for I refuse to buy a bird that has been pumped full of added liquid—and this seems to be the case with all birds that have these built-in thermometers. I also don't buy a bird advertised as "self-basting" because the processor has shot into it a syringeful of sodium tripolyphosphate mixed with cottonseed oil. The thermal self-basting method we use in our kitchen involves no chemical additives, is very easy, and has produced superior results for us for 30 years, and I have no intention of abandoning it.

One of our neighbors when we lived in California's San Joaquin Valley in the early 1940s was Milton Reiman, a commercial turkey grower whose ranch produced about 300,000 birds a year. Milt was generous with his flock; he presented his neighbors with turkeys at fairly frequent intervals, and being a gourmet as well as a grower was always interested in seeing that his prize birds would be properly cooked. Milt taught us how to cook turkeys by the thermal self-basting method at a time when food experts and home economists were recommending short cooking at high temperatures. It was about then, too, that the metal foil makers exercised their influence in magazine advertising offices with the result that the cooking writers whose works appeared on the editorial pages suddenly discovered that turkey could now only be cooked if it was swathed in foil.

Nothing could be simpler to use or produce a better turkey for the table than the method of thermal self-basting. Simply rub the bird with oil or butter, soak a big square of cloth in the same fat, and drape the bird with this cloth after it's put in the roasting pan. The cloth must be tucked in all around, and must touch the bottom of the pan, for the thermal method depends on capillary action. As the top of the cloth dries, capillary action

5. When using the thermal self-basting method described in the text, a big piece of cloth is soaked in oil or butter and draped over the bird in the roasting pan, as shown above. The cloth must touch the bottom of the pan, as it acts like a wick to pull up the fat-rich pan juices and distribute them evenly over the turkey. When this cooking method is used, no basting, preliminary searing, or final browning of the turkey is required, and the skin, while crisp, will be tender instead of leathery.

draws fresh fat from the pan's bottom, including as cooking progresses the natural fat that has cooked out of the turkey. It distributes this fat evenly over the bird's body. The result is a turkey with a skin that's nicely browned but not converted into leather, a skin the carver can penetrate easily. Under the skin, the flesh is moist, never dry and stringy. The turkey needs no other basting. Cook it 1 hour at 350 degrees, reduce temperature to 225 degrees, and cook 20 minutes per pound. That's all there is to it.

Except for professional chefs and maîtres d'hôtel, I can count on two or three fingers the number of my own friends who really enjoy carving, and perhaps a half dozen who profess no pleasure in carving, but do the job in workmanlike style. Even a lot of my hunting companions, who wield their knives with great efficiency in camp when cleaning, skinning, and quartering out an elk or deer, draw back from carving at table, though in my experience butchering calls for a nicer skill and a great deal more knowledge of anatomy.

However, the number of my carving acquaintances grows

slowly larger, and I seem to find an increasing interest in the art. This is all to the good, for carving at table lends a nice personal touch to a meal. It's an ancient and honorable art. At one time, kings and nobles took great pride in their carving skill, and in a later time royalty delegated the job to noblemen of their courts as a special mark of distinction. It wasn't until relatively recent years that carving in regal and noble houses was delegated to a professional, and even then the title of Household Carver was held by a noble of the court whose duty it was to see that the professional carried out his job satisfactorily. Even well into this century, the host did the carving at table, and the last tutor under whom an English gentleman's son studied was one who trained the fledgling in carving.

Now the custom of carving at table is returning, though a lot of hosts still shy away from the idea. Many of these, I'm pretty sure, are reluctant to carve because both the movie screen and the boob tube periodically show comedy scenes in which a host makes a fool of himself by trying to carve. Based on my own observation, the noncarvers fall into two groups. One is made up of those who lack confidence in themselves, the other of men who hesitate to adopt the custom because they think doing so will tag them as show-offs.

There's another and perhaps more cogent reason why some men hold back from at-table carving; it's a reflection of an attitude rooted in the U.S. ways of life. During the three decades ending in the 1930s, class-lines in this country were drawn more self-consciously than in later years, after a major depression and a pair of world wars had homogenized our social structure. In pre-1930 America, to the great middle-class majority, leisurely dining and customs such as carving meant a display of ostentatious wealth and snobbery. It shouldn't have been this way, of course, but it was. Looking back, I recall only one or two homes in my parents' circle of dining-out friends where meats weren't carved in the kitchen and brought to the table ready to serve, as was the practice in our own home.

My introduction to carving came in my very early teens, when I got my first job, as flunky in one of the neighborhood bakeries which at that time flourished in every city. The bakery was in a working-class neighborhood, and in the tradition of the

European immigrants who lived around it, many of the residents brought in their weekend roasts to be cooked. The roasts went into the big wood-burning oven as the fires died away after the last batch of about 500 loaves of bread came out. I remember this very well indeed, because my jobs included carrying in from an outdoor woodpile the fuel needed to keep that oven going while the bread was being baked.

There were always a number of hams among these private baking jobs; these the master baker swathed with a thick crust of dough to be cooked on heavy metal baking sheets. The hams, I came to understand, were for the lunches carried by the men to jobs and by children to school; fast-food establishments were unknown, then, and few schools had cafeterias. Many of the ham customers asked the bakery proprietor to carve the hams for them, and there came the inevitable day when I was alone in the shop and was requested by a patron to carve the ham she'd come to pick up.

At that time, I didn't know an aitch-bone from a drumstick, or understand the difference between right and left hams; all I knew was what I'd picked up by watching my boss carve. In those days, flunkies didn't argue with customers any more than they did with the boss; there wasn't any out for me except to try. I was struggling along, doing the best I could—which wasn't very good—when the proprietor returned and rescued me. Later, he gave me a few lessons, and I've since discovered that carving is like riding a bicycle; once you've acquired the knack, you never forget how to do it.

To the reasons given a few paragraphs back for the hesitancy of some men to pick up a carving knife, afterthought brings still another. A lot of fellows, I suspect, have the idea that carving is a ritualized performance, subject to a lot of firm dos and don'ts, like swinging a golf club, or is governed by some sort of protocol that can't be varied the fraction of an inch. This isn't the case, though. There are alternate methods of carving virtually every cut of meat, all of which are perfectly proper and correct, and the method you choose to use will cause no lifted eyebrows from those looking on.

It's true that there are some cuts of meat and some species of fowl that are best attacked at specific points, or carved in only one manner. These are very few in number, and in all cases the methods are dictated by commonsense; the anatomy of the animal or bird makes them the easiest approach to carving that specific section. You have equal latitude in selecting your carving tools. If you're an orthopedic surgeon, you might decide that a surgeon's scalpel and dissecting shears are the tools you find most comfortable to use. But there's no "must" about any knife or fork or other carving aid, though here again commonsense indicates that you select a knife that's long enough for the job of spanning a joint of beef or a turkey's breast instead of a stubby knife with a 3-inch blade that would make a lot of hacking necessary to get across a chunk of meat 8 or 10 inches thick.

About 99 percent of my own carving, whether in the kitchen or at the dining table, is done with a 10-inch roast slicer that has a thin, almost straight blade and a pointed tip. The knife was made during the late 1920s by J. A. Henckels Twinwerke at Solingen, Germany, and I bought it sometime in the early 1930s. Since then I've tried perhaps a dozen knives, including blades from Sabatier in France, Sheffield in England, Puuko in Finland, Gerber in the U.S., as well as blades forged in other Solingen plants and by a good cross-section of U.S. makers. Always, I go back to the Henckels knife, simply because it's one that feels good in my hand.

Now, I'm not suggesting that you rush out and buy a duplicate of my favorite, and that the use of it will automatically and at once endow you with masterful carving skill. I doubt you'd find a duplicate of my knife, unless in an antique shop, and even if you did turn one up it might not suit your hand or wrist. There are many very good knives made, by the manufacturers mentioned above and by others, and trial and error is still the best way to find the one that fits you perfectly. Once you do find that knife, cling to it. You may never find another like it.

Habit and familiarity with my favorite carving blade may be the reasons why I've never found an electric knife with which I've felt comfortable. Being so accustomed to an almost weightless blade makes the electric knives I've tried seem unduly heavy and rather clumsy. Those who begin their carving experience with electric knives all seem to like them, but I can see some pitfalls in their use. Habit and familiarity work both ways. Electric knives are suited for carving and no other purpose, and those who use them exclusively, getting no experience with regular blades, may have difficulty in using conventional knives in the preparation of raw meats, where electric knives are of no use whatsoever.

Certainly electric knives are better than the flood of junk knives on the market. Some are very expensive junk, especially those that are sold in fancy "presentation sets." You've probably got one or more of these sets kicking around, and may even have tried to use them. Your lack of success may in fact be one of the reasons why carving bugs you—if indeed it does. Or, you may, like me, feel more at home with a knife that isn't pretty, and feel inhibited about taking it to the dinner table to use in front of guests. Don't be bashful. If a knife fits you, use it anywhere. My old carver is far from being fancy—in fact, it's rather shabby—but it goes to my table regularly.

Along with your carving "presentation set" you may have gotten a pair of poultry shears. About the only time you'll use these is when you want to divide a duck or some other game bird into halves by cutting the ribs along the spine and then shearing the breastbone lengthwise. It's actually just about as easy to take the breasts off a duck as it is to split the carcass. Poultry shears were used a lot in years past, when game fowl were plentiful, but they're more a curiosity than a necessary accessory today.

Nor will your carving be helped greatly by the use of a special fork. If it pleases you to use the fork that came with your beautiful silver-handled carving set, you might as well get some good out of the set, because it's an odds-on bet the knife isn't going to be very useful. The important thing about a carving fork is intangible: your familiarity with it. If you don't know almost by instinct where the tips of its tines will be when buried in a piece of meat, there are going to be times when you'll spoil your knife blade by sawing on a tine of the fork. And though I've tried the heavy U-shaped carving forks with truncated handles, I'm not convinced they're of much value. Any cut of meat tough enough to require being anchored by brute strength is going to be too tough to eat, and a roast big enough to

Poultry shears, distinguished by their curved serrated blades and spring-loaded handle, are most useful when carving geese or ducks, which have deeply buried leg and wing joints and very tough tendons. They are also handy for halving the carcasses of ducks and small upland game birds. Use them if you have them, but you can get along quite well with a sharp knife.

be pierced by their oversized tines is heavy enough to hold its place on a platter while being carved.

What really matters is the sharpness of your knife. Backtrack a few pages if you need to, and study the methods of sharpening knives illustrated there. The same kind of attention given kitchen knives should also be paid to a knife used for carving. And don't be bashful about taking the steel with you to the table to use just before you start cutting, and at any time between slices when you feel the edge of your carver growing a bit dull.

One more thing you'll want to do. Before you begin carving any meat or fowl, remove any garnish or other foods that are on the platter. A roast or fowl will often be surrounded by baked potatoes or half-buried in parsley. Be a strip-tease artist and take it off. Put garnishes on a service plate, where they'll be out of your way.

Some meats ought to be served from a second platter, even though many carvers simply transfer the slices to dinner plates as they're cut. But when two kinds of meat come from the same cut—white and dark meat from turkey, rare and brown meat from a leg of lamb, for instance—it's a lot easier to do all the carving before serving, so your guests can have a bit of both kinds if they wish. In the case of turkey, a second small platter will certainly make carving the drumsticks and thighs a lot easier; at least by using one you'll have room in which to wield your knife and a place to rest the big bones after they've been cleared of meat without cluttering up the main platter.

Although the accompanying pictures illustrate all key carving procedures step-by-step, not every cut of meat is shown because so many meats are carved in basically the same fashion. To help you locate the sequences dealing with specific cuts, consult the following list, which is not alphabetized, but grouped according to the similarity of carving styles used.

Beef

Rolled roast: Boneless; carve at right angles to the grain of the meat, cutting straight downward to take off slices.

Tenderloin: Boneless; carve like a rolled roast, but make cuts at a slight right-hand angle to produce larger slices.

A rolled roast is carved in uniform slices at right angles to its long dimension. Any strings or skewers used to hold the meat in place during cooking are removed in the kitchen.

Bottom round roast: Usually boneless; carve at right angles to the grain; cut several slices from the near side with the handle of the blade at a slight left-hand angle, then from the far side with the knife's angle reversed. If the roast is cooked bone-in, stand on end and carve like a standing rib roast. If the meat has been boned before cooking, carve like a rolled roast.

1. A bottom round or rump roast is usually boneless. Rump roasts taken high on the animal may have a section of hipbone in them, and these are carved like a standing rib roast (pictured later). In carving a boneless bottom round, take the first slice off along one side, as above, the knife slanted slightly from the outer edge to the center of the roast.

2. Take succeeding slices off with the knife angled to produce cuts that are slightly thicker at the outer edge than in the center.

3. After several slices have been taken off, the pieces of meat are large enough for each slice to be divided into two portions.

Heel of round or Pike's Peak roast: Contains a long piece of gristle on the bottom. Carve like a bottom round roast, ending the cut at the gristle, and free the slices by cutting along the gristle with the knife blade roughly parallel to the platter.

Rump roast: If boned, carve like a bottom round; if bone-in, like a standing rib; if preboned and rolled, like a rolled roast.

1. A heel of round or Pike's Peak roast usually has a gristlelike piece of soft bone running most of its length; in the picture above the end of this bone is seen just to the right of the carver's knife hand. Take the first slice off with the knife slanted from edge to center; the slice ends at the top of the bone.

2. Make the next slices parallel to the first; end them when the knife reaches the bone.

3. Hold the knife parallel to the bone and slice horizontally along the bone's top to free the slices.

4. When several slices have been removed from the near side of the roast, begin carving the far side of the face at an angle of about 60 degrees to the first cuts. Then, take slices alternately from each of the two faces; this produces uniform portions and relieves the carver from having to divide big slices and from having to carve evenly across a very wide meat-face.

Chuck roast: May have different arrangements of bones, depending on the section of the shoulder from which it came. Remove the bones by cutting along their edges, between bone and meat, lift bones out, push the meat pieces together, slice with the grain. This is really a job best done in the kitchen; the slices can be assembled on a clean platter and taken to the table after carving.

1. Chuck roasts should really be carved in the kitchen. The first step is to remove bones and to take out the areas of bone or fat or gristle, as above, which defy neat carving. All bones are removed before any slicing is done. Slide the knife along the bones, parting them from the meat. A knife with a short flexible blade is better for this cut of meat than a long carving knife.

2. When all the bones have been removed, push the sections of the roast together neatly and cut uniform slices across it; the carving in this case is done with the grain of the meat.

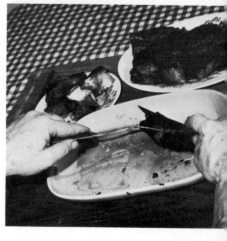

3. As the slices are carved, transfer them to a small clean serving platter. This is the procedure used in carving all steak cuts, though since the prime cuts such as T-bone have only a single bone, the steaks can readily be carved at the table.

Sirloin steak: Bones are in different arrangements in different sirloin cuts—pinbone, flat bone, and wedge bone. Remove bones in the kitchen and carve like a chuck roast. Or, cut along the bones and take slices by carving with the grain from bone to edge of meat.

Porterhouse steak: Carve like chuck roast, above.

T-Bone steak: Carve like chuck roast, above.

Flank steak (London broil): Boneless; carve on a board rather than in the platter, for the knife must be held almost parallel to the carving surface. Take off thin slices, carving with the grain.

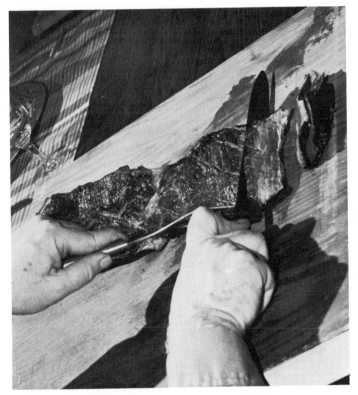

Boneless steaks such as London broil, which comes from the flank, should be carved on a flat board, as a platter's rimmed edge makes proper carving difficult. The slices must be carved with the knife almost parallel to the meat's surface, as shown above.

Standing rib roast (prime rib): Usually carved with the roast standing on end. The chine end of the ribs should be at the carver's left. With the knife blade roughly parallel to the platter, cut horizontally with the blade slanted slightly downward, the blade just above the bone. Take the next slice off in the same manner with the blade touching the bone. Start the third slice below the top rib, the knife blade following the bone and slanted slightly upward. Remove the top rib bone; the butcher will in preparing the roast have sawed the ribs free of the chine. The next slice is taken at right angles to the meat, to even up the surface of the roast. Then, repeat the procedure from the beginning to carve out each rib. The slices will be very slightly wedge-shaped. Those attached to the ribs are freed by running the knife along the bone after lifting the rib free. The alternate method is to carve with the roast chine bone down on the platter; the cutting angles are the same. Most carvers find it easier to work with the roast in a standing position, as this allows them to locate the bones very easily, and to keep an eye on the knife's angle at all times. When carving with the chine side on the platter, the ending of the cuts must be made with the knife held at an awkward angle, almost vertical.

1. When carving a standing rib roast—prime ribs— the bone side should be toward the carver with the tips of the ribs to his left. All carving is done with the knife horizontal. The first cuts are made straight across the top of the roast, as above, until the first bone is reached.

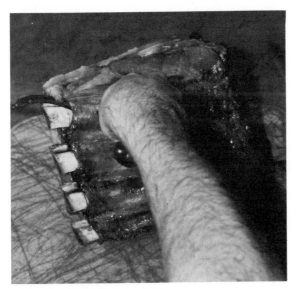

2. On reaching the topmost rib bone, the knife tip is tilted down and a slice taken with the blade sliding along the rib; the slice will be a bit thicker at the back than it is at the edge along the bone.

3. In making the next cut, the base of the knife is moved below the bone and the tip slanted upward. In cutting, the edge of the knife should stay in contact with the bone. This slice is removed from the roast with the bone attached and the bone cut away before serving; the slice will be thicker at the bone edge. The procedure for slicing the remainder of the roast simply repeats the cycle.

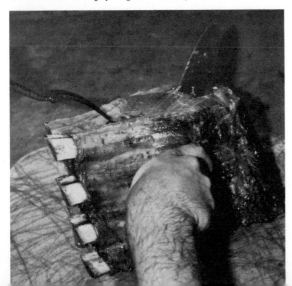

Veal

Rolled roast: Same carving method used with beef.

Rump roast: Same carving method used with beef.

Center leg and arm roast: Same method used with beef bottom round.

Breast: Have meat on the platter bone side down, the rounded edge of the roast away from the carver. Beginning at the carver's right, cut thin slices with the blade traveling at a slight angle downward to the left; cut to the bone. When the high arch of ribs is reached near the roast's center, begin carving from the left and angle the knife blade slightly to the right. When all slices are cut, free them by sliding the knife along the bones parallel to the platter, cutting horizontally.

Loin: Same carving method used with pork loin, below.

Crown roast: This is just a strip of the loin formed into a circle; cut between the ribs as you would a pork loin, taking care to keep the slices parallel.

Leg: Same carving method used with ham.

Lamb

Rolled roast: Same carving method used with beef.

Breast: Same carving method used with veal.

Crown roast: Same carving method used with pork loin.

Rack or loin: Same carving method used with pork loin.

Leg: Have the shankbone at the carver's left, the curved side of the leg uppermost on the platter. With a folded towel to keep the left hand cool and clean, grasp the shankbone in the left hand and lift the roast slightly, letting it rest with the butt end on the platter. Make a slanting cut from left to right about 2 inches from the point where meat starts on the shank, angling down to meet the bone, then make a vertical cut at right angles to the first cut and meeting it at the bone; lift out the wedge freed by these two cuts and set it aside. Start slicing from left to right, beginning at the wedge, cutting downward with the knife at a slight left-hand angle. When several slices are cut, free them by running the knife along the bone, horizontally, from

1. Carving a leg of lamb begins with placement of the platter; the shank of the roast should be at the carver's left.

2. With a napkin protecting the left hand from heat and fat, the carver picks the roast up by the shank and gives the leg a quarter-turn toward himself. The first cut is made about 2 to 3 inches below the top of the shank meat, at a right-hand angle to the bone.

3. Connect the second cut with the first by slicing straight down to the bone. The wedge of meat produced by these two cuts is removed to make room for the knife.

4. Working from left to right, as shown above, the carver cuts uniform slices, all cuts being made straight down to the bone.

5. Free the slices by cutting horizontally along the bone.

6. When enough slices for a first serving have been taken from the top of the leg, it is turned over and the carver begins taking long thin slices parallel to the bone.

7. After each two or three slices, the bone is rotated slightly to keep the slices uniform in size and shape. A portion should contain both a slice from the top of the leg and some of the browner meat from the bottom.

left to right. Continue carving, freeing the slices periodically, until the upper section is cleared. Rotate the bone to bring the uncarved half uppermost, and cut long thin slices parallel with the bone, carving horizontally from right to left. Give the bone a slight turn after each two or three slices to clear it evenly. Halve these slices before serving. A portion usually consists of some meat from each side of the leg.

Saddle of Lamb: A seldom-seen but princely special-occasion cut; it includes both hind legs and a portion of the lower loin. There is a T-shaped bone running through the saddle. Its top-bar should be at the carver's left, the platter slanting slightly toward the right. Make the first cut along the backbone and free the loin sections by running the knife along the ribs from the backbone to their tips; remove these portions to a separate platter. Carve the legs parallel to the bones as described above for carving the bottom of a leg roast, but make the horizontal slices all around the legs of the rack. Carve the haunches by making thin cuts across the grain at a slight angle until the bone is touched and free the slices by running the knife horizontally along the bone as described for the first cuts off a single leg, above. A portion should include some meat from loin, leg, and haunch.

Pork

Loin: Any loin roast from any commercial meat animal is nothing but a string of chops that haven't been separated. When you buy a loin roast, be sure the butcher saws through the chine (backbone) between each rib; then the carving job is quite simple. Have the loin on the platter with the bones facing the carver, the chine side down. Carve across the grain, cutting straight down between each rib, keeping the slices of even thickness.

Crown roast: Same carving method used with veal crown roast.

Butt roast: Same carving method used with beef rump.

Boston butt roast: A boned butt; carve in straight slices, cutting downward across the grain.

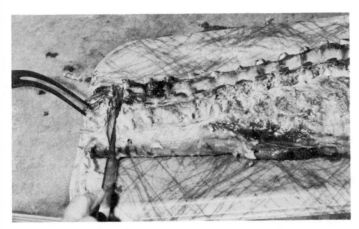

A loin roast of pork, lamb, or veal can be prepared for cooking in two styles. In the roast pictured, the chine (backbone) has been removed from the ribs; it is easier to carve a roast prepared this way with the ribs up. In the second method of preparation, the chine is left on the roast, but is sawed between each rib, and roasts made ready this way are more easily carved standing in the platter, chine-down.

Carving any loin roast from a small animal is a simple matter of slicing down between each rib, keeping the slices uniform in thickness. A crown roast is a loin roast formed into a circle, and the procedure for carving it is the same as for a straight loin.

Leg roast: There are two, upper leg and lower leg. The upper leg is carved by the same method used with beef bottom round. The lower leg is carved much like a ham—which it is, of course, the shank section—by carving across the grain to the bone and freeing the slices by running the knife horizontally along the bone, parallel to the platter. Look at the picture on page 157 of the ham with the bone superimposed to see how the bones lie inside a leg of pork.

1. A ham is always placed on the platter fat side up. If the ham is a right-hand one, as is the one pictured, the shank will be at the carver's left; a left-hand ham will have its shank at the carver's right. Either can be carved in the fashion illustrated by the pictures that follow, with the carver working from left to right on a left-hand ham, or the carver can begin slicing from the shank end, beginning the slices about 4 to 6 inches from the meat end, at the point where the knuckle joint begins. Either method yields slices that make a serving portion; hams carved the old-fashioned way, standing on edge, yield embarrassingly big slices that must be halved to serve. In beginning to carve the ham shown above, locate the hipbone with the carving fork or tip of the knife and make the first cut horizontally along the hipbone to a depth of 3 to 4 inches. The next cut, made downward at right angles, connects with the horizontal cut, and the wedge of meat produced is removed to make room for the knife.

2. Having removed the wedge, begin cutting slices of uniform thickness, cutting straight down to the bone; free the slices by sliding the knife horizontally along the bone at their bottom.

Ham: Skin the ham. Check the position of the bones in a ham by referring to the picture on page 157. The ham in this picture is a right-hand ham, if that's bothering you. To carve: Have the shank end at the carver's left, the ham on the platter skin side up. Use the tip of the knife to find the angle at which the hip joint slants; cut along the joint with the knife roughly parallel to the platter, making a cut about 2 to 3 inches deep. Cut straight down to meet the horizontal cut, and remove the wedge the two cuts have freed. Begin slicing from right to left, cutting across the grain straight down to the bone. After cutting three or four slices, free them with a horizontal cut, the knife following the bone. Repeat until enough slices have been cut. Usually, slicing the top of a ham this way will yield enough slices to serve an average dinner party. To complete slicing, turn the ham over, turn the platter end-for-end. Starting about 3 to 4 inches from the shank end—which is now at the carver's right—remove a wedge and slice as described above. Clearing the bone of all meat is a kitchen job; the knuckle joint must be passed by with several almost-vertical cuts along it, and neat carving ends at the hip joint, which must be cleaned with a small utility knife to remove all meat from it.

3. After several slices have been removed and the angle of the thighbone is apparent, make a deep cut horizontally along the bone, and subsequent slices will be easier to remove. Once the horizontal cut has been made, carve several slices at once to speed up service.

4. Continue slicing, making horizontal cuts as needed and carving down to meet them, until enough slices have been taken for a first serving. For photographic purposes, the slices in the pictures are thicker than would usually be made.

Wild Game

Venison roasts are carved in the manner described for lamb; all antlered animals have skeletal structures practically identical with that of sheep. The difference is one only of size. Small game such as rabbits and squirrels are not usually carved at the table; the procedure for handling them is given in Chapter VI. The bone structure of buffalo, which are still categorized as wild game, resembles that of beef cattle, though the bones are much larger. Bear hindquarter and loin roasts have essentially the same bone structure as their equivalents from beef, and you're not likely to encounter a bear forearm roast, since the meat from a bear's forearms is very tough-fibered and should be ground for sausages or meat loaf.

Poultry

Turkey: All trussing cords and skewers should be removed in the kitchen. With the turkey breast up on the platter, remove drumstick and thigh as a unit by cutting between thigh and body with the knife butt to the carver's right; cut as deeply as possible during the last stage of the cut, slanting the knife blade in toward the bird's body to open the hip joint. Hold the tip of the drumstick with the left hand (use a napkin to protect against heat and fat) and pull outward and down on the leg while cutting. Make the second cut below the thigh joint, just in front of the tail, pull the leg down to expose the hip joint, and slip the knife tip into the joint to sever the tendons. Put the leg section on a separate platter for attention later. Next, cut almost horizontally into the breast at its base, pulling the wing aside with the left hand, and cutting around the upper wing joint. Pull the wing forward to expose the joint—it's easier to do this if the carver moves to stand at the right of the platter—and slip the knife tip into the joint to sever tendons. Put the wing on the opposite side of the platter; it will not be carved unless you want to take off the upper joint as a second "drumstick." With the carving fork inserted at the bottom of the breastbone, begin carving the breast at its highest part; some like to do this with

1. It doesn't make a bit of difference which side of a turkey you carve first. The procedure is exactly the same. Most commercial growers remove the tip of one wing from turkeys when they are chicks, and my preference is to begin on the side that has a full three-joint wing. Begin by grasping the tip of the drumstick in your left hand, using a napkin to protect yourself from heat and fat. Pull the leg away from the side of the bird, cut down and inward toward the back of the turkey to reach the hip socket.

2. Lift the leg for your second cut, slice forward and inward from the tail, cutting as far back of the thigh as possible, and cut until your knife touches bone.

3. Pull the leg down as far as possible to expose the ball-and-socket joint where thighbone and hipbone connect. There is a tendon in the center of this joint. Sever it by inserting the knife tip into the joint with short stabbing strokes. You'll know when the tendon has been cut, for the leg will part from the body. Cut straight down from the hip joint to sever the strip of flesh that still attaches the leg to the carcass. Put the leg on a small platter.

4. Cut into the body above the wing joint at the bottom of the breast. The knife tip should be well under the turkey's back. Pull the wing away from the body and cut as deeply as possible.

5. Pull the wing forward, toward the neck, to expose the shoulder joint. It, too, has an inner tendon that must be severed with the tip of the knife. After severing the tendon, cut down from the opened joint to part the strip of flesh that still attaches the wing to the body. Put the wing aside on the platter with the leg; don't clutter up the carving platter and cut down on your work space.

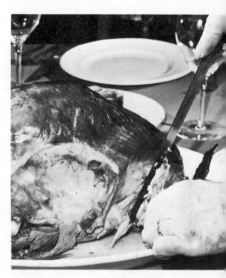

6. Take a thin slice from the breast just below the point where it reaches its greatest sidewise curve. Start the cut midway between breastbone and neck, hold the knife high enough to miss the breastbone, and let the upper edge of the slice run roughly parallel with the line of the breastbone.

7. Start each succeeding slice a bit lower on the breast and carve with the knife at an angle that produces slices a bit thicker at the bottom than at the top. You should get 8 to 10 slices from this area of a turkey's breast. To show clearly in the photograph, the slices are being carved thicker than they would normally be.

8. After slicing enough breast meat for a first serving, take dark meat from the leg. Carve it on a small platter. First, cut down between drumstick and thigh to expose the joint, hold the thigh firmly on the platter with knife or fork, and bend the drumstick down to reach the joint. Sever the inner tendon and cut through the remainder of the connecting flesh.

9. Hold the drumstick at a slight angle and carve oval-shaped slices from its sides. Turn it after each slice or two and carve from a fresh section of the leg. Carve the thigh in the same manner, or remove the bone and carve into uniform slivers with the grain of the meat.

upward cuts, some choose to cut downward. After taking off several slices, move down the breast and hold the knife at an angle to the body that will produce gently tapered slices of breast meat. When enough white meat has been carved, divide thigh and drumstick on their platter, cutting down at the joint with the drumstick held upright. Hold the drumstick at a slight left-hand angle and take oval-shaped slices, cutting almost parallel with the bone and rotating the leg slightly between cuts. When the drumstick has been cleared of meat, follow the same procedure in carving the thigh section, or, if you wish, hold it flat with the fork and slice lengthwise at a sharp angle, knife parallel to the bone. A usual serving consists of some pieces of both breast and dark meat from the leg or thigh. When the carving has been completed, use the tip of the knife to cut away the skin of the cavities so the dressing can be removed with a spoon.

Capon: Carve like a turkey.

Chicken: Generally the wings are removed first; this allows the carver to cut off more meat with the more-desirable drumstick-thigh section. The breast is then carved in the manner described for turkey, and the drumstick and thigh are divided and carved.

1. When carving chicken, take the wing off first; the cut is the same as that made in removing a turkey wing. This will produce more meat from the legs.

2. Begin as far forward on the breast as possible when making the cut between body and leg that will expose the hip-socket joint, and follow the hipbone with the edge of the knife as the cut is being completed. Then hold the leg flat with the fork while inserting the knife-tip into the hip socket to sever the inner tendon. Cut straight down to free the leg.

3. More portions of breast meat will be produced if you begin to carve at the tip of the breastbone. Slice downward and take pieces that taper slightly inward toward the body from the top of the breast.

4. Separate thigh and drumstick and carve the drumstick in the same manner as when carving turkey. A chicken's thigh is more easily carved by holding it flat on the plate with the fork and cutting slivers parallel to the bone. When the bone is reached, it can easily be removed with the tip of the knife and the remaining thigh meat carved.

Goose: There are some differences between the bony structure of waterfowl and those of turkey and chicken. On a goose, the drumstick and thigh meat is not usually carved, being on the tough side. To carve: Remove the wing tip joint, cut through at the juncture of tip and pinion. Remove the drumstick and thigh as a unit; cut close to the body and go deeper than you think necessary to reach the thigh joint, which is high on the bird's back. When the joint is exposed, sever the tendons with the knife tip and set the piece aside. Make one long cut along the keel (in other birds it's called the breast-bone), cutting along the upright keelbone down to the ribs. With the knife horizontal and roughly parallel to the platter, cut from the curve of the breast to the keelbone, taking out a thin wedge about 2 inches wide at its bottom. Slice the breast

1. Geese and ducks yield only dark meat. Their bone structure differs slightly from that of landfowl in that their legs are shorter and the wing-socket and hip-socket joints are deeper in their bodies. Their skeletons are almost cylindrical and covered evenly, with less flesh concentrated in the breast area. The wings and legs of a goose and duck are often reserved from being served, but to carve them the legs must be removed in order to take slices from the rear of the carcass. The wingtips are removed in the kitchen, but the upper wing joints are left on both for the sake of appearance and to keep the bird level on the platter. To take off the legs, cut down and inward at the point where the legs join the body. Hold the tip of the leg with a napkin protecting the left hand, pull the leg down and away from the body, and make the first cut as shown above, then cut behind and in front of the leg, pull it farther downward, and reach into the hip socket with the knife point to sever the leg tendon.

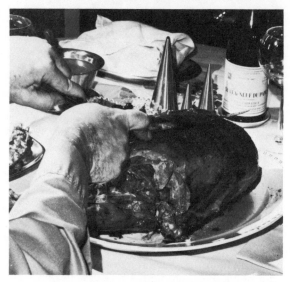

2. Insert the tip of the knife at the neck end of the breast beside the breastbone—in geese, often called the "keel"—and cut lengthwise along the bone; make the cut down to the ribs.

3. Turn the platter to put the body of the duck at right angles to the carver. All the rest of the carving is done with the knife horizontal and roughly parallel with the bird's body. Starting 1½ to 2 inches to the right of the keel, cut to the keelbone to produce a wedge; remove this piece and set aside.

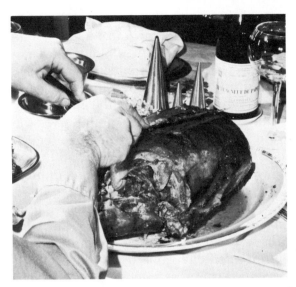

4. Carve serving slices by cutting from the curve of the breast toward the bone, tapering the cuts slightly to produce long ribbon-shaped slices.

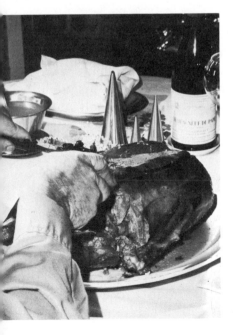

5. When the bottom of the keel is reached, begin the slices down the curve of the body and bring the knife blade upward slightly. The entire side of a goose is covered with a good layer of flesh, and can be sliced almost to the point where the bird's back begins.

lengthwise, working from the curve at its side toward the keel-bone, to produce long fairly thin slices about 2 to 3 inches wide. Work down the breast, toward the wing, and when the base of the wing is reached turn the platter end-for-end and repeat the procedure for the uncarved side: remove wing tip and leg and thigh, then slice the breast lengthwise. This is the easiest way I've discovered to carve a goose at the table; it eliminates the job of removing the wing from the body, and produces neat, evenly sliced serving portions. However, you will still have plenty of meat left, for a goose's skeleton is almost cylindrical and the flesh covering it is evenly distributed over breast, sides, and back. Complete carving in the kitchen, after your guests have dined to repletion and gone home. As for those drumsticks and thighs, take the meat off them and use it ground in a pâté or spread where it can be rendered chewable by grinding.

Duck: Carve in the same fashion as a goose, or remove the legs before the birds come to the table, and take off the breasts whole and carve them across their short dimension into neat slices.

Game Birds

Wild ducks and geese are carved in the same fashion as their domesticated cousins, though the smaller species of wild ducks may simply be cut into halves. This is a job for poultry shears; cut lengthwise, with the breastbone in one half and the spine in the other. Teal are usually served whole, one bird (two, if you're lucky) being a portion. Reed and marsh birds such as jacksnipe and small upland birds such as quail and doves are served whole. Roast pheasants are carved like chicken, but the drumsticks and wings are not commonly served.

Fish

There's really no carving involved in serving a large whole fish. The flesh of fish is arranged by nature in layers, and after it has been cooked any serving utensil can slip between the layers and part them without a knife being necessary. The key to easy table service of a big fish is advance preparation, and until you've gotten the knack of working quickly in removing skin and bones from a fish, this preparation is best done in the kitchen.

With the fish on a working platter or board, lift away the skin from the uppermost side and discard it. Slide the spatula along the back from tail to head, working the blade on top of the dorsal fin and lifting with a fork or second spatula to lift the flesh gently. Next, slide the spatula along the fish's body in the slit that has been opened, lifting with the fork, and slipping the spatula along the fin spines and ribs to the belly. The flesh will part from the bones very easily. When the top layer of flesh is freed from the bones, use two spatulas to lift off the top layer and transfer it to the serving platter; put it on the serving platter skin side down.

Lift the backbone from the remaining half-fish and remove all the fin spines. The head will come away with the backbone. Turn the unskinned half-fish over and remove the skin, then lift it as you did the first half, placing it neatly on the half already transferred to the serving platter. You're now ready to sauce the

1. Preparing a big fish for easy table service is best done in the kitchen. You will need a working platter or board and a serving platter. First, lift the fish out of the poaching liquid by the ends of the cheesecloth and put it on the working platter.

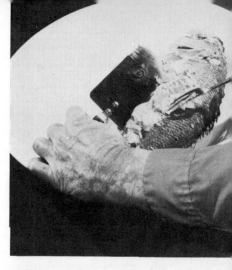

2. Skin the side that's uppermost. On a properly cooked fish, the skin will lift away from the flesh very readily; use a fork and spatula to fold the skin back.

3. When the skin is off the top half of the fish, gently work the fork and spatula along the back, between the flesh and the spines of the dorsal fin. Lift with the fork, slip the spatula into the body following the spine and rib bones; these will part readily from the flesh. Free the entire upper layer of flesh this way.

4. Use two spatulas to lift the upper layer of flesh and transfer it to the serving platter. Put it on the platter skin side down; to do this, rest the edge of the flesh on one side of the platter and tilt fish and platter together. There may be a few spines from the anal fin that have been lifted with the flesh; be sure to pull these free and discard them.

5. With fork and spatula, work the backbone and ribs free from the bottom half the fish, and discard them. Remember, cooking destroys the membrane that holds the spines of the fins together; they must be lifted out separately. The head will come off with the backbone, and unless you're preparing a set-piece trout or salmon that is to be glazed with aspic, discard the head.

6. Turn the bottom piece of flesh over on the working platter and skin it as you did the top piece. Then lift the piece of bottom flesh with two spatulas and transfer it to the serving platter, placing it on top of the first half. You now have a boneless fish body on the serving platter.

7. Garnish the fish, or sauce it, and serve. You will not need a knife; use a long-bladed serving utensil and simply work it across the body of the fish to remove serving-sized portions.

fish, or to garnish it with lemon and parsley or endive, and take it to the table. Divide the fish with the serving utensil into the size portions required, beginning at the head.

Carving's really no big hassle, if you have a truly sharp knife and have done a little homework in learning the anatomy of the meat being carved. The first few efforts are the hardest, so make these when dining *à deux* with Her, or experiment in the kitchen. You'll learn, among other things, that the bigger the cut of meat or the bird, the easier it is to carve. A big roast anchors itself on the platter and needs only a bit of steadying with the carving fork, while a small one will skid and slide and require a firm hand to hold it in place. A turkey is easier to carve than a chicken, a goose easier than a duck. So, if you've got the idea of starting with small cuts or birds and working up, reverse the procedure: start big and work down.

Since easy carving starts in the kitchen, a few basics of roast meat and fowl cookery are given in the recipes that follow, as well as a pair of basic recipes for preparing a large fish.

Roast Beef, Sauce Robert

6- to 8-pound bottom round or Pike's Peak roast	3 tbsp minced onion
1 tbsp peanut oil	2 tbsp butter
1 tsp peppercorns	1 cup red wine vinegar
2 tsp salt	3 tbsp fresh lemon juice
	½ cup dry white wine

Wipe the meat well, rub it with the oil. Crack peppercorns coarsely and press into the fat. Dust with salt. Cook uncovered in a preheated 375-degree oven for 45 minutes, reduce oven temperature to 250 degrees, cook 15 minutes per pound for rare, 20 for medium rare or 25 for well done. About 30 minutes before the end of cooking time, siphon fat from the roasting pan and discard. Sauté the onion gently in the butter until golden brown, stir in the vinegar and lemon juice, simmer about 5 minutes. Pour over the roast, let cooking time come to an end. Remove roast to a warm platter to rest at least 15 to 20 minutes before carving; this gives the meat time to firm up and reabsorb juices. While the roast rests, scrape the roasting pan well and drain the juice into the blender. Swirl the wine in the pan to deglaze, drain the wine into the blender. Blend 30 to 45 seconds at HIGH speed. If no blender is available, pass the sauce through a sieve, rubbing it with a wooden spoon to break up the semisolid bits from the pan, and reheat briefly. Serve the sauce in a sauceboat, passing it to be spooned over the meat as it is served.

London Broil

About 2 pounds beef flank, about 8 by 12 inches	1 tsp salt
	¼ tsp freshly ground pepper
	Large dash cayenne
2 tbsp olive oil or peanut oil	1 tsp fresh lemon juice
1 large clove garlic, mashed	

Trim any excess fat from the meat, pound gently with the flat face of a meat mallet or the flat of a cleaver, score into a diamond pattern on both sides with shallow cuts. Combine all remaining ingredients, rub well into both sides of the steak, let stand 1 to 2 hours. Broil 4 to 5 minutes per side about 6 inches below the broiler with heat set high. Remove to a carving board, carve and serve as explained on page 175.

Roast Veal Breast, Southern Sauce

5- to 6-pound veal breast	¼ cup minced sweet onion
Cooking oil	½ tsp salt
½ cup pure peanut butter	⅓ cup fresh lemon juice
(the kind without lard in	
it)	

Sear the meat in hot cooking oil over high surface heat; use just enough oil to film the pan's bottom. Combine the remaining ingredients and rub generously over the meat. Cook uncovered in a preheated 300-degree oven, cook 1¼ to 1½ hours, basting with pan juices two or three times. Transfer meat to a hot platter, let rest 10 to 15 minutes before carving; see page 178 for carving procedure. Strain the pan juices through a coarse sieve into a sauceboat, spoon a little of the juice over each serving of the meat.

Stuffed Rolled Veal Breast

5- to 6-pound veal breast, boned	3 sprigs parsley, chopped
1 cup coarse dry breadcrumbs	3 or 4 celery tops with leaves
	½ tsp crumbled thyme
	⅓ cup dry white wine
2 tbsp grated sweet onion	1 egg
3 tbsp chopped mushrooms	½ tsp salt
2 slices fat bacon, chopped	¼ tsp freshly ground pepper

Spread the breast out flat, combine all remaining ingredients, and spread them over the meat. Roll like a jelly roll and tie with string or hold outside edge in place with skewers. Rub lightly with cooking oil or butter, put in a lightly oiled pan, cook 30 to 40 minutes in a preheated 350-degree oven, turning once to sear evenly. Reduce oven heat to 225 degrees and cook 15 minutes per pound of meat. Baste once or twice with pan juices or butter.

Leg of Lamb, French Style

5- to 6-pound leg of lamb	1 large carrot, peeled and grated
6 or 7 cloves garlic, peeled	½ cup dry white wine
⅓ to ½ cup peanut oil	2 cups chicken stock
1 onion, 2-inch diameter, chopped	

Prepare the lamb by trimming off all but a thin layer of fat. Do not cut off the shank bone. With a thin, sharp knife, make small openings evenly distributed over the meat and slip a clove of garlic in each one. Rub the surface of the meat with oil, put on a rack in a shallow roasting pan, cook 15 to 20 minutes in a preheated 400-degree oven, reduce heat to 225 degrees and cook 12 minutes per pound for rare, 15 minutes per pound for medium-rare. This roast cooked this style should be either rare or medium-rare. Baste occasionally with the reserved oil. Midway of cooking time, scatter the onion and carrot on the bottom of the pan. At the end of cooking time, transfer lamb to a carving board or ovenproof platter, reduce oven temperature to 125 degrees, and return lamb to oven, leaving the door open. Let it rest at least 20 minutes to reabsorb juices and firm up. Meanwhile, prepare the sauce. Drain liquid from the pan into a bowl, put pan on low surface heat, swirl the wine in it, stir and scrape pan to remove bits clinging to sides and bottom. Drain into the bowl with the juices taken from the pan earlier, then strain the bowl's contents into a saucepan through cheesecloth. Twist the cloth to squeeze out all juices. Add stock to saucepan, simmer over low heat 10 to 15 minutes, stirring often. Put lamb on platter, strain sauce into sauceboat, spoon a bit of sauce over each serving of meat as it is carved.

Crown Roast of Lamb, Stuffed

8- to 12-rib rack (loin)	1 egg
Cooking oil	½ cup milk
2 cups coarse breadcrumbs	1 tsp crumbled rosemary
½ cup grated onion	1¼ tsp salt
½ cup grated carrot	¼ tsp freshly ground pepper

Have the butcher saw the chine between each rib. When ready to cook, rub the meat with oil, form it into a circle with the rib bones outside. Trim excess meat from the tops of the ribs so they stand ¾ inch above the flesh. Combine all remaining ingredients into a stuffing, put in center of the crown, mound neatly; rub extra oil on the outside of the roast. Cover the tips of the rib bones with bits of foil or heavy brown paper that has been soaked in cooking oil. Cook in a shallow roasting pan, 30 minutes in a preheated 400-degree oven, then reduce temperature to 225 degrees and cook 20 minutes per pound. Transfer to warmed serving platter, let rest 15 to 20 minutes before carving. Carving procedures are on page 183.

Tipsy Roast Pork Loin

6-pound pork loin	1½ cups liquor: brandy, Cognac,
2 tsp salt	Bourbon, rum (your choice)
½ tsp freshly ground pepper	8 large potatoes
½ tsp ground cloves	4 firm red apples (or onions, if you
Bay leaf	prefer)

Trim excess fat from roast. Combine salt and pepper with cloves, rub well into meat. Put the roast in a shallow platter, pour the liquor over it, let stand 2 to 3 hours, turning three or four times so all surfaces will come into contact with the liquor. Drain, reserving any liquor remaining in the platter. Cook on a rack in a shallow roasting pan in a preheated 350-degree oven for 2½ hours; test by running a skewer into the meat: if juices run clear with no tinge of red or pink, the roast is cooked completely. Peel potatoes and parboil them 5 minutes, drain. If apples are used, core them; if onions, score the stem ends with an X-cut so they will hold their shape. Remove pork to platter when cooked; it should rest 20 minutes. Skim loose fat from pan, put potatoes and apples (or onions) into pan juices, return to oven and cook 25 to 30 minutes, turning once or twice. Pour liquor from marinade over meat and flame. Garnish platter with potatoes and apples (or onions) after draining them. Serve a potato or apple with each portion of meat. Carving procedures are on page 183.

Roast Stuffed Turkey

18- to 20-pound turkey, shop-cleaned
Butter: ¼ cup for a fresh bird; if frozen add ½ tbsp per pound

Stuffing:

8 cups dry breadcrumbs	1 tbsp dry crumbled sage
3 cups cornbread cubes	½ tsp dry crumbled rosemary
¾ cup walnut or pecan meats	1 tsp freshly ground pepper
	1½ tsp salt
1 cup sweet onion, chopped	¾ cup melted butter
1 cup celery, chopped	3 to 4 cups dry white wine
½ cup minced parsley	1 cup chicken or turkey stock
½ tsp dry crumbled basil	3 eggs, lightly beaten

To prepare the turkey, remove giblets from cavity, boil in lightly salted water for stock. (Giblets can be added to dressing unless part of the dressing is to be frozen; freezing causes giblets to become bitter.) Remove any shop trussing from bird; remove neck if this has not been done. Wipe both cavities thoroughly with cloth or paper towels, wipe outside of bird well. If a frozen turkey, reserve ¼ cup butter and use the remainder to rub into the cavities, dividing it between them.

To make dressing: Combine dry ingredients, including seasonings, in a big mixing bowl. Combine liquids by beating lightly, pour slowly over dressing mixture while stirring it so the liquids will be absorbed evenly. Stuff breast cavity and truss—see illustrations on page 155—then body cavity, and truss legs. Rub bird thoroughly with butter. Melt remaining butter and in it soak a large square of clean white cloth. Put bird in roasting pan, spread cloth over it, tucking the edges and ends of cloth well down, into contact with bottom of pan. Cook in a preheated 350-degree oven for 1 hour, reduce temperature to 225 degrees, continue to cook until the bird has cooked at 225 degrees 20 minutes per pound. No basting is required. Remove turkey to warmed platter; it must stand 20 to 30 minutes to reabsorb juices and let its flesh firm up. During this time, make the gravy:

1 cup flour	1 cup stock (from giblets)
1 cup milk	Salt and pepper as needed

Put roasting pan over low surface heat, scrape and stir; put flour and milk (which must be cool) into jar, close jar tightly, shake until they form a smooth mixture. Combine with stock, add slowly to the pan juices while stirring. Cook until gravy reaches the consistency of thick cream, taste and adjust seasoning with salt and pepper as needed. Carving procedures are on page 188.

Roast Chicken, Pan Gravy

Roasting chicken, 3 to 4 pounds	1 clove garlic
¼ cup butter	3 pieces celery tops with leaves
1 tsp salt	½ tsp dry crumbled tarragon
¼ tsp freshly ground pepper	¾ cup dry white wine

Wipe chicken inside and out, cream together butter, salt, and pepper, rub bird with this inside and out. Put garlic, celery, and tarragon in cavity. Truss (procedure given on page 155). Put in roasting pan, drape with butter-soaked cloth, letting cloth touch bottom of pan. Cook in a preheated 225-degree oven 25 minutes per pound. Transfer bird to heated platter; it should rest 15 minutes before carving. Skim loose fat from pan juices, pour wine into pan over low surface heat, stir well, scraping to dislodge loose bits, strain gravy through sieve into sauceboat. Carving procedures are on page 188.

Stuffed Boned Chicken

Roasting chicken, about 3 to
    4 pounds
¼ pound salt pork
½ cup chopped onion
¾ cup chicken stock

2 eggs, lightly beaten
3 to 4 cups cooked rice
¼ tsp freshly ground pepper
Butter or cooking oil

Bone the chicken according to procedure explained on page 148. Blanch the pork by trimming off salt rinds and plunging into boiling water 5 minutes; drain and chop coarsely. Combine pork, onion, stock, rice, pepper; stuff the bird with this, being sure to work the stuffing up into the wing-bone and thigh-bone cavities. Close the back seam by sewing or with skewers. Pat and press the chicken into its original shape; no trussing is required since there are no tendons to pull the legs and wings out of the position in which you place them. Rub well with butter or cooking oil, put in roasting pan, drape with a cloth soaked in butter or oil, being sure the cloth extends to the bottom of the pan. Cook in a preheated 225-degree oven for 25 minutes per pound. Transfer to heated platter, let rest 20 minutes. Carve like a rolled roast, in equal slices across the body, after removing wings and drumsticks.

Baked Fish

Whole fish of about 4
    pounds; it can be a
    bass, cod, snapper,
    whitefish, etc.
2 tsp salt
1 cup chopped scallions
2 tbsp peanut oil

Very large pinch cayenne
1 cup minced onions
2 tbsp fresh lemon juice
¼ cup fine cracker crumbs
4 tbsp butter
¾ cup dry white wine
3 or 4 lemon slices, seeded

To be ready for cooking, the fish must be cleaned, scaled, fins removed, and washed thoroughly inside and out; the head and tail should be left on if your pan is big enough. Sprinkle fish inside and out with salt, let rest about 15 minutes. Sauté the scallions lightly in peanut oil, cook about 3 minutes, until they just begin to soften. Stir cayenne and lemon juice into scallions, spread half the onions on a shallow baking dish long enough to hold the fish, cover fish with remaining onions, sprinkle with cracker crumbs and dot with butter. Pour the wine into the baking dish, and cook in a preheated 325-degree oven for 15 minutes. Remove, arrange lemon slices in overlapping layers on top of the fish, spoon some of the pan juices over it, return to oven and cook 20 to 25 minutes, until flesh flakes easily. Serving procedures are on page 199.

Poached Fish

(Not all fish are suitable for poaching. Avoid excessively oily fish such as striped bass, any of the herring family—which includes tuna—and sturgeon. These are best baked on a rack that will allow the oil to drip from their flesh and be discarded. Large fish are best for poaching; choose such varieties as salmon, trout, steelhead, black bass, halibut, sea trout, sole, flounder, pompano. Steaks from large fish can also be poached.)

Court-bouillon for poaching:
1 bottle dry white wine
2 quarts cold water
1½ cups sweet onion,
    minced
Pinch salt

1 cup peeled minced carrot
Bouquet garni: 6 sprigs parsley, 3
    celery tops with leaves, sprig
    thyme, 3 peppercorns

Bring all ingredients to a boil in a saucepan, reduce to simmer, cook 30 minutes. Remove bouquet garni. Strain through cloth into a clean jar. If not all used, this can be kept stored in a closed jar in the refrigerator for several weeks.

To poach:
Before cooking, the fish should be cleaned, scaled if necessary, and side and bottom fins removed. The head and tail should be left on if possible. Fold the fish in cheesecloth, leaving a good length at each end, so it can be lifted out without breaking. Put on a rack in a pan deep enough to allow the court bouillon to cover the fish completely. Pour cold court bouillon in the pan

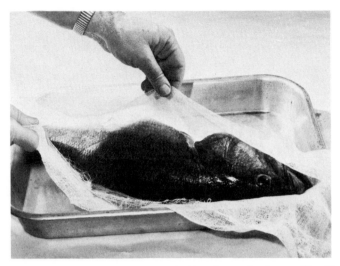

When poaching a fish, leave the head attached; it will add flavor. Wrap the fish in cheesecloth, leaving about 8 to 10 inches extra length at both ends.

to cover the fish. Bring to a boil over high heat, reduce at once to simmer; the simmering should be very slow, the liquid should not bubble, but the surface should shimmer gently. Cook 4 minutes per pound, timing from the moment boiling stopped and simmering began, Lift the fish from the pan with the ends of the cheese-cloth, unfold to a platter. The fish can be served hot or cold, with a sauce, or the skin and bones can be removed by the procedure shown on page 199, and the fish coated with aspic or a *chaudfroid* sauce.

Remember, the recipes in this section are basic procedures that can be followed in cooking cuts of meat, fowl, or fish similar to those used as illustrations. In most recipes, veal and lamb are interchangeable, and stuffings given for use with meat dishes are equally suitable for fowl or fish. Recipes for cooking ducks and geese will be found in Chapter VI.

V

Cooking Outdoors

When she points out that outdoor cooking is your job, what She's really telling you is, "I'd like to pretend I'm one of the guests, this time." She's still willing to share, to do her part in getting things ready and helping you here and there, but She expects you to carry the main load. In fairness, She deserves it, especially if your entertaining has usually been of the kind that's loaded Her down with most of the extra work. So let's leave Her out of this chapter almost entirely, and consider outdoor cooking and hosting outdoor dining as being a man's show.

You may or may not enjoy cooking and eating outdoors. Some people don't get any lift out of breaking away from the walls that enclose most of us most of the time; others find al-fresco meals so pleasant that backyard and patio cooking and dining have become one of our chief national pastimes.

Now, if you don't enjoy cooking and eating outdoors, don't do it. Don't let yourself be forced into something you don't like, just to keep in style. On the other hand, don't turn your back on it until you've tried it. This chapter is intended primarily for the fellow who hasn't tried it, the novice outdoor chef. If you're already a smoke-cured veteran, it might repeat a lot of things you already know. At the same time, it might also have in it a few ideas you haven't encountered yet.

Before going any further, let me risk being boringly repetitive, like one note played on the single string of a small violin, and unload on you a pet peeve to which I've referred before in print on several occasions.

Don't call your patio grill a "barbecue," and don't call all outdoor cooking "barbecuing." To do so marks you either as a novice or as one who's woefully uninformed. Unless the meat served is cooked in an underground pit over dying coals, both meat and coals covered with the earth that came from digging the pit, it's not barbecue. Meat cooked over an open fire on a metal grid is grilled; if cooked on a spit, it's roasted; if cooked buried in live coals, it's baked.

In spite of the labels tagged on bottles and the names attached to printed recipes, not all meat sauces used in outdoor cooking are "barbecue sauce." In fact, no prepared commercial sauce that I've ever tasted qualifies as such, because a barbecue sauce must be one that will flavor meat while it's being cooked and also be tasty when applied to meat after it's cooked. A sauce to be used in barbecuing—or in grilling, roasting, or baking outdoors—should be made of ingredients that won't be reduced to their chemical constituents by heat. Most manufactured sauces contain preservatives and additives that react unfavorably when kept hot too long. In many bottled meat sauces the only solid ingredients come out of a laboratory test tube, and really don't belong on meat at all. Read the labels.

Authentic barbecuing still survives in areas where there's more space than people, but in thickly settled neighborhoods barbecuing is almost impossible. Digging a pit in a city would require cracking through the basement slab of a high-rise; in a suburb it would mean excavating part of a lawn on which tender—and expensive—care has been lavished. Patio cooking is something else; you can do that anywhere you can find enough open space to accommodate a small grill, and don't run afoul of city ordinances that prohibit open burning.

Don't laugh at that remark about open burning; it's not a wisecrack. Early in the 1960s, when Los Angeles created its first smog-control authority, one of the first acts of the pinhead bureaucrats manning the commission was to draw up an ordinance prohibiting the use of outdoor cooking grills on smog-thick days. The law never did get on the books because a bevy

Patio cooking can be done anywhere you can find enough space for a small grill. Heavier grills are usually equipped with wheels, like the two at left above, and the others are light enough to be lifted and carried from place to place. The grill at far right doubles as a smoke cooker.

of outdoor chefs heard about it and bombarded the City Council with letters pointing out that the smoke from backyard grills didn't contain the air pollutants—hydrocarbons and their kin—that auto exhausts and factory smokestacks were pouring into the air.

As this is being written, the energy crunch is making news headlines, and it's not beyond the realm of possibility that we might see a "voluntary" ban on using electric or gas-fueled grills at some future date. Brownouts in large areas of the nation periodically bring requests for reduced use of power, and it could come to pass that outdoor cooking grills might suffer some sort of restriction if they burn electricity or use natural or butane gas.

If you have a grill that burns either, cling to it as long as the bureaucrats will let you. If you're buying a new one, though, get the charcoal-burning kind. And learn not to depend on starter fluid to help you kindle your briquettes; it's made from petroleum, you know, and we might see the day when it's bootlegged, as liquor was during Prohibition. There's not likely to be a shortage of charcoal, though, or of the pressed-wood "logs" that many outdoor chefs favor for big permanent grills. Charcoal briquettes are made from logging wastes and trash woods; pressed-wood logs from sawmill chips and sawdust. These raw materials would be wasted otherwise.

You can cook anything over charcoal that you can cook over a gas or electric grill, and vice versa, so don't worry about the recipes at the end of this chapter being unsuitable for use regardless of the kind of fuel your outdoor cooking facilities employ. In fact, you can cook them indoors on the kitchen range and they'll taste just as good.

While we're on the subject of fuel, let's also get a misconception straightened out. The purpose of charcoal used in outdoor cooking is to provide heat, not to season foods cooked over it. Let the naive and uninformed enthuse about "the delicious flavor of hickory-cooked meat." What they're saying is that they know so little about outdoor cooking that they've gotten it confused with the smoke-curing of meats. Smoke-curing is a process of preservation, not a style of cooking. It requires the use of an enclosed area, a room or cabinet or even a compartment, in which meats such as ham or bacon are suspended to dry out. The smoke in which the meats are bathed during drying, and the flavor it imparts to them, are both accidental by-products of the fire that provides the small amount of evenly controlled heat needed to do the drying.

Hickory came into use for smokehouse meat-curing only when the supply of more desirable woods had been depleted. This was soon after meat-smoking became a big-scale commercial operation instead of a matter of individual farmers curing a few hams and sides of bacon from their own hogs. Early gourmets turned up their noses at ham or bacon smoked over anything but sweet fruitwoods or corncobs, but there weren't enough fruitwoods or corncobs to supply the commercial packing houses as their curing expanded. Packing houses actually smoked hams and bacon during this era, instead of giving them a "smoky flavor" with chemicals brushed on and injected into the meat.

When the better woods got too scarce and expensive to use, hickory remained. Hickory is a trash wood. It isn't suitable for use in building or in making furniture, and while hickory trees produce flavorful nuts, their wood isn't good for much except burning. So the big commercial packers adopted hickory for their smokehouses, and began selling the idea to their customers that no wood could compare with it for smoke-curing meats.

Like a number of commercially promoted myths, hickory-smoked meat became an article of faith. As the years passed and the number of ham and bacon buyers who'd never seen a smokehouse came to outnumber those who had, the hickory myth somehow got transferred to embrace all outdoor cooking as well as meat-curing. It's firmly embedded in our national folklore today, and there are a number of firms perpetuating the legend by packaging hickory chips in bags or boxes and selling them to the naive to be scattered over cooking coals and impart "that good old hickory flavor" to meats cooked on outdoor grills. Newcomers to the art are convinced that some kind of wood producing a pungent smoke must be used in addition to good clean-burning charcoal in order to flavor grill-cooked foods.

One of my acquaintances, who leads an otherwise blameless life, uses chips of wet mahogany on his outdoor cooking grill. These do impart a very distinctive flavor to the meats he cooks, but it's an acquired taste, and I still prefer my meat to taste like meat instead of like a piece of furniture that's endured a catastrophe. Some of your guests may share this prejudice, so instead of wasting money on packaged trashwood chips, why not put it to better use? Like, say, a bigger steak or an extra case of beer, and do your cooking over plain unvarnished coals? If you must add a flavor to the meats you cook on a grill, sprinkle herbs on the glowing coals.

Beginning outdoor chefs often get bugged by the job of building charcoal fires. They get angry and frustrated because briquettes don't burst into flame when a match is touched to them, and resort to copious sprinklings of naphtha fire-starting liquids. A foolish few even use gasoline to start their grill fires; you'll recognize them by their blistered faces and singed eyebrows. Admittedly, charcoal isn't the easiest fuel to light, but it's a lot easier to start a briquette fire than it is to start one of green, wet wood in a forest. You need only one simple piece of equipment and a kind of kindling that's available everywhere for free.

A lot of outdoor-supply stores now stock the kind of fire-starting utensil that's been my faithful standby for years. You can buy one, but all you need to make your own is a tall fruit-juice can, a hammer, a nail, and ten minutes' time. Take both ends out of the can with the can opener. Brace the inside of the

Punch holes all around the bottom section of a tall can to make a chimney that allows you to kindle briquettes in your grill with a minimum of effort and without using starting fluid.

can against a piece of scrap wood and use the nail as a punch to pierce the can with a dozen or so small holes. If you've got an electric drill, it'll do a neater job. Stagger the holes around the bottom section of the can, leaving about three inches of one end unpunctured. This is your chimney. It won't last forever, but it doesn't cost anything to make a new one.

For kindling, find a corrugated-cardboard shipping carton, the kind stores receive by the hundreds every week, and will give you free. Be sure it's corrugated cardboard. The spaces between corrugations act like tiny chimneys to bring oxygen to the flames when such cardboard is burning, and the glue used in forming the cardboard is highly flammable. Tear about 10 or 12 square inches of this cardboard into inch-wide strips and crush the strips in your hands to compact them and wrinkle them up.

Put your pierced can, holed-end down, in the middle of your firepit. Push the cardboard strips down to the bottom of the can; don't pack them in firmly, they need air to burn. You'll need a layer about 3 inches thick. Now, fill the can level full of charcoal briquettes. Strike a match, tilt the can, and light the cardboard at the bottom. It'll catch at once. Wait a minute or so to give the flames time to take hold; you can tell how they're doing, for when they're well ablaze smoke and flames will begin pouring out the top of the can. Unless there's a breeze, you may have to speed the process by blowing on the bottom of the can, or fanning it to create a better draft.

Soon the briquettes in the top of the can will begin to settle down. Add a few more, and when the topmost briquettes begin to glow redly, lift the can straight up with a pair of pliers or your meat tongs. Use a fire rake to spread the burning briquettes in an even layer over the bottom of the firepit. Charcoal briquettes must be in contact with each other in order to burn, so don't heap fresh fuel on your coals; push fresh briquettes into them from the outer edges. Later, when you've got a solid bed of glowing coals, you can pile fresh briquettes on top to make a deep layer for cooking.

Patience is required when building a bed of coals with charcoal. It takes a certain amount of time—weather conditions such as humidity and wind have something to do with this—to form a proper bed of cooking coals. Restrain your eagerness to begin cooking until all the small flames the charcoal will create at the beginning have burned out, and your briquettes glow red. Then, and not until then, should you begin to cook.

For tending your fire, you'll need a few simple tools. Children's toy garden tools, the kind sold in sets in toy stores, make the most satisfactory ones you could hope to find. Use the rake or hoe to spread briquettes evenly and push them around as needed. The shovel saves your hands from getting dirty while you're cooking; use it to add fresh fuel. You'll also need a way to control hot spots that stray drafts will create and to douse flare-ups caused by hot fat dripping from your grid onto the coals. For this, the most efficient tool is another child's toy, a small plastic water-pistol of the type that shoots a small jet of water with pinpoint accuracy for short distances.

You need only a few drops of water to reduce a patch of white-hot coals to the orange-red hue that's best for most grill-cooking. Fat flare-ups are a bit more difficult to control, especially if you're grilling a fatty meat like pork or using a basting sauce that contains oil, as so many do. Dissolve a teaspoon of baking soda in a cup of water and fill your pistol from this. The addition of soda makes even a tiny jet instantly effective. (Incidentally, when filled with a mixture of household ammonia and water in equal parts, one of these little pistols is a very effective and totally legal weapon to use against stray dogs and muggers.

Children's toy garden tools are ideal for fire-tending in grills. Don't forget the water pistol; it's indispensable for dousing flareups caused by hot fat dripping onto the coals.

These little toys are accurate up to about 15 feet, and a jet of ammonia in the face will send either man or beast into quick retreat.) Back to the grill, if you get a big flareup of fat that the water jet can't control, sprinkle it generously with salt.

One of the keys to successful and easy outdoor cooking is having a way to control the distance between your firepit full of coals and the grid on which the food rests. Almost all modern grills have this feature, either a lever that lifts the grid or some kind of chain and pulley device that can be used to adjust the grid and spit or the firepit itself. There's a very wide array of portable and semi-portable grills available today, and a little shopping will certainly turn up one that will meet your individual requirements for size and flexibility and will fit into the space you have for cookouts.

There are so many variables in outdoor cooking that it's dangerous to try to be precise when writing about it. Grills don't have kitchen-range conveniences like thermostatically controlled ovens and surface burners with heat adjustments. Over coals, cooking times must be adjusted to the heat a given grill puts out, and learning to judge just how hot your bed of coals really is requires a bit of practice.

Color is the best guide for judging a bed of coals in terms of the heat it's putting out. Dark coals give low heat, orange-red the medium heat that's best for most cooking, bright yellow or white coals a high heat that might be useful for searing, but will char food exposed to it for more than a few moments. My interpretation of dark, orange, and bright yellow might not correspond with yours, though. One of us might be colorblind, or we might just react differently to what we see. And fuels vary, too; a bed of very small briquettes will produce hotter heat at a darker color than will one made up of bigger briquettes.

More accurate than color-judging is measuring the effective radiated heat of a bed of coals by using the palm of your hand as a thermometer. Except for welders and others whose jobs require them to handle hot objects, most of us have a pretty uniform pain level. Hold the palm of your hand 8 to 10 inches above your cooking coals. If you can keep it there seven seconds or longer, you have dark coals and low heat. If you must pull your hand away in four to six seconds, your coals are emitting medium heat; two to three seconds, high heat. Don't overdo this test. You're not trying to prove how tough your hand is, you're testing a cooking fire. Pull your hand away the instant the heat becomes uncomfortable.

Now, let's deal with a few generalities. Thin cuts of meat, chops from veal or lamb and thin beef cuts, should be grilled over medium heat; pork chops over high heat. The ideal way to grill thick steaks—a steak 1¼ to 1½ or 2 inches thick is best for grilling—is to use your adjustable grid. Sear the steaks on both sides with the grid almost touching medium-hot coals, then raise it until the meat is about 6 inches above the coals to finish cooking. Searing is an essential step in cooking steaks; it seals the meat's surface and keeps its flavorful juices from escaping.

Use this technique in spit-cooking red meats, too. Let the spit revolve for five to ten minutes with the meat almost touching the coals, then raise it to a height of 10 inches or so to finish cooking. Remember that the bigger and thicker the roast, the lower the heat ought to be and the longer the cooking time. Fowl, in contrast to red meats, shouldn't be seared, but kept 10 to 12 inches above the coals for the full cooking time, at heat just a bit below medium.

Chickens cooked on the grid should be split in half, and

cooked bone-side down during the first two-thirds of the total cooking period and basted often. This allows the basting sauce to penetrate into the flesh more effectively than would be possible if the sauce had to penetrate through the almost impervious inner membrane that lines a bird's cavities. And, by cooking longer on the bone side—which isn't eaten— you'll have better control of browning the skin, which usually is eaten. Fish, which are usually grilled because they're difficult to hold on a spit, should rest 10 inches or so above moderate coals. You can tell when a fish has been cooked by the bubbling of its skin; when the skin starts puffing, turn it or take it off the grill.

When you're spit-cooking, do make provision for catching the juices that run from roast or fowl. These contain the essence of the meat's flavor, and are an invaluable base for a swiftly made sauce. You can arrange a drip pan by clearing a space in the firebox directly under the spit, putting it in place after the meat begins to yield its juices so that you'll know precisely where the pan should go. You don't need a big container, for the dripping from a spit-cooked roast or bird is usually confined to a very small area. When the juice begins to run, which will usually be ten to fifteen minutes after cooking starts, put your pan in place. This also eases your job of fighting flare-ups. Use the drippings for basting; there's no better sauce for any meat than its own juices.

Do your basting with a swab, not a brush. Make the swab by winding a strip of cloth 3 or 4 inches wide around one end of a dowel or some similarly shaped length of unpainted wood. Tie it in place with string. Use the swab once or twice, snip the string, and throw the cloth away. This makes it possible to use a fresh swab when you change sauces and saves the job of cleaning a brush. Baste meats often, whether you're cooking on the grid or on the spit. Open-coals cooking is a dry method, and frequent basting results in moister, tastier meats.

You really need only one or two simple tools for grill-cooking. One is the swab, the other is a set of tongs. Never use a fork to turn meats being grilled. They open holes through which juices escape, and undo all the searing you've done to seal them in the meat. Oddly, the makers of outdoor cooking

Do your basting with a swab rather than a brush, and whether you're spit-cooking or grilling, baste often as the meat cooks.

A turner and spoon with long handles are needed if you do pan-cooking or stewing on your grill, but the truly important tool is a set of tongs. The fire rake at right is added to some sets of outdoor cooking utensils, and baffles novices at the art who can't figure out its function.

sets never seem to have learned this. These sets usually have a knife, fork, spoon, sometimes a pancake turner and maybe a fire rake, but seldom tongs. If you use a griddle on your grill, the pancake turner is handy; if you use a Dutch oven or cook in pots, you'll use the spoon. But throw the fork away and forget you ever saw it if you want to produce fine, juicy meat from your outdoor grill.

Unless you have a fire-tending passion that verges on pyro-
mania, or your outdoor grill is fueled with electricity or gas,
you'll want to confine your patio cooking to grilling and spit-
roasting. Cooking dishes such as stews and soups and beans in a
wilderness camp where a fire is kept burning most of the time is
one thing; cooking such dishes in your patio or backyard is
another. There really isn't much point in running out to add
briquettes to your grill every few minutes, when the kitchen
range is so close and handy. Save your grill for the uses to which
it's best suited; use it to cook meats, and as a sideline, some
other dishes that can be cooked at the same time, but do stews
and soups and anything that needs long cooking in the kitchen.

One of the more pleasant aspects of dining outdoors is the
relaxed informality of such meals. Up to a point, you can throw
protocol out the window—or, more aptly, over the fence—and
serve just about anything you please in any style you choose.
Stop short of one thing, though. Spare your guests the indignity
of paper plates and plastic utensils. There's enough low-priced
informal dinnerware around to make it easy and economical to
assemble a complete service for a dozen—plates, cups, knives,
forks, and so on—without breaking the bank.

Melamine and similar plastic dishes are acceptable for
outdoor dining anywhere but at the White House, Buckingham
Palace, and similar castled dining halls. Paper plates and cups
are abominations of modern living. The plates get soggy, the
cups always burn the lips of the unsuspecting who try to drink
hot coffee from them. If you think enough of your guests to invite
them to your home, they certainly don't deserve to be sen-
tenced to struggle with paper plates and plastic knives and
forks. And the good food you cook deserves better, too.

Outdoor meals certainly shouldn't be elaborate, but neither
should they be plain bread-and-meat affairs. You'll want to
serve a big crisp salad, which can be prepared in the kitchen
and the dressing added at the outdoor table just before serving.
While the cooking's going on, you'll also want to offer your
waiting guests some kind of drinks and nibbles.

A good combination with which to begin a warm-weather
outdoor meal is hot nibbles and cool drinks. Here's where you
can get some mileage out of an hibachi. Set up a small table away
from the main dining area; on it put the hibachi, a sheaf of small

skewers—bamboo skewers are best because they don't need insulation and can be thrown away after being used—and a platter or several plates of grill-it-yourself nibbles. Let your guests amuse themselves by heating their own; this will keep them occupied and out of your way while you're busy tending to the main course on the grill.

For the nibbles, you might provide shelled shrimp, scallops cut into bite-sized chunks, small cherry tomatoes, skinned pearl onions, and beside the hibachi, a bowl of cubes cut from firm, flavorful sourdough bread. Have two, perhaps three, containers of soft herbed butter on the table, each flavored with a different herb, each with its own stiff brush to anoint the nibbles before they're cooked. Or, since the dinner's outdoors and you don't have to worry about carpets, serve some of the appetizers that you might not want to offer indoors. If you feel ambitious, you'll find in the recipe section a bread that can be baked directly on the grill or on a hibachi; you can mix the dough in advance and let the guests do their own baking, too.

Beer is the perfect go-with for outdoor dinners. It can be served with pre-dinner appetizers and with the meal itself. So can pitchers of Sangria, and its white-wine equivalent, Spritzer, which is simply white wine and club soda mixed like a highball. Jug wines are ideal for outdoor service. You can decant them into small individual carafes, or let your guests pour directly from the jug. Chill beer and white wines in a washtub or wheelbarrow heaped with crushed ice.

How far you want to go in planning the main course is between you and Her and the family budget. As you read this, meat prices may be in the same state of fluctuation they are as it's being written, but having survived through a depression and several inflationary-deflationary cycles, I've learned that only one thing is certain: food prices are never stable. So plan your menu in the light of existing conditions; if steak's too high, serve something else.

By "something else" I don't mean ground-meat patties. The worst possible choice you can make in selecting meat to be cooked on an outdoor grill is ground meat. This is like slandering Good Old Mom and the Flag, but the cruel fact is that successful open-fire grilling of beef requires searing it properly, and because of the torn-up structure of the beef from which they're made, ground-meat patties simply cannot be seared without creating a charred, unpalatable crust. There is no powder, no liquid, no paste, that can be put on a ground-meat patty to make it searable. To a lesser, but still important extent, this is also true of thin beef cuts that have been mangled in the "tenderizing machine" found in most butcher shops.

This needn't rule beef or beefsteaks out of consideration. When properly prepared in advance, chuck, flank, and other lower-cost beef cuts can be cooked as steaks very successfully. Marinate them in wine with onions and herbs, in wine vinegar diluted with water and herb-seasoned, lemon juice—any liquid that's naturally acid—and if you drain the meat well, wipe it dry, and anoint it lightly with oil or butter it will sear and brown as nicely as porterhouse or T-bone. Do, however, avoid commercial meat-tenderizing preparations. In its wise beneficence, the Federal Food and Drug Administration, that watchdog of our health, still allows the sale of meat tenderizers based on sodium nitrate or nitrite, which are both toxic and carcinogenic.

At their best, which really isn't very good, meat tenderizers free of noxious substances are based on one of two enzymes: bromelin, which is extracted from pineapple, and papain, which comes from the papaya plant. These are harmless substances, but meats on which they're used become mushy because both these enzymes attack the muscle fibers as well as the connective tissues. Naturally acid liquids such as wines and vinegars work selectively to soften only the connective tissues; these tissues are what make meat tough.

There are many other meats you can cook in addition to beef. Lamb, veal, pork, fowl, fish, are all excellent when grilled. A stuffed beef heart cooked on the spit makes a good one-dish meal. Kidneys grilled over coals are prize morsels. Chicken and turkey can be spit-cooked whole; broiling chickens and squab turkeys can be split and cooked in halves on the grid. You can get turkey pieces—legs, breasts, thighs—if you don't want to cook a whole bird. Almost any kind of meat is suitable for kabob cookery.

If you're wondering why nothing has been said about that great American illusion the frankfurter or hot dog, there are

Many kinds of vegetables can be cooked along the edges of your grill while the meat course occupies the center section.

good reasons. First, a frankfurter cannot be cooked, it can only be heated. Its flavor is locked in when it is manufactured, and cannot be changed by cooking. The only scope a cook has in serving frankfurters is to supply several different kinds of condiments and seasonings to mask the sausages' bland, uninteresting taste. Second, frankfurters are more expensive than prime beefsteak in terms of meat content; today's frankfurter can legally contain as little as 30 percent beef and still be labeled as an "all meat" wiener; the other meat can be chicken skins, and even the beef can be tripes, lungs, snouts, and other slaughterhouse offal. The 70 percent of the wiener is milk curd, soybeans, and water. If these two reasons aren't enough, sodium nitrate and sodium nitrite, already mentioned, are what makes wieners look red, no matter what substances they contain.

To move on to more appetizing subjects, the meat course of your outdoor dinner really needn't be a problem. Neither should vegetables. Quite a number of vegetables can be roasted along the edges of the grill while the meat course cooks in its center. Summer squash, zucchini, eggplant, and mushrooms are some of these. Brush them well with oil or butter and turn them often so they will cook evenly. Fresh corn in the shuck can be roasted this way as readily as it can be cooked buried in coals. Strip back the shucks and remove the silk, drop in some butter, pull the shucks back in place, and secure them with a twist of wire. Turn often, of course.

Because no two grills present precisely the same cooking conditions, it's impossible to give cooking times for vegetables prepared this way; the vegetables also vary in freshness and water content and therefore react to heat differently. Do some experimenting to find out the characteristics of your grill, and establish average cooking times.

A number of fruit desserts can be prepared in the fashion described for cooking vegetables. Oranges and grapefruit, halved and sweetened with honey or grenadine or flavored with a liqueur or sweet sherry, will warm nicely in their skins; put them on the grill to heat while dinner's being eaten. Or, as the cooking coals subside, put on the grill a pan containing soft-skinned fruits such as peaches and apricots, or cherries, grapes, or berries, in a flavored syrup. Let them poach as the coals die while you and your guests dine, and they'll be just right to pass when the meal's ended.

You can bring out a cake from the kitchen, or a pie or fruit cobbler. If you own a hand-cranked ice-cream freezer, stir up the cream mixture in advance, fill and ice the freezer, and have it waiting when your guests begin arriving. Invite them to take turns cranking while they enjoy their pre-dinner refreshments and you prepare the entrée. You've got to know your guests pretty well before using this somewhat sneaky way of making ice cream or sherbet, but a lot of them may cherish nostalgic memories of having turned a freezer crank during childhood— or have heard their elders recalling this painfully pleasant form of anticipatory exercise—and will enjoy participating.

After or with dessert, serve camp-style coffee, brewed on the grill while dinner's being eaten. A surprisingly large number of people have never tasted old-fashioned boiled coffee, and it takes second place only to the drip coffee made as described in Chapter III. Those who have become victims of the delusion that "instant" coffee bears some resemblance to real coffee will be both surprised and delighted when they taste camp coffee for the first time, and the pleased expressions on their faces will be your reward for brewing it.

Camp coffee must be made in the old-style coffee pot, the kind great-grandma used. These pots are made of enameled steel, have a big flat bottom and sides that slope gently toward the top. They have no innards, require no filters or other accessories. These pots have staged a remarkable comeback; once almost impossible to find, they're now prominently displayed in most homewares and outdoor equipment stores. They aren't expensive; our 16-cup pot cost less than $5 when bought in 1972 to replace one that after more than 20 years of service had finally sprung a leak.

Brewing coffee in these pots is simplicity itself. Fill it to within an inch of the level where the pouring spout starts, using cold water. Add the coffee: one level tablespoon per cup and one "for the pot." Put the pot on the grid, or if you're in a hurry, directly on the coals. After ten or fifteen minutes, steam will begin pouring from the spout. Another five minutes and the coffee will begin to bubble audibly. Let it rest until a steamy froth gushes from the spout, then remove it from the coals and at once pour in a cup of cold water to settle the grounds. (An eggshell does the job equally well.) The grounds will drop to the bottom within a minute or so, and you can pour fine, fragrant coffee into your guests' cups.

To taste its best, camp coffee should be brewed in an old-fashioned enameled-steel coffeepot.

Having carried your imaginary patio repast to its successful conclusion, let's look at a few recipes for dishes that you might want to serve when the meal is translated into reality.

Basting Sauces and Marinades

Steak Sauce

1 clove garlic
2 shallots
3 tbsp peanut oil
½ cup tomato juice
1 tsp salt

3 or 4 drops Tabasco
1 tsp dry crumbled herbs, your
    choice of thyme, oregano,
    basil, sage, savory, rosemary

Mash the garlic and shallots into a paste, combine them with the oil, blend in the remaining ingredients.

Wine Basting Sauce for Beef

1 cup dry red wine
3 tbsp tomato paste
2 tbsp peanut oil
2 tsp dried crumbled
    oregano

2 cloves garlic, mashed
1 tsp salt
½ tsp fresh ground pepper

Briskly stir all ingredients into a smooth mixture.

Butter Basting Sauce for Veal or Lamb

⅓ cup melted butter
4 shallots, mashed
2 tbsp white wine vinegar

1½ tsp dry crumbled marjoram
¾ tsp salt
Dash freshly ground white pepper

Blend butter and mashed shallots, combine with other ingredients.

Minted Basting Sauce for Lamb

⅓ cup olive or peanut oil   3 tbsp minced fresh mint leaves or
⅓ cup melted butter   2 tbsp dry crumbled mint
Pinch of salt   leaves

Stir all ingredients together.

Tart Basting Sauce for Pork

½ cup dry white wine   1 tsp salt
3 tbsp white wine vinegar   Dash freshly ground pepper
1 tsp dry crumbled sage or
   oregano

Stir all ingredients together.

Basting Sauce for Chicken

½ cup pure peanut butter   2 tbsp soy sauce
¾ cup boiling water   1 clove garlic, mashed
1 tsp hot chili powder   ½ tsp fresh lemon juice
2 tbsp dark molasses

Beat together the peanut butter and boiling water; blend in
remaining ingredients.

Tenderizing Marinade

2 cups wine (use red for beef,   ¼ tsp dry crumbled basil
   white for veal or lamb)   3 or 4 cracked peppercorns
2 cups water   1 tsp salt
2 tbsp Cognac or brandy

Marinate tough cuts 4 to 6 hours, turn occasionally to make
sure all surfaces of the meat come in contact with the liquid. Drain
meat well, wipe dry, rub with oil or butter before cooking.

Dry-Meat Marinade

½ cup peanut oil   3 tbsp fresh lemon juice
¾ cup dry vermouth   1 crumbled bay leaf
2 tbsp brandy or Cognac   ¼ tsp salt

Use this marinade for dry meats such as lamb and small game.

Grill Bread

1 cup milk   1 tbsp sugar
2 tbsp butter   1 tsp salt
2½ to 3 cups flour   1 pkg dry yeast

Heat milk, melt butter in it. Combine 1 cup of the flour (without sifting) in a mixing bowl with the sugar, salt, and dry yeast; do not dissolve the yeast in water, just blend it with the other dry ingredients. Put 1 cup of the warm milk in the bowl with the flour and beat until blended. Add ½ cup more flour while continuing to beat, 2 or 3 minutes. Mix in remaining flour by double tablespoonfuls, using enough to make a firm dough. Turn dough out to lightly floured board. Knead until smooth and elastic; if the dough is unduly soft and spongy, add a bit more flour while kneading. Put dough into a well-greased bowl, turn it to bring the greased side up, cover with towel, let stand to rise in a warm place. At a temperature of 85 degrees, rising should take 45 minutes to 1 hour; the dough should double in bulk. Punch down the dough to liberate bubbles, turn out on floured board and knead 5 to 10 minutes. Form into a ball, let rest 15 minutes, then divide into 12 smaller balls. Press each one flat; they should form circles 5 to 6 inches in diameter. Store dough on a baking tin covered with waxed paper until ready to cook. To cook, place dough circles directly on bars of grill over medium heat. When puffy and browned on both sides it is ready to eat.

Kabobs

Almost any food that's firm enough to stay on a skewer after it's been cooked is a suitable candidate for kabob cooking. Kabobs are most easily cooked over an hibachi. Bamboo skewers are better than metal because they don't transmit heat to the hands.

Suggestions for pre-dinner nibbles to be grilled: small onions that have been marinated in white wine vinegar with a touch of Tabasco; eggplant cubes marinated in olive oil; cherry tomatoes; strips of green or sweet red pepper; small mushrooms rubbed with an herbed butter; shrimp rolled in minced dill; quartered scallops marinated in lemon juice.

To make herbed butter, simply blend the herb or herbs with softened butter and chill until firm. You can blend such liquids as lemon juice with butter this way, too. Offer it with raw vegetables.

Grilled Herbed Steaks

3-pound piece boneless   Butter
    rump or chuck, 1½ to 2   ¼ cup crumbled herbs: basil,
    inches thick   thyme, oregano; your choice
Tenderizing marinade

Marinate meat 2 hours, turning several times. Wipe dry. Rub with butter, spread herbs on waxed paper, press steak into them on both sides. Grill, cooking to desired degree of rareness.

Boned Grilled Leg of Lamb

4- to 5-pound leg of lamb   Basting sauce—chef's choice
Dry-meat marinade

Bone the leg of lamb (procedure given on page 157); spread the boned meat on a firm flat surface, and pound with the side of a meat cleaver or the flat face of a meat mallet to flatten. Marinate 2 to 3 hours, turning several times. Drain, wipe dry, rub with oil before putting on grill. Cook to desired degree, basting frequently.

Grilled Spareribs

10 to 12 pounds spareribs; allow about 2 pounds per serving, since spareribs are 60 percent bone
2 cups tomato sauce (canned)
1 cup strong black coffee
1 cup red wine vinegar
1 tsp chili powder
3 cloves garlic, mashed
½ cup grated sweet onion
1 tsp Worcestershire sauce
1½ tsp salt
1 tsp freshly ground pepper
6 or 8 drops Tabasco

Trim excess fat from ribs. Combine all remaining ingredients and marinate the ribs 2 hours, turning occasionally. Drain well. Grill about 20 to 25 minutes per side, depending on the thickness of the ribs at their base. While they cook, baste the ribs with the marinade. Before serving, use a heavy-bladed butcher knife or cleaver to divide the ribs into individual sections of one rib each. Serve with sliced boiled potatoes, sour pickles, and sliced raw onion.

Grilled Chicken Halves

Allow ½ chicken per portion
Butter or peanut oil
Basting sauce for chicken

Wipe birds well after splitting carcasses into halves, rub on both sides with butter or oil. Grill about 20 minutes bone-down, basting often, then turn and grill 10 to 12 minutes until skin is nicely browned, basting.

Grilled Deviled Bones

15 to 20 pounds beef shank
    and forearm bones, cut
    about 3 inches long
3 tbsp dry mustard
1 tsp cayenne

2 tsp salt
1 tsp freshly ground pepper
1 tbsp Worcestershire sauce
2 to 3 tbsp dry red wine
¼ pound butter

Most butcher shops will save suitable bones and saw them into the required lengths. Wipe bones with a damp cloth to remove splinters and meal from sawing. Combine the dry seasonings with wine, blend into the butter. Spread this on the bones, especially the ends, and grill 20 to 30 minutes. Turn often. Serve with toast or firm bread and provide each guest with a thin knife to be used in extracting the marrow.

Grilled Fish Steaks

Steaks 1 to 1¼ inches thick
    from salmon, halibut,
    etc.; allow a half or
    whole steak per portion,
    depending on size
Butter

½ cup dry white wine
1 tsp paprika
1 tsp salt
¼ tsp freshly ground white
    pepper
⅓ cup fresh lemon juice

Wipe the steaks; do not remove skin. Rub each side well with butter, put on grill. Combine remaining ingredients and baste with resulting sauce. Cook 4 to 7 minutes per side over medium-low heat. The steaks are ready to come off the moment the skin can be slipped free. Remember, retained heat will continue to cook the fish for several moments after they're off the grill.

Grilled Black Bass

4- to 5-pound bass (or trout or
    other fish)
½ cup lemon juice
⅓ cup butter

1 tsp capers
1 tsp dillseed
½ tsp salt

When the fish is cleaned, leave on the head and tail and dorsal fin, but remove the side and bottom fins. Scale if necessary. Using a sharp-tined fork, puncture the fish at several places and angle the fork to make small openings into which a bit of lemon juice can be dribbled. After treating both sides, let the fish rest 5 to 10 minutes. Cream the remaining lemon juice into the butter, add capers, dillseed, and salt, put this in the fish's cavity, and close the cavity with a skewer. Grill 8 to 12 minutes per side, depending on body thickness; when the skin begins to puff and form bubbles the fish is done. Or, test by slipping a knife into the back beside the dorsal fin where the body is thickest; twist the knife gently, and if a clean liquid flows the fish is cooked.

Grilled Vegetables

Vegetables with skins that suit them to be grilled whole are: yellow and acorn squash, summer squash, eggplant, onions, green and red bell peppers, mushrooms. These should be lightly rubbed with oil or butter before putting on the grill. Hard-skinned squashes with sweet flesh, such as Hubbard and butternut, should be quartered, the seeds and strings removed, and the flesh rubbed with butter and cinnamon or allspice. The shucks on corn should be pulled back far enough to remove the silk and a blob of butter applied, then the shucks smoothed back in place and secured with a twist of wire. Put vegetables at the ends and sides of the grid, where the heat is less intense, and turn often. To serve them, cut open, slash the flesh deeply, add seasoned butter.

Eggplant and green tomatoes can be sliced, dipped in batter, and grilled without a pan. For the batter, combine 1 egg, 1 tbsp milk, ½ tsp salt, 3 to 4 tbsp flour, beat until smooth. Cook 3 to 4 minutes per side.

Spit-Roast Squab Turkey Cacciatore

6-pound squab turkey	2 large sweet onions
½ cup butter	1 sweet green pepper
1 tsp salt	12 button mushrooms
1 tsp dry crumbled basil	¾ tsp paprika
2 firm-ripe tomatoes, about 4 inches in diameter	2 tbsp dry red wine

Well in advance of cooking, cream ⅔ of the butter with the salt and basil and freeze it. Wipe the turkey thoroughly with a damp cloth inside and out. Close the breast cavity by pulling the loose flap of neck skin smoothly over the back, secure it with skewers. Quarter the tomatoes, drain them of juice and seeds; peel and quarter the onions; clean the pepper and cut it into chunks. Put tomatoes, onions, pepper, mushrooms, and the chunk of frozen butter in the body cavity and close the cavity with skewers and lacing. Truss the bird by procedures given on page 155. Cream together the reserved butter, paprika, and wine, rub the bird with this; use any remaining for basting. Balance the turkey on the spit, cook over medium coals about 1½ to 2 hours. Baste with drippings. Test by thrusting a small skewer into the joint between drumstick and thigh; if the liquid that flows runs clear, with no tinge of pink, the bird is cooked. Serve some of the stuffing with each portion.

Spit-Roast Pork Tenderloin

4-pound pork tenderloin	2 tsp dry crumbled rosemary
1 tsp salt	¼ tsp freshly ground pepper
½ cup Rhine wine	

Pork tenderloin is usually the piece the butcher takes home for himself, so if you can't find one buy a 6- or 8-rib section of loin, bone out the eye, and trim of excess fat. (Use the ribs left to cook as spareribs.) Balance the meat on the spit, with a drip pan below it. Cook 1¼ to 1½ hours. Combine the remaining ingredients and baste with them until they're used up, then baste with drippings. Slice to serve.

Spit-Roast Kidneys

6 pair calf, lamb, or beef   3 to 4 tbsp flour
    kidneys   1½ tsp dry crumbled thyme
2 cups flat beer   ¾ tsp powdered cloves

To prepare the kidneys: split, trim away all fat, tubes, and membranes, plunge into boiling salted water for 5 minutes. Drain well, wipe dry. Combine beer, flour, and seasonings. Thread kidneys on spit. As soon as they get warm, brush them with the beer mixture. Brush on more occasionally as the spit turns; the mixture will form a crinkly crust on the kidneys. Cook 10 to 15 minutes, depending on the size of the kidneys.

Grill-Cooked Fruits

Oranges and grapefruit can be grilled without using a pan. Halve the fruit, remove seeds, spoon over each half a bit of bar syrup, grenadine, sherry, or port. Put at the edge of the grill or over dying coals. Bananas can also be grilled in their skins. Take off one skin section along one side, lay them on the grill with the peeled section up, score deeply, spoon on a bit of dark rum.

Cook apples, apricots, pears, peaches, grapes, plums, cherries, and berries in a shallow pan over dying coals. Halve the fruits, remove cores or pits or seeds, pour over them some cider or red or white wine sweetened with bar syrup or grenadine or Maraschino Liqueur. Let them poach during dinner; baste once or twice, or turn the fruits in the pan once or twice.

Old-Fashioned Ice Cream

6 egg yolks   ¼ tsp salt
1⅓ cups sugar   1 vanilla bean, split, or 2 tbsp
1 quart light cream   vanilla extract
                                 2 cups heavy cream

Beat egg yolks lightly. In the top of a double boiler, combine the yolks, sugar, light cream, salt, and vanilla bean. (If extract is used, add it later.) Cook with constant stirring until the mixture coats the stirring spoon. Remove from heat; if vanilla bean was used, remove it; if extract is used, add it. Stir in the heavy cream, pour into the freezer can (you need a 3- to 4-quart freezer) and put in the freezer pail. Set dasher in place, pack crushed ice and rock salt around can, using 5 parts ice to 1 part salt. Crank until the dasher becomes very hard to turn; 15 to 25 minutes. Remove dasher, scraping the ice cream that clings to it back into the freezer can. Plug dasher opening, drain liquid from freezer pail, pack with more ice and salt, mounding it over the top of the freezer can. Cover with newspapers or a gunnysack, and let the ice cream set up for about 30 minutes, or until ready to serve it.

Makes about 2½ quarts. For a fruit ice cream, add the fruit before beginning to freeze.

Outdoor cooking can be as simple or as complicated as you want to make it. My own rule is to reserve the more complex dishes for the kitchen, and keep the patio cooking as straightforward as possible. If complexities are avoided, one chef can prepare a meal for eight or ten on the grill and enjoy doing it.

VI

Cleaning and Cooking Fish and Game

Hunting and fishing aren't everybody's thing. For all I know, you might be against either or both, or you may live in an area where there's no opportunity to get out in the field with shotgun or rifle, no lake or river or ocean close by where you can drop a line. The odds are about even that you do indulge in some form of these activities, and even if you don't you at least have some friends who do and who're generous enough to share with you the results of their outings.

If you're active in the outdoors, you may not need the information in this chapter. In that case, you're invited to skip it. If you're totally turned off by the idea of hunting or fishing, you might be tempted to skip it, too, thinking you'll never be called on to skin and cook a rabbit or to clean and prepare a fish. However, sooner or later somebody to whom you can't say no is going to give you that rabbit or fish, or a brace of duck or pheasant or a piece of venison, and then you'll be faced with two choices. You can toss the gift in the garbage pail and lie to your friends about how much you enjoyed it, or you can refer to this chapter, cook the gift of game, and actually relish the unique flavor brought to your table by wild meat or freshly caught fish.

While gifts from your outdoor-type friends will vary somewhat according to the region in which you live, some types of
game are so widely distributed that they can be considered
universal. You'll probably never get anything exotic; most of
your windfalls will be small game, or venison, or fish. But
unless She's an unusual wife, a diamond in the diadem of
domesticity, the first thing She'll do will be to make it clear to
you that it's your responsibility to prepare, perhaps to cook as
well, any kind of furred, feathered, or finned foods that come
your way. After you've made the game kitchen-ready, She
might agree to cook it, but it's almost equally likely that the
cooking as well as the preliminary preparation will be your job,
too. Surprise Her, then, by accepting the challenge.

Not that this chapter will equip you to deal with every kind
of creature that walks, flies, or swims. The subject's too big to fit
into the number of pages I've got left; it's a book in itself. As a
matter of fact, I wrote such a book a few years ago—*Cooking
Over Coals*—and if you're interested in outdoor dooking and in
cooking wild meats, you might refer to that one.

What we'll try to do here is hit the high spots, lay down a
reasonably straight path that you can follow, and cover the
generalities of preparing and cooking the kinds of game animals
and birds and fish that you're most apt to encounter. If you're
equipped with a bit of basic information that applies to a number of species and situations, you'll be pretty well able to use
your own ingenuity and imagination to apply the basics of
which you're sure to specific situations that would baffle you
otherwise.

Nonhunters seldom give much thought to the differences
between wild and domestic animals. These are consider-
able, whether the animals are small, like rabbits and squirrels,
or big, like deer. Pound for pound, a wild animal or bird will
have twice to three times as much muscle tissue on its body as
will one that spends its life confined to a pen or cage. The wild
creature has to scrounge for food during most of its waking
hours. It has to run from its enemies and chase its prey, and
generally is too busy for lazy hours of lounging.

Wild creatures eat what they can find in order to survive,
and the foods they find generally aren't the kind that pad their
bodies with layers of fat. Animals and birds in the wild often

drink water very sparingly; some get most of the moisture they need from their foods, and may drink from a stream or pond once a day or even less frequently. As a result, their flesh is lean, well muscled, and very dry. This must be kept in mind when you're preparing wild meats for cooking, and must be kept in your awareness during the cooking itself.

Generally speaking, the frying pan is the enemy of good wild-game cookery. This is true of small game and large, birds as well as animals. When cooked quickly, over high heat, wild meats shrink, get tight and tough, come out of the skillet dry and stringy. After it's been skinned, a wild rabbit may look just like one that's been cage-bred and has never put its paws on bare ground, but it's not the same. You can safely fry a domestic rabbit, but if you fry a wild one you're apt to break a tooth when you try to bite into it. This is equally true of pheasant; cleaned and plucked, a pheasant might look like a small chicken with underdeveloped drumsticks, but even if it's cooked by the Colonel's secret recipe, it won't come out like a chicken.

You wouldn't want it to, of course. One of the great pleasures of cooking wild game is preserving its distinctive flavor—a sort of concentrated essence of the outdoors—that domestic animals don't have. Some people don't enjoy the taste of wild meats—or say they don't, because it was once a fashionable fad to scorn them. A surprisingly large number of those who profess to dislike game meats have never tasted any. This bit of information I've gathered over the years by conducting a totally unscientific survey.

Whenever I hear somebody remark that they can't stand the taste of wild meat, I make an impolite nuisance of myself by questioning them. I try to find out whether their dislike is based on personal experience, belief in fables, or blind emotional reaction. Roughly one-fourth of those whose prejudices I've probed eventually have admitted that they've never tasted wild game. A bit more prodding uncovers the fact that about half these people have carried into adult lives a childhood trauma, usually traceable to having at an early age seen what they still call "cute little animals" or "beautiful wild birds" displayed, bloodstained and bedraggled, by an older relative returned from a day of hunting.

Shocked by their first close-hand encounter with death,

most of the individuals in this group recall that they refused to eat the game they saw after it reached the family table, and have been refusing to eat wild meats ever since. Most of them grow angry when, after their story's been told, they're asked if they refuse to eat chicken on Sunday, turkey at Thanksgiving, or beefsteak or leg of lamb or pork chops. None of them likes to be reminded that all these meats come from animals that are killed and converted into neat impersonal cuts of meat or carcasses in the butcher shop. The thing is that many who object to the idea of eating wild game have never seen a turkey beheaded or a steer or sheep or hog slaughtered and butchered out. And there's always the fact that domestic animals are seldom as "cute" or "beautiful" as wild ones.

Questioning the remaining three-quarters of those who say they don't like game meats almost always uncovers that at some time or other they've been served badly handled or badly cooked game. It's been my misfortune to have shared their experience. I've had venison from deer that weren't bled and cooled quickly and were draped over a pickup fender or closed up in an airtight car trunk during a day or more of hot driving. I've swallowed some venison that's been contaminated by gall, and some pheasants that were put into an unventilated rubber-lined pocket of a hunting coat and carried around in the warm sunshine for several hours before being drawn.

Nobody will claim that badly handled, badly cooked game meats taste delicious. They don't. They taste terrible. But a lot of individuals who've experienced the bad taste of neglected game think this is the "wild flavor" they've been told to expect in game meats. This is why so many people will make the blanket statement that they can't stand the "wild flavor" of venison or pheasants or ducks, and will refuse even to taste game dishes made from meat that's been carefully handled and expertly cooked.

Strangely, few people refuse to eat wild fish—fish that come from waters that have never been hatchery-stocked, or from the ocean. It's much harder to get sentimental over a fish than it is a deer or bird. You can't follow its bounding form through the brush or watch it in flight. And fish is cooked badly much less frequently than game meats; fish signal their deterioration to the world, while it takes the nose of an expert to detect signs that a game bird or animal has been mishandled and its flesh has turned sour. In some cases, detection before the meat is cooked is literally impossible, because it's the heat of cooking that completes the process which began with the failure of a hunter to clean his game properly and to protect it from excessive warmth.

There's really nothing you can do to salvage wild meat that's gone sour. If you encounter some and don't discover it until after the meat's been cooked, all you can do is shrug it off, call it bad luck, and eat scrambled eggs instead.

There are a number of things you can do to improve the flavor and tenderness of wild meat before it's cooked. One step often overlooked by those unacquainted with raw meat is hanging. Even small animals benefit from a brief period of aging, and so do upland game birds. The hanging time needn't be excessive—a couple of days for rabbit or squirrel, three days for pheasant or chukkar, two for quail. Select the coolest spot you have outside the refrigerator, wrap the carcass loosely in an open-weave cloth, and let it hang. It *must* hang, by the way. If laid on a table or shelf, the portion of the meat from which air is shut off will begin quickly to decay.

Contrary to the belief of many, refrigeration and freezing have no aging effect on meats. Cold delays the process of tissue breakdown, which is the purpose of hanging any meat to age. The colder the air surrounding the hanging meat, the slower this breakdown occurs. Extreme cold will virtually stop the breaking-down of tissue, but will not stop it completely. After the hanging period ends a bird or animal can be refrigerated or frozen, but never freeze or refrigerate first and hang afterward. This accelerates the multiplication of the bacterial organisms that cause aging as well as the bacilli that carry salmonella and staphylococcus. Once wild meat—or any meat, for that matter—has been put into refrigerated or frozen storage, it should be cooked at once after being removed from its cold resting place.

Whether aged by hanging or not, do marinate game to soften the connective tissue that makes meat tough. In wild meat this tissue is a bit harder than in other meats. In Chapter V you'll find several marinades, and any of them is suitable for use with wild meats. All of them will reduce to some degree the "wild" flavor. If you value this taste, skip marinating, and after it's aged, cook your game in a fricassee or stew. If it is to be oven-cooked, use a closed roasting pan and follow a recipe that includes a liquid of some sort in the pan during cooking. Certainly you should marinate any wild meat that is to be grilled or spit-roasted. Remember that wild meats respond best to long, slow cooking at low temperatures.

Fish should never be cooked for long periods. Even when a fish is being poached, the cooking time is short when compared to the time required to cook a stew of red meats. This is because the structure of fish flesh is totally different from that of mammal and bird flesh. Under a microscope, red meat looks like a lot of long thin strings wrapped longitudinally into bundles; the wrapping between the bundles is the connective tissue. The flesh of fish under a microscope looks like overlapping shingles on a roof; it is made up of thin short fibers arranged in layers, and fish have no connective tissue in their bodies.

Cooking for extended periods only makes red meats grow softer and more tender; it makes fish grow tough and stringy. A well-cooked fish is one that's still moist when removed from the pan; cooking will continue for several minutes by the heat the flesh retains. This is the reverse of what happens to red meats, which are soggy when first taken from the pan and need to be allowed to rest a few minutes so the tissues can become firm and the juices drawn from them by heat can be reabsorbed.

Most hunters and fishermen are very nice fellows, and usually thoughtful. They'll seldom bring you a bird that hasn't been field-drawn, an animal that hasn't been gutted and usually skinned, a fish that hasn't been cleaned. Only a thoughtless or lazy few will show their lack of good outdoor habits by bringing you as a gift game that's not prepared, or at least partly prepared, for the table. Those few will always be around, though, so let's begin with the assumption that you neither hunt nor fish and don't know thing one about getting any animal, bird, or fish ready for the pot or about cooking them after the preliminary steps in cleaning have been completed.

Small Game

All the small edible animals that you're likely to encounter are handled in pretty much the same fashion. They'll probably be rabbits or squirrels, though in some sections you might run into a possum, which isn't skinned at all, but scalded and scraped like a pig. Both rabbits and squirrels are much easier to clean after they've been skinned. Your first step is to slip your knife into the skin just in front of the hind legs and make a circular cut that parts the skin like a belt all around the body. Hold your knife at right angles to the carcass and use the first half-inch of its tip to make the cut; this ensures that you won't go too deeply and damage the flesh.

Slide your forefingers in the slit, get a good grip on the skin, and pull the forward section toward the head, just as though you were taking off a glove by turning it inside out. The skin will peel away cleanly as far as the neck and paws. Cut off the neck and the forepaws just behind the fold of skin, and discard them with the skin. Next, strip off the skin from the hindquarters in the same manner, and when you make the cut parting the skin from the carcass take off not only the hindpaws, but cut as well around the genitals and anus.

A thin membrane will be left holding the intestines in the carcass. Slit this from the breastbone to the anal cut and scoop out the intestines and everything that's attached to them. Cut them free at the stomach opening, separate and save the heart and liver. Then reach your forefingers up into the chest cavity and pull out the lungs, and give an extra tug to yank the windpipe free. You may need to do a bit of cutting from the neck end to part the windpipe from the tissues surrounding it.

Most small game will have been brought down with a shotgun, so you'll want to check the skinned carcass carefully, looking for the discolored spots that mark pellets. Not all the pellets bruise the flesh around the spot where they penetrate, so look closely at the carcass to be sure you haven't missed any. Dig the pellets out with the tip of a knife. Check the body cavity, because a pellet may have penetrated an intestine and caused fecal matter to leak out. If so, cut away the tissues that are stained. Wash the carcass, and it's ready to be disjointed, unless you plan to cook the animal whole.

1. Rabbits and squirrels are skinned and cleaned by the same method. Hang the animal by its hind legs, circle the skin just in front of the hindquarters with a shallow cut, and pull the skin down over the forequarters.

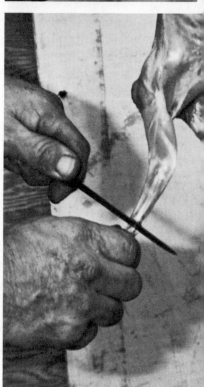

2. Cut off the head, severing the neck close to the body, and cut off the forepaws above the skin.

3. Take the skin off the hindquarters just as you did off the forequarters.

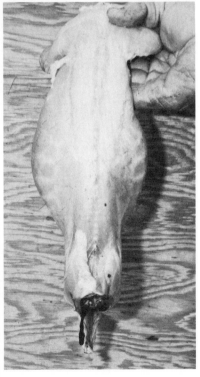

4. After skinning, clean as outlined in the text.

1. First step in disjointing a rabbit—or a squirrel—is to cut just back of the forelegs; cut down at the angle shown, through the shoulder.

Dividing up a rabbit or squirrel into cooking portions takes ten minutes of your time and a sharp knife. With the forequarters facing you, cut just back of the forelegs to remove legs and shoulder joint. Next, slice along the last rib from the breastbone forward; cut through the spine, then cut along the breastbone, open the chest, and split the piece by cutting through the ribs on one side of the spine.

Move halfway down the body and cut down through the spine again, then make a similar cut just in front of the hind legs; split these two pieces lengthwise with a cut along the backbone. Finally, take off the hind legs at the hip joint and split the saddle along the spine, cutting lengthwise. This method of cutting divides the rabbit into 12 pieces, each one containing about the same amount of edible meat. This is how you'd divide a rabbit or squirrel for a dish from which individual pieces would be served. For a stew or fricassee, you might

2. Slice along the last rib, angle the cut forward as it is being made, and cut through the spine.

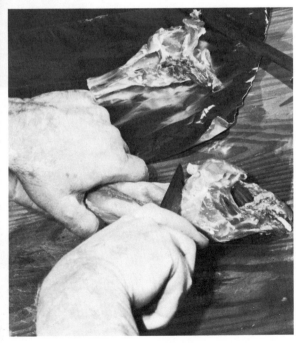

3. Cut lengthwise through the rib section at the breast, spread it open, and slice along the backbone, cutting through the ribs.

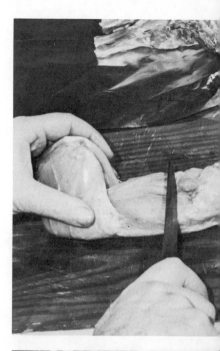

4. Cut down through the center of the body, severing the spine, and divide the section into two pieces by cutting lengthwise at one side of the backbone.

5. Cut off both hind legs by slicing through the body just in front of them; then, after splitting the section of body, cut the legs off the saddle.

6. Finally, split the saddle lengthwise. This method of cutting yields 12 pieces for skillet or stewpot. If you're cooking a stew, 14 pieces are more desirable than 12; split the forelegs away from the shoulder and divide the hind legs at the center joint.

want to divide the forelegs from the shoulders and the hindlegs from the thighs, which would give you four more pieces, or 16. A squirrel is cut up in the same manner, though its smaller body will probably yield only one center body section instead of two, for a 10-piece total.

A thoughtful cook, when preparing stews and fricassees of small game, will drain the meat out of the pot during the last few minutes of cooking and slip out all the bones. This takes little time and virtually no effort, for if the dish is well cooked the meat and bones will be at the parting stage anyhow, and a knife won't be needed to separate them. Then the meat can be returned to the pot for a final few minutes of simmering and everybody will enjoy the stew more, since there'll be no bones to worry about.

Venison

All venison is of a family, whatever species of antlered game it might come from. You won't have to deal with an entire carcass unless you hunt yourself, in which case you'll know how to take on the butchering job. If your friends bring you venison, it'll probably be in the form of steaks, chops, or roasts, which won't require any attention other than cooking. Use the dry meat marinade on page 231 to tenderize and add moisture to the meat. Cook it as you would veal or lamb—with ingredients that add still more moisture.

Wildfowl

All wildfowl are divided into two groups: upland game birds, which include pheasant, partridge, quail, grouse, and doves; and waterbirds, which takes in ducks and geese as well as the reed and marsh birds like jacksnipe and woodcock and other members of the snipe and curlew families. The reed and marsh birds are in a gray zone between true waterfowl and upland birds; they're also increasingly scarce as urbanization along our shorelines fills their natural habitats to provide fresh sites for new suburbs, shopping centers, and factories. You aren't likely to see many of these birds unless you hunt them yourself; in many areas it's illegal to shoot them and in other places the seasons are short and the game limits small.

Upland game birds should be cooked like small wild animals—by braising and stewing, using recipes that extend their flavor into dishes that a number of people can enjoy. Waterbirds—ducks and geese—run to fat; most of them not only have a layer of fat under their skins, but their tissues are also fatty. It follows logically that you'll use different methods of cooking them. Upland birds need to have moisture and fat put into their flesh, waterbirds should be cooked in ways that remove or minimize their fat.

Good hunters always field-draw their birds at once after bringing them down. This means removing the intestines, but leaving the lungs and other organs in the carcass. Since hunters are also pretty generally aware of the need for hanging birds for a brief period before they're cooked, most of them will leave the plumage on. The birds should be completely cleaned before hanging them. Your hunting friends, then, will either bring you field-drawn birds or birds that are cleaned, aged, and plucked. The latter present no problems of preparation, and instructions for hanging have already been given.

You'll naturally make it your first order of business to find out whether the bird is field-drawn or fully cleaned. If the only opening in its abdomen is a small slit, it's just been field-drawn, so before you hang it, open up the cavity and get all the rest of the innards out. While you've got the cavity open, spread it and check for discolored tissues caused by the penetration of shot pellets. Cut away any such areas, because sometimes pellets will pass through the body of a bird shot at close range and in passing through the intestines will carry fecal matter into the flesh. As a final step, wash the cavity and wipe it dry, rub it with vinegar, and dry it again. Then it's ready for hanging.

When the aging process—some like to call it ripening—has ended, it'll be time to pluck. This is a somewhat tedious business. There are several kinds of wax preparations that can be melted and poured over the feathers, or the bird can be dipped into them. The wax is then left to harden, and in theory is pulled away in neat strips or sheets, bringing all the feathers with it. It's really not all that simple, and by the time you've heated the wax, applied it to the bird, and waited for it to harden, you can have the bird plucked the ordinary way.

There's a gadget designed to be used in an electric drill, very much like those used by commercial poultry processors, that does a faster and cleaner job. It's a rubber cylinder with rows of short rubber "fingers" that whisk feathers off in short order. However, unless you're faced with the prospect of cleaning birds regularly, you're better off taking the birds to a poultry shop, where they'll use their machine to pluck it for a small fee. If your neighborhood abounds in small boys, there's usually one who'll do the plucking for a fee equal to what you'd pay the poultryman.

Hand-plucking really isn't all that bad. It's fun in camp, when a lot of hunters are gathered around doing the same job, swapping tall tales and sharing a drink or two while they work. Done alone, it gets a bit tedious, but it takes no special skill or knowledge. Just grab a handful of feathers and pull, and keep grabbing and pulling until the bird's bare. Don't do the job indoors, or you'll have a mess that defies cleaning up.

Once plucked, the bird's ready to be put in the refrigerator until you're ready to cook it, or wrapped for freezer storage, or cooked at once. Incidentally, if you freeze game birds be sure to check your state's laws as they apply to wild-bird storage; in some states there's a time limit after the season closes, in some it's illegal to keep them in your freezer after the season ends.

Fish

One hard-and-fast rule applies to fish of all species: get them from the water to the pan as soon as possible. Every minute that a fish out of water is left uncooked removes a fraction of its flavor.

Freshness was no problem to primitive man; he ate his fish raw as soon as it was caught. In various later periods and cultures, the aristocracy and the wealthy assured themselves of fresh fish by keeping them in a pond or in vats of running water. A few—a very few—deluxe restaurants still do this, but whether in a restaurant or a home kitchen, a truly fresh fish is a rare object today.

A lot of people dread cleaning fish because they think it's a messy job. It isn't, if you know how to do it. Those who haven't learned usually go about the cleaning chore backwards, and then it does become a messy task.

Here's the quick, easy way. Have ready a knife that's razor-keen right down to its tip. Hold the fish in your left hand. If you haven't washed the fish, it won't be slick or slimy. If it is slick, put salt on your left hand, and that will cut the film and enable you to hold the fish firmly. Insert the tip of the knife in the fish's vent; don't let the blade go more than a quarter-inch deep unless the fish weighs over 10 pounds; then you have to go just a hairsbreadth deeper.

Make one cut from vent to jaw tip. Still using the tip of the knife, make a cut on each side of the lower jaw that will slit from the jaw tip to the top of the gills. Follow the jawbone at the beginning of this cut, and curve it along the bony rim of the gills to the point where the fish's neck would be if fish had necks.

When the membrane has been cut on both sides of the jaw and head, sever the thread of membrane that is still attached to the tip of the jaw. With your left thumb, force open the jaw and lower gill rakers—these are the white spiny formations that curve along the back of the fish's mouth. With the jaw wide open, you can see a place inside the mouth at the top where the gill rakers are attached to the skull. This is gristle. Cut between the roof of the mouth and the gill rakers, severing the small strip completely.

Put your knife aside. With your right thumb, pull the bottom gill rakers down through the bottom of the jaw. Get a firm grip on the fish's head, your thumb pressing against the roof of its mouth, your fingers wrapped around its head. Take the gill rakers in your other hand and pull them back toward the tail. All the intestines will come out in one connected string. Cut around the vent to free them from the body of the fish, then discard them.

Spread the body cavity open, and you'll see a line of blood under a thin membrane along the fish's backbone. If it's a small fish, one under 3 or 4 pounds, scrape the membrane and blood away by running your thumb along the backbone from the back of the cavity toward the mouth. If it's a big fish you'll probably have to slit the membrane with your knife to scrape the blood out. Now, you can wash the fish. Get all the blood out, pull off any loose threads of tissue in the cavity, and cut off the bottom and side fins. The whole job should take two minutes—much less time than you've spent reading how to do it.

If you're cleaning a small panfish or a trout, your fish is ready to be cooked. If it's a big black bass out of warm water, cut out the gill plates and the fins and cut away the flesh around them for a distance of about a quarter-inch from the joint where fins join body. This is where algae collect on warm-water fish; you can't wash these areas clean and unless they're cut out your fish will taste muddy or mossy. If you've got a big fish that needs to be scaled, and you're near a source of piped water, lay the fish on a flat surface outdoors and run a swift fine jet of water in a zigzag pattern from its tail to its head; the water will lift the

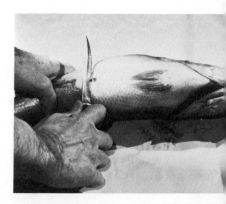

1. To clean a big fish the easy, quick way, first make a shallow cut just back of the vent; slant the knife slightly toward the head.

2. Slip the knife into the vent and make a slit along the belly. The cut should be very shallow, just deep enough to penetrate the cavity without touching any of the internal organs. Cut from the vent to the end of the body, severing the gristly section that comes to a vee just under the gills.

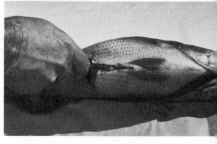

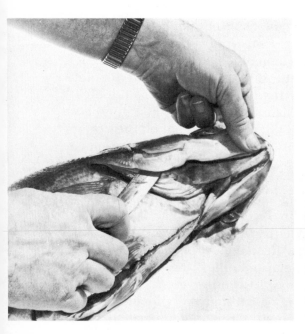

3. A bony plate called the operculum is located back of the fish's cheek connected to the head by a thin membrane. The back edge of the operculum is connected to the gills. Slide the tip of your knife into the membrane near the top of the head, and cut between cheek and operculum on both sides. At the tip of the jaw, a piece of gristle connects the tongue to the jawbone; cut through this gristle to free the tongue.

4. This cut is necessary only when you're cleaning a fish that goes above two pounds; on small fish it can be omitted. But a big bass like the one pictured, or any fish of three pounds or more, will have a tough piece of bone just at the gill opening. Cut behind this bone from each side of the belly slit to the point where the bone tapers away, which will be near the center of the fish's body.

5. Open the jawbone and pull the tongue back toward the fish's tail. On both sides of the tongue are spiky gill rakers—one is just above the middle of the knifeblade in the picture. The gill rakers are connected to the fish's spine by a strip of flesh at the top of the mouth. Hold the jaw area open and cut through this strip, freeing it from the backbone.

6. Put your knife aside for a moment. Get a good grip with your left hand on the fish's head, with your right take hold of the tongue and gill rakers and pull them back toward the tail. All the intestines will come out in a single connected string. Make a cut around the vent, connecting with the first cut made in the cleaning, and the intestines will come free, to be discarded. Along the backbone at the top of the cavity there is a membrane that extends the length of the cavity and traps the fish's blood. Slit this membrane and wash out the blood and bits of spongy tissue. Be sure to get all the blood. An old toothbrush will help get into the corrugations along the backbone. Then, pull the membrane free from the cavity's sides, and discard it.

7. Cut off the pectoral fins, which are just behind the gills on the body, and the pelvic fins, which are on the fish's belly. This is most easily done by taking off both fins on one side with a single cut, as illustrated. It's very important to do this when cleaning warm-water fish, for algae collects at the base of these fins and cannot be scraped away. This is what gives improperly cleaned fish what most people describe as a "muddy taste."

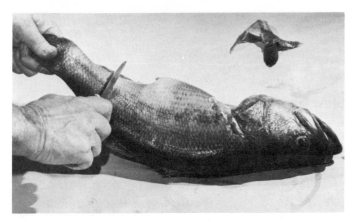

8. Warm-water and deep-sea fish must be scaled; cold-water fish such as trout don't need this treatment. Use the back of your knife or a regular serrated fish-scaler, or if you're near a hydrant, do the job outdoors using a jet of water as described in the text. When scaling, of course, you work from tail to head, as shown.

scales out of the body and wash them away. If you scale the fish in the field, you'll have to scrape the scales away with the back of your knife or use a scaler.

Some fish can be reduced to fillets without being cleaned, if you do the filleting job at once. Have a long sharp knife with a thin blade ready to use. Make a diagonal cut back of the gills, slanting from the head to the belly. With the fish lying on its side, cut into the body just ahead of the tail. Hold your knife parallel to the working surface and slice toward the head of the fish; you'll begin with a half-moon of flesh freed from the section in front of the tail. Grasp this half-moon in your left hand and lift it gently upward while you keep the knife moving along the fish's backbone to take off all the flesh on one side of the fish in a solid slab. Turn the fish over and repeat.

To skin the slabs of flesh, lay them on a flat surface with the cut side down. Nick the skin at the tail end, cutting between skin and flesh until you've freed a flap of skin big enough to grasp in your fingers. Lift the skin and cut along the line it makes between skin and flesh. When you've got an inch of skin freed, roll it into a cylinder in the direction of the head, and keep rolling as you slide your knife along the underside of the skin all the way to the head. The fillet's now ready for the pan.

To help you enjoy that fish—and the animals and birds we dealt with earlier in this chapter—suggested recipes follow.

Small Game

Rabbit Stew (usually called Brunswick Stew)

2 or 3 rabbits
1½ pounds uncooked ham
   cut in ½-inch dice
1 gallon cold water
2½ tbsp salt
1¼ tsp freshly ground
   pepper
2 pods hot red pepper
Bay leaf
3 sprigs parsley

Sprig of fresh thyme
2 cups fresh corn or canned
   whole kernel corn
6 red-ripe tomatoes
2 cups okra sliced in ½-inch
   rounds
1½ cups fresh or frozen lima
   beans
2 cups uncooked rice
¼ cup butter

Cut the rabbits into stewing-sized pieces—page 248—and put them in the water-filled stewpot with the ham. Add salt, pepper, bay leaf, parsley, thyme; simmer until the meat begins to get tender, add corn, tomatoes, okra, lima beans, rice. Let simmer until all ingredients are tender, then fish out bay leaf and pepper pods, stir in butter. Do not add more water unless absolutely necessary; a Brunswick Stew should be so thick it can be eaten with a fork. Serves 12 to 14.

Brewmaster's Rabbit

2 rabbits, cut up for stewing
1 tsp salt
½ tsp freshly ground pepper
3 tbsp peanut oil
3 potatoes, peeled and
   halved
1 sliced sweet onion

1½ cups flat beer
2 pods hot pepper
1 tbsp brown sugar
1 clove garlic, minced
½ cup cold water
3 tbsp flour
½ tsp salt (approximately)

Rub rabbit pieces generously with salt and pepper and brown in oil; cook very slowly over low heat, turn often to brown evenly. Add potatoes and onion, beer, pepper pods, sugar, and garlic. Cover pot and simmer until meat is tender. Strain solids from pot, discard pepper pods, remove and discard rabbit bones. Combine water and flour by shaking in a sealed jar, add to pan juices, stir until smooth, taste and adjust seasoning with salt as required. Return solids to pot, cook long enough to reheat them.

Serves 8 to 10.

Rabbit in Red Wine

½ cup chopped sweet onion
1 clove garlic, minced
¼ tsp dry crumbled rosemary
3 tbsp butter
1 rabbit cut in stewing pieces
1 tsp salt

Large dash freshly ground pepper
Bay leaf
1 cup dry red wine (use a very
    heavy wine such as Barolo)
½ cup light cream

In the stewing pot, brown the onion, garlic, and rosemary in the butter; drain from pot and brown rabbit in the remaining butter after dusting the pieces with salt and pepper. Return onion mixture to pot, add wine and bay leaf, cover and cook over very low heat until meat is tender, 45 minutes to 1 hour. Drain rabbit from pan, remove bay leaf, bring liquid in pot to boil, cook until reduced to about ½ cup. Stir in cream, return rabbit pieces to heat. Drain rabbit to heated platter, strain saucer into sauceboat, pass with rabbit.

Serves 8.

Squirrel Pot Pie

2 squirrels cut for stew
⅓ pound salt pork
½ cup flour
1 tsp salt
½ tsp freshly ground pepper
½ cup dry white wine
½ cup grated carrots
1 recipe pâté crust for a two-
    crust pie; ½ recipe if only
    a top crust will be used

2 cups sweet onion, chopped
1 clove garlic, minced
2 cups firm-ripe tomatoes,
    seeded, skinned, and drained
4 tbsp chopped parsley
½ tsp dry crumbled thyme
2 stalks celery chopped with
    leaves
2 bay leaves

Rub squirrels with salt pork, then cut pork in ½-inch cubes, blanch in boiling water, drain, and sauté in heavy skillet until crisply browned. Drain pork from skillet, reserve on paper towel. Combine flour, salt, and pepper and rub squirrel pieces with it. Brown over very low heat in pork fat, drain. Measure fat remaining in pan, return 4 tbsp. In a jar, shake remaining seasoned flour with wine to form a smooth mixture. Pour into fat in skillet over low heat, stir until smooth and creamy, add 3 cups cold water, stir to blend, remove at once from heat. If a two-crust pie is being made, line an oiled baking dish with half the pâté crust rolled to ¼-inch thickness. If the pie is single-crust, omit this step, transfer rabbit to baking dish, add pork pieces and remaining ingredients, pour sauce from skillet over them, cook in a preheated 350-degree oven 30 minutes, remove, roll out crust, put over top of dish, slash in two or three places, brush with water or egg white to glaze, return to oven to bake 15 to 20 minutes, until crust is brown.
Serves 8 to 10.

Braised Squirrels

2 squirrels cut for stew	3 finely minced shallots
1 tsp salt	1 cup sliced mushrooms
½ tsp freshly ground pepper	½ tsp dry crumbled thyme
2 tbsp butter or peanut oil	¼ tsp dry crumbled marjoram
¼ cup brandy or Cognac	½ cup dry red wine
2 cups chicken or beef stock	1 tsp cornstarch
1 cup grated sweet onion	

Rub squirrel pieces with salt and pepper, brown in butter over very low heat. Drain butter from pan, heat brandy, pour over squirrel pieces and light. Let flames burn out, then add all remaining ingredients except cornstarch. Cover pan, simmer at very low heat until squirrel pieces are tender, 45 minutes to 1 hour. Dissolve cornstarch in cool water, stir into pan, simmer until pan liquids thicken.
Serves 8.

Venison

Venison Steaks, Chops, Cutlets

8 venison steaks, chops, or
    cutlets, ¼ to ½ inch
    thick
2 tbsp lard
3 shallots, chopped coarsely
1 cup dry white wine

1 cup homemade sour cream
1 tsp salt
¼ tsp freshly ground pepper
½ tsp dry crumbled sage
¼ tsp dry crumbled rosemary

Heat a heavy skillet, using no fat. Test skillet by dropping a few drops of water into it; when the drops dance and vanish within 10 seconds or so, the pan is ready. Sear each piece of venison quickly, no more than 10 to 15 seconds per side, pressing the meat firmly to the pan. Sear one or two pieces at a time, removing the seared pieces to a plate. Remove pan from heat. When it has cooled a bit, return to medium heat, and in the lard sauté the shallots until they are quite brown. Fish out and discard the pieces of shallot. Add the liquids and seasonings to the pan, stir, put in the meat. Cover pan and cook 30 to 35 minutes over low heat until the meat tests tender.
    Serves 8.

Roast Venison

6-pound haunch or
    forequarter roast
Thin slices pork fat
2 cups dry red wine
2 tsp salt

½ tsp freshly ground pepper
⅛ tsp cayenne
8 peeled potatoes
8 2-inch-diameter sweet onions
3 whole cloves

Put roast on a rack in a deep roasting pan, cover the top of the meat with thin pork slices (if no pork fatback is available, use blanched salt pork or bacon and reduce the amount of salt to 1 tsp), and cook with the pan uncovered in a preheated 350-degree oven 30 minutes. Combine wine and seasonings, remove pork pieces from roast, pour the wine mixture over the roast. Add potatoes, onions, and cloves to the pan, reduce oven temperature to 300 degrees, cook 40 to 45 minutes, basting often with pan drippings. Remove meat to platter to rest before carving, put potatoes and onions around meat. Strain pan juices to a saucepan, skim off loose fat, reduce by boiling, pass with the meat as a sauce.

Serves 8 to 10.

Wildfowl

Pheasant au Vin Blanc

1 pheasant, disjointed	1½ cups chicken stock
1 pound fresh mushrooms	1 cup dry white wine
1 thick slice bacon	½ tsp salt
2 cloves garlic	1 tsp tarragon leaves (about 4)
2 tbsp butter	Freshly ground white pepper
2 tbsp peanut oil	2 tbsp cornstarch

Wash and wipe dry the pieces of pheasant, quarter the mushrooms lengthwise. Sauté the bacon until very brown; when it first begins to yield fat to the pan, add the garlic. When garlic browns, remove it and the bacon from the pan. Brown the pheasant pieces lightly over low heat, drain from pan to oiled casserole dish. (It's optional, but flaming the pheasant pieces with Cognac or brandy at this point is a nice flavoring touch.) Warm casserole briefly in oven, put in butter and peanut oil, stir, add broth, wine, salt, tarragon, pepper. Cover casserole and cook in preheated 350-degree oven 35 to 40 minutes, until leg pieces of pheasant test tender to a fork. Dissolve cornstarch in 2 tbsp cool water, add to pan, stir, return to oven for about 5 minutes, until sauce thickens.
Serves 6 to 8.

Pheasant Valois

2 pheasants, disjointed	Bouquet garni: celery tops,
1 tsp salt	thyme, parsley, bay leaf
¼ tsp freshly ground pepper	2 tbsp butter
1 carrot, peeled and sliced	1 tbsp peanut oil
1 large onion sliced thickly	1½ pounds mushrooms
2 cups chicken stock	2 cups homemade sour cream
1 cup dry red wine	Freshly grated nutmeg

Rub the pheasant pieces with salt and pepper, put the carrot and onion pieces on the bottom of a deep heavy saucepan, to cover it, put the pheasant pieces in, add stock, wine, and the bouquet garni, cover the pan and simmer over very low heat 1 to 1½ hours, until the pheasant is very tender. Remove the pheasant pieces, skin, take out bones, reserve meat on a plate, discard skin and bones. Strain the cooking pan's contents into a bowl, discard solids, reserve the liquid. In a saucepan, combine butter and oil, sauté the mushrooms; if they are very large, slice or quarter them. Drain the mushrooms and reserve with the pieces of pheasant. Pour the reserved cooking liquid in the saucepan; there should be about 1½ cups. If not, add a bit of stock. Bring to a boil, reduce to simmer, combine nutmeg and sour cream and stir into the liquid. Do not allow to boil. When the sauce has thickened, put the pieces of pheasant and the mushrooms in it to heat. Transfer to a tureen, serve by ladling over boiled or steamed rice.
Serves 8.

Quail Chef's Style

8 quail	8 large mushrooms, sliced
2 to 3 tsp salt	1 cup minced fresh parsley
1 to 1½ tsp freshly ground	½ cup minced watercress
white pepper	1 tbsp Cognac or brandy
½ cup butter	1 cup chicken stock
1 cup minced sweet onion	1 tbsp fresh lemon juice

Bone the quail; the technique is the same as that given on page 148. Lay the birds flat and pound them gently with the side of a cleaver. Combine salt and pepper and rub into the birds, brown them in a skillet over medium-low heat, using half the butter. Remove the browned quail to a warmed casserole dish, cover. Add the reserved butter to the saucepan, sauté the onion until it begins to soften, add the mushrooms, and continue cooking until the onions are browned nicely. Spread the onions, mushrooms, parsley, and watercress over the quail in the casserole. Pour the liquor in the saucepan, swirl the pan to blend it with the remaining butter, pour in the stock and lemon juice, simmer 3 to 5 minutes, pour over the birds in the casserole. Cover the casserole and cook in a pre-heated 375-degree oven 15 to 20 minutes, until the dish is warmed.

Serves 8.

Quail Cooked in Cases

8 quail	½ cup peanut oil
1 cup ground uncooked ham	8 large outside cabbage leaves
1 cup parboiled rice	1½ cups Rhine wine
3 shallots, minced	½ cup light cream
1½ tsp salt	Freshly grated nutmeg
⅛ tsp freshly ground pepper	1 tsp cornstarch dissolved in 1
2 tbsp paprika	tbsp cool water

Bone the quail; procedure is the same as that given on page 148. Combine ham, rice, shallots, half the salt, all the pepper. Stuff the quail with this mixture, close the backs by sewing or with small skewers. Combine the reserved salt and paprika, rub the quail with the mixture, brown them in the peanut oil over very low heat. Wrap each bird in a cabbage leaf; if the leaves are thick and stiff, soften them by dropping them into boiling water for 2 or 3 minutes. Use cocktail picks or skewers to hold the leaves in place. Put the cased birds in an oiled casserole dish, pour in the wine, cover, and cook in a preheated 350-degree oven 30 to 35 minutes. Remove the birds, remove and discard the cabbage leaves, put the quail breast-up on a warmed platter. Strain the liquid from the casserole through cloth into a saucepan, add the cream and nutmeg, simmer it without boiling for about 5 minutes, stir in the dissolved cornstarch, cook until the sauce thickens. If the sauce is grainy and coarse, stir into it 1½ tsp butter and beat briskly. Serve the birds on thick toast slices, some of the sauce poured over them.

Serves 8.

Wild Duck in Port Sauce

2 large wild ducks	2 cups Port
¼ cup butter	2 to 3 tbsp Triple Sec or Cointreau
½ cup chicken stock	Salt

Wash and wipe the ducks, rub them well inside and out with butter, put in a roasting pan on a rack, cover, cook 30 minutes in a preheated 375-degree oven. Combine stock, wine and liqueur. Uncover the pan, pour this liquid over the ducks. Reduce oven temperature to 300 degrees and continue to cook about 20 minutes, basting with pan juices several times. When the legs of the ducks test tender to a fork, remove them to a warmed platter. Remove pan, skim loose fat from the liquid in it, put pan on surface heat and bring to a boil, stirring and scraping it. Taste sauce and adjust with salt as needed. Strain sauce into a sauceboat, pass with the meat when the ducks are carved and served.

Serves 8.

Roast Wild Duck Normandy

1 large wild duck	2 to 2½ cups coarse breadcrumbs
2 tart apples, peeled and	1 to 1½ cups fresh apple cider
cubed	¼ cup Calvados or applejack
1 cup walnut meats	1 tsp salt
	1 egg

Remove the wingtips before cooking. Combine apples, walnuts, breadcrumbs, cider, Calvados or applejack, salt, egg. Stuff the duck, close cavity incision, pull flap of neck skin across back and secure with skewers. Cook on a rack in a preheated 375-degree oven for 30 minutes, reduce oven heat to 300 degrees and cook an additional 20 to 25 minutes, basting frequently with pan drippings. The bird is ready to be served when the legs test tender. Let rest 15 minutes before carving. Serve some of the stuffing with each portion of meat.

Serves 6.

Roast Goose

8-pound goose
4 slices bacon, chopped
1 large sweet onion,
    chopped

3 stalks celery, chopped
1 small turnip, peeled and grated
1 tbsp salt
1 tbsp vinegar

Take off the wingtips, pull the flap of neck skin smoothly over the bird's back, and secure with skewers. Combine bacon, onion, celery, turnip, salt, vinegar; put into cavity, close cavity by lacing between skewers. Put goose on a rack in a roasting pan, cook in a preheated 375-degree oven for 30 minutes, reduce oven temperature to 325 degrees, and continue to cook for 2 hours while basting often with pan juices. Let the bird rest on a heated platter for 20 minutes before carving. The stuffing provides flavor only and is not served.

Serves 8 to 10.

Wild Goose Cassoulet

8-pound goose
1½ pounds large white
    beans
Cooking fat
1 pound small hard sausage
    (chorizo)
¼ pound bacon rind

3 large sweet onions
2 large firm-ripe tomatoes
Bouquet garni: ½ carrot grated, 3
    cloves, 1 bay leaf, 1 clove
    garlic
1 tsp salt

Disjoint the goose; procedure is similar to that on page 143. Soak the beans in cold water at least 4 hours, drain. Brown goose pieces in fat. Cut sausages in 1-inch lengths, chop bacon rind coarsely, quarter onions and tomatoes. Put beans in a large deep casserole dish or roasting pan; bury the pieces of goose, sausage, bacon rind, onions, and tomatoes and the bouquet garni in the beans, dust with salt. Fill casserole with cold water to cover ingredients. Cover and put in a cold oven, set temperature at 300 degrees. After 1 hour reduce to 250 degrees and continue to cook 2 to 3 hours. Do not uncover casserole or add more water. Remove the bouquet garni before serving.

Serves 12 to 14.

These are basic recipes for wild game. The chief ingredient in most of them—the meat itself—is pretty much interchangeable; recipes that are based on rabbit can be used to cook squirrels, and vice versa, and most of the small-game recipes are also suitable for the cooking of upland birds. Ducks and geese can also be swapped around in the recipes for their preparation. At first glance, game cookery might seem a bit complicated and involved, but the recipes are easier to prepare than they are to read. Anyhow, wild game's an increasingly scarce commodity, and it's worth a bit of trouble to serve it at its best.

APPENDIX:
EQUIVALENT MEASURES AND SUBSTITUTIONS

3 teaspoons = 1 tablespoon; 16 tablespoons = 1 cup; 1 cup = 8 ounces

DRY MEASURE

1 teaspoon = $\frac{1}{8}$ ounce = 3.5 grams

1 tablespoon = $\frac{1}{3}$ ounce = 10 grams

1 cup = $3\frac{3}{4}$ ounces = 114 grams

LIQUID MEASURE

1 teaspoon = $\frac{1}{6}$ ounce = 5 grams

1 tablespoon = $\frac{1}{2}$ ounce = 15 grams

1 cup = 8 ounces = 250 grams

(These are not laboratory-precise, but practical kitchen equivalents.)

FOOD CAN SIZE IN CUPS

Buffet = 1 cup; #1 = $1\frac{1}{3}$ cups; #1 tall = 2 cups; #2 = $2\frac{1}{2}$ cups; #2$\frac{1}{2}$ = $3\frac{1}{2}$ cups; #10 = 13 cups.

SUBSTITUTIONS

Thickening sauces and gravies: 1 tbsp cornstarch = 2 tbsp flour.

Sweetening: 1 cup honey + $\frac{1}{3}$ tsp baking soda = 1 cup sugar; when substituting, reduce total liquid in recipe by $\frac{1}{4}$ cup.

Shortening: 1 tbsp butter = $\frac{4}{5}$ tbsp pork fat or $\frac{2}{3}$ tbsp chicken fat or $\frac{7}{8}$ tbsp lard or $\frac{1}{2}$ tbsp beef suet; when substituting animal fats for butter, increase the total liquid in the recipe by $\frac{1}{3}$ cup. No substitutions are given for margarine or the so-called "pure vegetable" liquid and solid shortenings because they cannot be recommended; almost all of them now contain an additive based on silicones which prevents them from blending with acid liquids such as lemon juice and wine in making sauces and gravies. So far, peanut and safflower oils have escaped being degraded by the addition of foreign substances.

Index

Note: Italicized page references indicate illustrations.